dance
OF THE
spirits

Sanjai Velayudhan

Dance of the Spirits

ISBN 978-93-52019-55-7

Cover: Tina Patankar
Photo Credit: Sanjai Velayudhan
Layouts: Chandravadan R. Shiroorkar
Typeset in Palatino Linotype
Printed at Dhote Offset Techno Krafts

Published in India in 2017 by Inkstate Books
An imprint of Leadstart Publishing Pvt. Ltd.
Unit 25, Building A/1, Near Wadala RTO,
Wadala (E), Mumbai 400 037, INDIA
T + 91 96 9993 3000   E info@leadstartcorp.com
W www.leadstartcorp.com

*Dedicated to my daughter, Nakshatra. For she believed in
me when none did!*

About the Author

Sanjai is an acclaimed marketing strategist and consultant for leading global brands. Having worked and lived in multiple countries, he is now settled in Bangalore. An alumnus of University of Leicester (CLMS), University of Delhi and Indian Society of Training and Development (ISTD), his true passions are History & Psychology. He perceives them as intertwined and believes that *'If you do not have a history, you do not have a future!'*

In short, an intellectual nomad, a secular radical and iconoclast!

www.sanjaivelayudhan.com
www.facebook.com/pages/Dance-of-the-Spirits
www.twitter.com/v_sanjai
www.instagram.com/sanjai.velayudhan

Acknowledgement

This work is the outcome of more than six years of research and writing. It would not have been possible without the encouragement and support of many people. I knew a few of them personally, but I didn't know many. The common thread that bound us together was the pride of being a Malayali and love for Theyyam performances. I take this opportunity to thank them all.

Let me start with Vandana Bijesh, who introduced me to her relatives and arranged my stay at their *tharawads* (ancestral homes) on multiple trips where they welcomed me and were generous hosts. Among them are K. Bhaskaran master, Radha Bhaskaran, the family members of the Kambrath *tharawad*, Trikarippur, Kannur, P. Suvarnan, Girija Suvarnan and the family members of the Makkuni *tharawad*, Azhikode, Kannur. They supported me whole-heartedly, even though they did not have to.

Thanks are due to Madhavan Velayudhan and Laila Velayudhan who, like every parent, thought that their child was the smartest. They brought me up with a lot of freedom and encouraged me to read books on diverse subjects.

Thanks to the inquisitiveness of Ishaan, my son. His 'childish' questions could surprisingly be thought-provoking and often prompted me to relook at certain portions of the work.

Last but not the least, Latha, my wife, for putting up with me as I swayed between ecstasy and agony, hope and despair. I don't think there is another woman like her.

Contents

PREFACE

Theyyam is the magico-religious ritual native to the Malabar region of Kerala.

Pre-modern Kerala was one of the most asymmetrical and hierarchical societies of the country with the despicable caste system practised with utmost severity. The members of the 'lower' castes and 'untouchables' lived in desperate conditions.

Over a period of time, the collective imagination of the oppressed lot gave birth to one of the most complex worlds of religious and cultural practices - Theyyam! People of those times found dignity in it. Their rebellion found a voice in these complex, spiritual performances.

Theyyam is a grand ritual, both terrifying and compelling. Combining the extreme emotions of religious fervour and fear, Theyyam offers its devotees what they craved for the most – hope. The power of Theyyam lies in its psychological and social context. It is not just another mask-dance but is actually the 'theatre of the oppressed'.

In reality, pre-modern Kerala, despite being a predominantly matriarchal society, was not kind to its women. Their struggles and sufferings were similar to that of the people of the lower castes. This is also their story.

Asatomā sadgamaya

Tamasomā jyotir gamaya

Mrityormā amritam gamaya

Oṁ śhāntih śhāntiḥ

From ignorance, lead me to truth;

From darkness, lead me to light;

From death, lead me to immortality.

Om peace, peace, peace.

(Brihadaranyaka Upanishad — I.iii.28)

bali tharpanam

Thiruvananthapuram was under the magical spell of the rain god that night. Heavy rains hammered relentlessly down the old roof tiles of the renovated house. The periodic sounds of the thunder were deafening; strikes of lightning flashed through the rain-blurred windows, methodically and menacingly. The air was damp and cold. Though it was quite late, sleep evaded me. The bedroom, with its closed windows, felt claustrophobic. Today, I was extra-sensitive to nature's stimuli. The din outside made me anxious. I got a sudden and strong urge to open the door and let in some fresh air.

Though the impulse to get out of bed was compelling, I resisted it. Lakshmi was deep in sleep, curled up in a foetal position. I could feel the comforting warmth of her body and her gentle breathing over my back. The slightest movement could disturb her. Normally a deep sleeper, these days she was hyper-sensitive to the slightest disturbance. It seemed she was subconsciously always on guard.

I do not remember when sleep finally overpowered me. The next thing I remember is Lakshmi shaking me gently to wake me up from deep slumber. I heard her say, "It's already 4.30 a.m. Don't we have to go to the temple?" I opened my eyes. The light in the room felt intense and blinding. My eyelids felt heavy. All I wanted to do was to return to sleep. I felt very tired, which was more psychological than physical.

Firmly persuaded by Lakshmi, I slowly got up and sat on the edge of the bed. She handed me a mug of tea with wisps of steam emanating from it. The aroma of the brew was strong. She sat next to me to ensure that I didn't go back to sleep. Her smile was comforting.

Lakshmi seems to have adapted fast. She is now a mellow, empathetic person. At least that is what she projects. That is a welcome change for me. I can relate to her better.

I was never an early-riser and vigorously resisted the idea of getting up before dawn. But then, today was not an ordinary day.

My eyes were transfixed on the windows. The heavy precipitation had tapered to a light drizzle, as though even God had finally exhausted his abundant supply of water.

For a land known for bountiful rains, climate change is beginning to play havoc. The destruction of forests and mutilation of nature in general has brought unalterable changes. Maybe, even God can't make much of a difference. Kerala is called 'God's own country'. Ha! A smile spread over my lips.

She reminded me, "We have to reach the temple on time, Krish." There was an urgency in her voice. Though her voice was gentle, there was a steely resolve in her words. I looked at her deep eyes. They seemed for a second to accuse me; "If it wasn't for your idiocies." I felt a sudden rush. The hot tea scalded my mouth as I quickly gulped it down.

As we stepped out of the house, around 5 a.m., I saw that my in-laws were already in the car, waiting for us impatiently. They were always together, like a deity and his consort. As soon as we sat inside, Lakshmi's father started the car. He was muttering to himself. For me, these were sounds of suppressed anger. If I weren't his son-in-law, he might have hurled the choicest of abuses at me. Old age seemed to be getting at him. Secretly, I liked that.

The roads seemed to have turned into shallow rivers due to the incessant rains and overflowing drains. The muddy water resembled strong milky tea.

I hated the monsoons. The persistent wetness and the overcast skies always managed to dampen my spirits. The inky sky was unusually dark. The night was engaged in a losing battle with the sun.

Time! Time is everything, I told myself. Victory and defeat are dictated by it. In an hour, the sun would win the battle. The victor and the vanquished will alternate their roles. The battle for survival is eternal!

As the car moved forward, Lakshmi glanced at me. She had an anxious look on her face. Last year had been very difficult for the both of us. It had revealed a new side of Lakshmi to me. I realised that she could not only withstand enormous adversities but could also be forgiving. I had possibly misread her all this time.

A reluctant smile spread across her lips, making her look more enigmatic. She was wearing a simple Kerala sari. Her damp hair was casually swept back in a typical *kulipinnal*. A couple of leaves of the sacred *thulasi* were tucked carelessly in her hair. As an ardent believer in the power of the Gods, she was the perfect antithesis to my atheism. Silence prevailed, conspicuous by its gloominess. I shifted my gaze and slowly rolled down the window in a metaphorical attempt to let despair out.

The early risers were going about their chores as usual. Newspaper and milk delivery boys, wearing ill-fitting, cheap plastic raincoats, were busy picking up their merchandise. They rode around in bicycles or motorcycles, oblivious of the messy roads that were the result of the previous night's pandemonium.

As we hit the main road, the old man started accelerating the car. He seemed to be in a hurry. The cold wind hit us hard. We passed new office buildings and tall apartment towers shrouded in concrete and glass. They dominated the skyline like muscular monstrosities. The traditional and older buildings seemed to be cowered in submission. The booming IT outsourcing industry had managed to change both the mental and physical landscape of Kerala, the land of bold and adaptable immigrants.

The Malayali diaspora is spread all over the world. Unlike the compulsions of their forefathers, today's ambitious and hardworking denizens have enough opportunities to prosper in their own homeland. The young want the best of both the worlds. The IT professionals travel the globe, earn handsome salaries in foreign currencies, acquire an accent, and return home to prosperous lives. Yes, Kerala is undergoing a rapid socio-cultural transformation.

Monumental architecture has always defined Thiruvananthapuram, one of the earliest inhabited places in the country. The land of the mighty *Venad* kings still has its fair share of old palaces, gateways and forts that remind one of the royal past. Their battle for survival against real estate sharks is not an easy one. Like hungry vultures anticipating the death of their prospective victims, many greedy people eagerly await their demise. In today's Kerala, not many seem to appreciate heritage buildings, nor understand their context.

I wonder if the grandeur of monuments such as the Padmanabhaswamy temple, which was the axis mundi of the political geometry of medieval times, can ever be matched by the modern structures. The recent discovery of a treasure worth billions of dollars in the secret vaults of the temple has only added to its aura. Architecture has always demonstrated its power to dominate the mind of the masses.

I have always harboured a strange fascination for the mysteries that history has to offer in plenty. Stories of archaeological finds still grab my full attention. I am in awe of the exploits of kings and conquerors. I like to spend time around old forts and monuments imagining myself as an investigator digging into the past, unravelling it's deep held secrets. I have always lived between the past and the present, spending a substantial amount of time analysing the bygone era. My secret desire is to be an archaeologist or a historian. No wonder, I have a strange fascination for detective novels. I do believe in the saying, 'If you don't have a history, you don't have a future!'

Lost in my thoughts, I didn't realise that we had reached Thiruvallam, where the temple was located, till Lakshmi nudged me. It felt as if we had taken ages to reach the destination, although the temple was only about seven kilometres from her home. The head priest himself was waiting for us; or more specifically, for my father-in-law who was a former Non-resident Indian and now a prominent, local businessman. Everybody knew the wealthy and politically prominent individuals in Kerala.

The priest, draped in white, was a tall man, about 80 years old. His slightly protruding belly betrayed the sedentary yet lucrative nature of his profession. The spreading tentacles of cataract gave his eyes a smoky look. The frame of the old- fashioned spectacles he wore on his pockmarked face had green patina. Like an obsessive-compulsive person, he continuously ran his left hand over his white chest hair. As the master of the temple and the custodian of its traditional rituals, he displayed the confidence of a messiah who had the power to invoke immense divine interventions. He looked as old as the temple itself.

The priest gave me a benevolent look and requested me to take a dip in the banks of the mighty Karamana river flowing adjacent to the ancient temple. We could hear the raging holler of the overflowing river. It seemed to be in a hurry to reach Kovalam where it would converge with the Arabian Sea. Originating from the Western Ghats at Agastyarkoodam, it hurtled through thick rain forests. The broken branches of trees and plants floating on it were perhaps the remains of its victims as the river rushed forward with gargantuan energy, destroying everything along its way.

As I stood near the river, I thought that water has always been the nucleus around which Kerala's political, religious and social life revolved. Trade, predominantly of spices, was the lifeline of the state. The seductive fragrance of its spices had spread across the globe, attracting not just traders from far way lands but also conquerors and evangelists. Water thus proved to be both a blessing and a curse.

The large amount of water in the river was due to the pre-monsoon rains, also called the 'mango showers' because they helped in ripening the fruit on the trees. The mango trees around the temple were in full bloom. Their crowns were coloured with yellowish-white flowers that grew on brand new red stalks.

The evergreen tree, which bore the king of all fruits, is hardy by nature. A true survivor of adversities. I still remember the grand old tree in my father's ancestral home in Palakkad. We children called it the 'grandfather tree' as it seemed to be as old as our strict, un-empathetic grandfather. He wouldn't let us throw stones at the tree to bring down the ripe mangoes that constantly tempted us with their succulence. Every morning, we had to scour for the fruits that had fallen from the tree. Many would have been nibbled on by the squirrels or pecked on by the birds.

What we feared the most were the weaver ants that stitched leaves together into small nests. If disturbed, these ants could bite with such vengeance! We would observe the ants walking in a line like disciplined soldiers on the branches with their translucent orange bodies glistening in the sun. All this from a distance, of course. Despite restrictions, we threw twigs and stones at the tree whenever grandfather went out for his routine walks. We always managed to gather enough mangoes to fulfil our gastronomic desires. Needless to say, my cousins and I invariably ended up with bloated stomachs and resultant diarrhoea. The mango tree has remained an important symbol of endurance and nourishment to me.

My flow of thoughts was interrupted by Lakshmi's call to stop procrastinating and come out after a quick cleansing. I slowly dipped my legs into the water. It was ice-cold and sent a shiver through my body. A little worried about the gushing waters, I sat on the granite slab and took the customary bath in the holy river.

The wind was blowing hard. While walking back to the temple's courtyard, the shivering became uncontrollable. I was sure I would end up with pneumonia. Lakshmi was waiting for me impatiently at the granite shrine dedicated to the deity *Parashurama*. She was behaving like her old parents. She wanted to complete the rituals before the auspicious hour passed. I stood beside her in front of the deity and prayed. I wanted forgiveness for my indiscretions and eternal peace for the departed soul of a woman I had known only for a few days.

Constant chants emanated from the old granite edifice. Though tradition dates the temple back to ancient times, archaeology establishes it around the middle of the 12th century. This is supposed to be the only temple dedicated to Lord *Parashurama*, who is considered as the sixth among the ten avatars of Vishnu. Ironically, for a God, he exhibited extreme anger and aggression as he annihilated entire enemy warrior clans. It would be termed genocide in modern times. He is closely associated with the myths about Kerala's origin, thus giving it the tag 'God's own country'.

There were a few other people praying with their heads bowed down. Akin to greasing the lord's hands for fulfilment of their prayers, they put soiled notes or coins in the *hundi*. The priest was conducting a special prayer. He constantly rang a small bell as if to get the attention of God. He held a brass plate with offerings including a bunch of flowers and brightly burning camphor. The old man seemed to be enjoying the ecstasy of celestial communion. He came out and extended the platter with the sacred flame pointing towards us. We put forth our palms around the flame, and then dabbed our faces with them. With a small spoon, the priest then poured out holy water into our cupped palms; we drank some and smeared the rest on our hair. Lakshmi took a pinch of holy ash from the platter and applied it on my forehead. I placed a few 100 rupee notes on the plate as an offering to the priest. I didn't want to disappoint him and wanted him to wholeheartedly participate in the subsequent rituals. His eyes seemed to twinkle at the sight of so much money.

The priest led us to the place where the *bali* was to be conducted. His face had turned sombre. This ritual was conducted for the peace of departed souls. His assistant had the accompaniments for performing the *bali tharpanam* ready. They included the *darbha* grass, cooked rice, paddy stalks, sandal paste, black sesame seeds and fresh flowers.

We sat on the white sand that spread like an endless

carpet. As the ritual began, my mood began to darken. The priest requested me to remember the departed. I wanted to recollect the memories of a smiling Maria, but the visual that rushed in was that of her bloodied face and cold gaze.

During the *puja*, I mechanically followed the instructions of the priest hoping that her soul would finally find peace.

This was an attempt to bid a final goodbye. Inadvertently, my eyes welled up. As I wiped the tears off, I noticed that the intensity of my emotions had agitated Lakshmi.

Memories of Maria were an elephant in the room. She remained the invisible partner in a twisted ménage à trois. Our marriage had survived only because Lakshmi felt partly responsible for triggering the tragic events that unfolded last year. She was the one who had spurred me to make that hasty trip to Kochi.

This *bali tharpanam* had a larger meaning for us. Lakshmi wanted a formal closure and I wanted redemption for my lapses and guilt for not having been there when Maria needed me the most. To forgive myself, I had to ensure that Maria's soul was at peace. This could also mean a fresh start for Lakshmi and me.

The priest asked me to make small balls of rice mixed with black sesame seeds and flowers. They were placed on flat stones called *bali kallu*. The ritual was entering the final phase. As instructed, I clapped my hands to invite the crows to accept the food. It is believed that the departed soul arrives in the form of a crow and partakes the offering. The *bali tharpanam* is considered successful if the crows eat the rice. It is assumed that only if the souls are satisfied with the purity of intention of the person, do they accept the offering, enabling the soul to attain *moksha* or salvation from the eternal cycle of rebirths.

The sky was being painted by the bright orange rays of the sun. I clapped loudly inviting the crows.

There were many birds circling above but none came down. I was worried and looked at Lakshmi. She whispered in her father's ears and he signalled for us to be patient. We waited for what felt like an eternity. The birds who served as proxies for the souls seemed to avoid the offering. I wondered if Maria hadn't forgiven me. Perhaps, I deserved her ire.

Frustration set in and I wanted to turn back but Lakshmi dissuaded me. She wanted to bury Maria's memories in the very sands of the temple. As we waited anxiously, a crow with unusually thick black feathers descended condescendingly and started walking slowly towards us. It looked at me intently as if its small dark eyes were gauging my candour.

It took a few steps slowly towards the rice balls. As I waited with anticipation, it stopped for a few seconds as though it was pondering. Was my mind playing tricks with me? Maybe it wasn't hungry or it didn't like the appearance of the food. Finally, much to our relief, the crow decided to devour the feast laid out. As it started pecking, a few more crows came flying down and the offering vanished quickly into their bellies.

I felt lighter. It was as though a great burden was taken off my heart. This was like a symbolic exorcism of tormenting memories.

The priest too seemed relieved and a smile spread on his erstwhile constipated expression. Lakshmi's father offered some more money to the priest as *dhakshina*. After thanking him, we quietly walked back towards the car. Lakshmi walked close to me and I threw my arms over her shoulder. This was a rare gesture of affection we displayed in front of her parents. Today, I didn't care. I wanted to feel the assurance of her touch.

As we sat in the car, our moods underwent a paradigm shift. As the parents and their daughter started chatting, I lay back on the seat. The traffic was still thin. The car moved ahead with incredible speed. It seemed like an escape from all ordeals.

My calcified belief system had softened a little in the last few months. From an ardent atheist, I was now open to accepting the nuances of religious beliefs. Was I the same person who used to denounce rituals like these as mere psychological dramas? Or was this new garb of spiritualism a mode of escape?

I still retain an otherwise rational mind but I am afraid to question the existence of spiritual beings. What could have caused this change of heart? Contrary to acceptable logic, my mind sometimes interprets last year's events as the outcome of a grand scheme planned by malevolent spirits.

Did they use Maria, Ajay and me as pawns to execute their grandiose strategy? Is that possible? Though I didn't completely accept this, the sequence of events seemed to strongly point towards such a possibility. I wasn't sure if spirits, allegedly a couple centuries old, could harbour and execute revenge with such clinical precision. But then, one could never tell.

As we reached home, Lakshmi suggested that we have breakfast. I desperately wanted sleep and solitude; so I promptly refused despite her insistence. I went upstairs to the bedroom. Lying on the plush bed, I pulled up the comforter to my face. Like a child, I felt a strange sense of security wrapped in it. Unlike last night, I waded into deep sleep soon.

While asleep, I sensed the temperature dropping despite being ensconced in the expensive comforter. I felt a hand touching my face tenderly. This feeling lingered for a few seconds. Fear ran down my spine and cold sweat broke out. I woke up but couldn't move. I wanted to scream but couldn't. I was not sure if I was asleep or awake when all this happened. Was it Maria? Had she come to bid me a final goodbye? A strong sense of anxiety gripped me.

I tried hard to push away the comforter and got up from the bed. The room smelled unmistakably of Maria's perfume. It was strong and overwhelmed me with nostalgia. My mind turned turbulent. I walked across the room trying to rationalise the experience.

Was this her way of assuring me that she did not hold me guilty? Was this experience the result of a collective integration of my grief, despair and anger? Did my mind conjure this up to offer the redemption that I was seeking? Was I deluding myself that Maria was happy and possibly leaving for her abode in heaven? My scepticism was countered by the strong smell of Maria's perfume still permeating the room. Or was that my mind playing tricks with me?

Can dead people roam the terra firma in the form of spirits? Can they haunt and possess human beings in their malevolent form?

Though never empirically proven to exist, human minds continue to believe in such beings. Many people claim to have had the 'experience' I just had. After the 'exposure', different people react differently. While many go back to their normal lives, many others cannot handle such a 'contact' and become a little unhinged psychologically. The irrational side of an otherwise rational human mind can indeed be perplexing!

I heard Lakshmi's soft footsteps as she came up the stairs. The strong feelings that had coiled around me like a constrictor began to loosen. I finally concluded that my mind had been playing tricks with me. Perhaps everything was the result of a tempestuous mind.

Lakshmi walked into the room and her first reaction was, "What is this smell? Like the fading fragrance of a woman's perfume. Smells like Chanel No 5." Her words seemed to confirm my fears. She looked at me. I gathered enough courage to say, "You and your imagination!"

She insisted that I take a hot shower. The ritual bathing on the banks of the river Karamana didn't account for much. Not wanting to be alone in the room, I insisted that she remain there. She said, "Make it fast. Ambika and her family have come for a visit. They are waiting to meet you."

It was then that I became aware of the noise downstairs. I could hear my daughter's laughter and her loud chatter.

I came out of the shower quickly. I noticed Lakshmi sitting on the bed, seemingly pondering the source of the fragrance. I liberally sprayed eau de cologne in an attempt to mask the fragrance and her suspicions.

I asked myself, "After all, who was Maria to me?" The relationship, though fleeting, had been intense. I had even contemplated a divorce with Lakshmi. Had we really been in love or was it just a deep kind of fascination? Or, as the old astrologer in Kannur had claimed, had Maria and I been mates in the previous birth? Were our lives intertwined in some ways? There would be no firm answers.

Joining Maria in her journey into the colourful, mysterious and fiery world of Theyyam had indeed proven to be a turning point in my life. Somehow, I began to feel free of the guilt that had been plaguing me like the proverbial heavy sack of bricks. I felt euphoric.

Ambika and her family were seated around the dining table talking to Lakshmi's parents. The clock indicated that it was way past lunch time. As I joined everyone, Ambika called out to Lakshmi, who was in the kitchen, "Hey I forgot to tell you. Remember I spoke to you about my cousin Malini who was desperate for a child? That she had even attended the Theyyam seeking divine intervention. Her wish was granted and she delivered a baby girl a couple of months ago."

That seemingly casual statement shocked me. Was it my child or did the Theyyam spirits bless Malini with a child? I would never know and that ambiguity was killing. After all, the serpent gods had not been lenient…

kochi

It was the sheer intensity of the bright sunlight that woke me up. It was way past midnight when I had gone to bed. The flight from Dubai had landed at the Kochi International

Airport quite late last night.

As soon as I checked in, out of curiosity, I had opened the heavy curtains that shielded the occupants of the rooms from the outside world.

All I could see were old street lights that unsuccessfully tried to throw light around the buildings across the road. A makeshift cart on the corner was still serving food. Light from a petromax flickered. A couple of SUVs were parked next to it and a small group of young people were having a very late meal. They must have been returning from a party or a movie. Kochi did have a nightlife, though it was restricted to a few affluent pockets. Stray dogs, the nocturnal lords of the roads, were running amok on the empty tar roads. Till the early hours, the roads were their empire. They would fight, mate and play all night but vanish as soon as dawn broke. Tired and sleepy, I turned my gaze away and returned to my secure, cocooned world.

Kochi was my home but I have no place to call my own. As he aged, my father, my *achhan*, became nostalgic about his ancestral home in Palakkad. He decided to settle there, against my protestations. He and my mother, my *amma*, seemed to have decided to spend the rest of their lives around the relatives who lived close by.

Kochi had better medical facilities and *achhan*'s old friends also lived in and around the area. Thus, in my opinion, Kochi would have been a better city for them to retire to but then they didn't listen to me. I felt hurt that they treated me as a kid with no worldly exposure. I had invested a considerable amount of money in renovating our old house. I wanted my daughter to spend her vacations there. But since they knew that I wouldn't agree, they did not inform me when they sold the house. It hurt me a lot. Since every call with *amma* ended in arguments regarding the relocation, I stopped the regular calls. It was Lakshmi who kept the communication going. I hadn't visited my parents for quite some time. An invisible iron curtain had descended between the parents and their child. I felt homeless. Kochi held so many memories of growing-up. I could never feel the same sense of longing with Palakkad. This was also the reason why I did not inform my parents that I would be in Kerala. Things had changed so much.

As I agonised, I had forgotten to close the curtains.

As soon as I woke up, almost instinctively I called room service for a pot of hot and strong tea. Bed-tea was my bad habit. Lakshmi had tried to wean me away from this, but old habits die hard. Though feeling lazy, I had to reluctantly get out of bed to close the curtains. The soft knock on the door indicated that my fix had arrived. When I opened the door, a well-dressed young waiter greeted me and walked in.

He made tea with no sense of urgency. The strong aroma of the fresh beverage made me impatient. He confidently interacted with me in reasonably flawless English. Before leaving, he said, "Have a great day ahead, sir!" The hospitality industry in Kochi was adapting to international standards quickly. I felt happy. I sank into the plush chair with the cup of tea.

Lakshmi had spent a lot of time choosing the right hotel for me. She could be very fussy when she wanted to. Her firm belief that I was incapable of being independent and was reliant on her for nourishment, advice and almost everything else, gave her a sense of security and importance. While it unburdened me from the nitty-gritties of life, it could also be stifling at times. She would often ask, "What will you do without me around? Can you live by yourself?" I would put on a naughty expression and reply convincingly, "You are my only addiction, darling! You are like a drug that I don't want to be weaned away from." That would make her happy. Very happy, though she would never admit to it.

I was 37 years old and she was just two years younger than me. Yet, she behaved like she had seen more life than me. Over a period of time, I learnt the hard and valuable lesson that as long as she was happy, it was easy to manipulate her. Need for praise was her Achilles heel. However, she seemed to be totally oblivious to this chink in her otherwise impregnable armour.

Ignoring my desire to stay in one of the heritage properties, Lakshmi had chosen a new five-star hotel right in the heart of the city. Though I had protested, as usual it was her wish that had prevailed. I had a penchant for history while Lakshmi loved the contemporary. In many ways, ours was a marriage of amicable contrasts.

I didn't have reasons to complain though. The hotel was managed by an international hospitality brand and was quite popular with the affluent western tourists. The young owners of the property were from an old aristocratic family known for its wealth and political influence. They had spent lavishly in creating tasteful interiors that highlighted the culture of Kerala.

The room was spacious, complimented by a king-size bed, fluffy pillows, and clean white bed linen. At home, I discouraged using white bed sheets or pillow covers as I was constantly worried about them getting dirty. On the contrary, I was allured by white apparel. I loved women in white as I associated it with sensual elegance.

The walls were painted in light green pastels; a few photographs were mounted on them symmetrically. Right across the wall, there were four large photographs that depicted the iconic Chinese nets, shot at different times of the day. These simple mechanical contraptions hold large horizontal nets. They use the cantilever technique with large stones tied with ropes as counterweights. The hurricane lamp suspended in the middle serves as a bait for the fish. The net is lowered periodically into the water and then lifted back. The unfortunate victims, oblivious to the trap in their own backyard, end up on the dining tables by the next day. They never even get a chance to regret their folly and none can ever back to warn their friends about the entrapment. So, even centuries after their arrival, the Chinese nets continue to be a successful fishing mechanism in Kochi. Its design seems to have withstood the vagaries of time. Just like the stories of Kerala.

The furniture in the room, including the tables, chairs and lamps, were from the colonial era. They were possibly sourced from one of the big antique warehouses located at the famous Jew Street. Refurbished with modern embellishments such as silk linen covers, these pieces from another era had been granted a new lease of life.

Just a couple of decades ago, Kochi had only a handful of star-rated hotels. Most of them were in and around the man-made Willingdon Island catering to mostly western businessmen and local elites. Over the last few decades, the muscular forces of financial prosperity and its intimate soulmate, social change, have been reshaping Kochi. Global brands have set-up their offices here, signalling her brave new global aspirations.

Slick marketing campaigns and roadshows by the Government of Kerala have made the state one of the most sought-after tourist destinations globally. Its clean beaches, green paddy fields, emerald backwaters, hill stations, forests, exotic wildlife, and rich folklore have been showcased to attract the well-heeled tourists. Ayurveda, the indigenous medical science of wellness and longevity, has become a prime attraction. The well-connected, urbanised Kochi gets her fair share of income from tourist dollars. Even historic buildings are being rapidly converted into heritage hotels and art galleries.

Called the Queen of the Arabian Sea, Kochi is mainly known for her deep ports, the Indian naval base, shipyard, and seafood exports. Coastal Kochi is dotted with factories that employ thousands of women, whose nimble fingers clean prawns for export. These prawns have created many millionaires. These exporters, with their large houses and imported fancy cars, form the business elite who influence the politics of the state. For people from the other parts of Kerala, Kochi is still the veritable land of opportunities.

It is IT outsourcing and software production that largely fuels contemporary Kochi, ensuring a steady stream of well-paid jobs. The money in Kochi is slowly acquiring a refined hue. It is one of the most happening places in India. As the inhabitants of Kochi, we were treated differently when we visited our relatives during vacations.

The low hum of the air-conditioner sounded like a lullaby urging me to return to sleep. I looked at the clock on the side table. It was 10.40 a.m. Gosh, it must be 9.10 a.m. in Dubai, I thought. Lakshmi must be wondering why I had not called her. Inarguably, she was the lord of the household. Despite being far away, I was still afraid of her wrath.

I have asked this question to myself many times. Despite being a go-getter and self-starter, why did I let her dictate my life? I don't think I ever found an answer.

I restricted my involvement to the most critical decisions and did not interfere in routine issues. She ran the household like clockwork.

There were many strong-willed women in my family who had to struggle against many adversities. Sometimes they lost, sometimes they won. But they always put up a strong fight. Having been used to strong females in the family, I didn't find Lakshmi's dominant personality to be odd. Deep inside, like other alpha men, I secretly liked the presence of a strong and independent person as my spouse. I pampered her with my psychological dependence. I didn't want a passive wife and she didn't want a domineering husband. In a Faustian bargain, she enjoyed the feeling of power and

I the resultant intimacy. It was a wish fulfilment akin to the Oedipus complex.

Lakshmi had been an entirely different person when we were courting. She loved listening to my past stories and current adventures. As she egged me for more details, I would sometimes make up stories to satiate her curiosity. I used to call her late in the nights after getting drunk and she would laugh at my naughty jokes. She had told me that she liked my playfulness and childlike demeanour. But, gradually, after our marriage, her matronly behaviour became pronounced and she seldom encouraged my playfulness. Maybe I too played a role in that transformation. In our transactions, she upgraded to the parent-ego state and I got down-graded to the child-ego state. But these quickly reversed when I lost my temper. Her ability to switch ego-states was possibly her greatest strength. She is a control freak who carefully disguises her needs under the garb of caring and affection. She loves to dispense tough love in a seemingly restrained manner.

She wanted to know where I was at regular intervals. Yesterday, I had called her as soon as I reached the airport, after I cleared security check, before boarding the aircraft from Dubai, and after landing at the Kochi airport yesterday.

Today being a Thursday and a weekend in Dubai, she must be sleeping late, hugging Meenakshi, our 12-year-old daughter. We call her Meenu at home. The choice of her name drew loud protests from Lakshmi's parents and other relatives. They felt that it was old fashioned. I liked the way it sounded and, therefore, remained adamant about it.

Meenakshi means 'the one with the eyes of the fish'. Lakshmi astutely kept away from the battle as we had a deal that I would choose the name if it was a girl and she if it was a boy. To sweeten the deal, I had also promised her a solitaire ring if blessed with a girl.

As she was being taken to the ward after giving birth, despite being very tired, Lakshmi indicated to me by touching her fingers that she hadn't forgotten my promise. Well, she had literally delivered hers. So, I had no reason to argue and got her a solitaire ring from the Tiffany & Co. outlet at the Deira City Center. I didn't hesitate to bargain despite the sales manager giving me a penetrating dirty look. I am sure sales managers were trained to sport that look but I pretended not to notice. Grudgingly, he agreed to a small discount.

I am a non-conformist among men in my love for shopping for jewellery, especially the exotic variety. Though I personally dislike wearing any, including my engagement ring, I liked to see it on Lakshmi. I make it a point to pick up jewellery for her from the countries that I travel to. Perhaps, this is my way of imposing my choices on her.

I have a fetish for nose rings. I had tried for almost two years to convince her to get her nose pierced. She had steadfastly refused, till one lazy weekend. Out of the blue she said that she wanted to get her nose pierced. I was surprised and asked her a couple of times, "Are you sure about this, Lakshmi?" She answered in the affirmative. She seemed to have made up her mind, possibly realising that this would give her another lever of control over me.

We drove to the iconic Gold Souk. She took her time choosing the nose ring at a reputed jewellery store. The manager of the outlet took us to the backrooms. The goldsmith suggested that we use a piercing gun that would be less painful but, she wanted the piercing to be done the traditional way using a gold needle. I looked at Lakshmi as he again warned us that it would be quite painful. She sat there with a determined look on her face. I couldn't bear to see her undergo pain. So I left the room. I personally have a low-threshold for physical pain.

She didn't scream or cry. As Lakshmi came out, my first reaction was to hold her hands and look at her nose. It was red. She simply raised her hand indicating to me to not ask anything. The look on her face was quizzical as if to say, "What all should I do for you?"

Her body language suggested that she definitely wanted me to know how miserable she felt and how much pain she had undergone to fulfil my fetish. She put on her classic 'I am the martyr' look. As we walked outside of the large bazaar, she held my hands and walked very close to me. She doesn't do this often. I suggested dinner and a late night movie. Unlike her usual self, she wanted to have a quick dinner and return home. She was unusually quiet.

After reaching home, Lakshmi freshened herself, changed into lingerie, and walked into the bedroom. I stood in the drawing room for a few moments not knowing what to do. Following my instinct, I went to the room. She had switched off the light and was lying on her back. As she saw me coming in, she slowly and deliberately opened the window curtains to let the pale moonlight in. The nose ring made her look like a temptress as the little diamonds caught the light and sparkled naughtily. She offered me her hand inviting me to join her and huskily said, "No condom tonight." I could feel the tremble in my body. The faint smell of her sweat mingled with her perfume was always the libido trigger for me. She pulled me towards her. As my hands caressed her body and moved towards her waist, she kissed me. She seemed to be in the heat.

We skipped the customary long foreplay. Her active participation drove me into ecstasy. She was unrestrained and surprisingly rough. She responded positively to my gentle bites around her nipples. In between, she wickedly whispered, "Are you on steroids tonight?" I replied, "Yeah, you." I think those words excited her more. For me, the feel of natural lubrication without the hindrance of latex was indeed a new experience. She seemed intoxicated and insatiable. We had sex three times that night.

The next morning, we woke up late and went out to a nearby restaurant for a leisurely brunch. She was unlike her usual self. She wanted to finish eating and return home. She walked with her hand around my waist. I could feel her hard nipples brushing the back of my arm. Maybe she did this deliberately. She continued to be in a state of arousal. We made love twice that afternoon. Though gentler than the previous night, it was equally exciting. We went to bed early that night, clearly exhausted from the carnal overload. We continued to have a healthy sex life but nothing matched the hunger and vigour of that weekend.

Both of us were under constant pressure from our parents to have a child. But we wanted to wait till Lakshmi's career as a clinical psychologist was established. As months went by, her parents became more impatient. They would often emotionally blackmail her saying, "So you want us old people to die without seeing our grandchild?" It was when she announced her pregnancy that I realised she was already planning a baby. So, had she faked her desire that weekend? I don't know. Perhaps it was the urgent and innate need to be pregnant that had played havoc with her hormones and behaviour.

Despite her confidence, Lakshmi had her insecurities about the fact that I worked closely with many beautiful and ambitious women. She didn't feel as beautiful or smart as them. As I travelled frequently on work, she secretly worried that my sex drive would weaken my resolve to be loyal. She aspired to be my only source of excitement and obsession. She loved the feeling of being my sole fixation, the erotic goddess who demanded constant propitiation in return for ecstatic pleasure. She was possessive as far as I was concerned. I thought she was like the woman in Billy Joel's number 'She's always a woman to me'.

The phone rang. It woke me up rudely from my train of thoughts. As expected, it was Lakshmi. I didn't answer it. The phone continued to ring. Then there was abrupt silence. After a couple of minutes, it rang again and I thought it prudent to attend to her call.

"Why did you not pick up my call?" There was a mix of worry and anger in her voice.
"I was in the washroom," I lied.
"So, tell me how is the hotel and how did your day go?" She wanted all the details.
"It's a great hotel. I woke up late and just had my tea. Nothing much has happened to report, madam."
She was offended. I wanted to tell her to leave me alone but just couldn't. So I asked, "How's Meenu?"
"She's still sleeping. Did you have your breakfast?" She was still curious.

"No. Not yet." Despite my rising anger, I said this gently.

"Go have your breakfast. It is already late." I didn't like her guiding my life like a remote control even as I was seeking liberty, albeit temporarily. For a change, I wanted to decide what I did.

"Okay. I will call you back at night," I replied and cut the call.

"Control freak!" I murmured to myself. As a sign of rebellion, I decided to skip breakfast. How would she know? I reasoned to myself.

I walked towards the large windows. They were my insulated gateways to the world outside, the world of the hoi polloi...the crowd I belonged to a few years ago. I cringed as I admitted to that. Kochi treated me differently now and I viewed her differently. I felt a cruel satisfaction as I now viewed the outside world as one of the 'ordinary folks'.

The arterial road and the battered bus stop looked as though they had been victims of the alternating twin forces of scorching sun and hard rains. The road had a fair amount of traffic. The large red local buses that looked like old boxes stopped very briefly at the stop and rushed out again in search of new passengers.

People patiently waited for the bus. Those standing outside the confines of the bus stop used umbrellas to protect themselves from the harsh sun. We Malayalis have an innate desire for fair skin and live in mortal fear of melanin. My tanned complexion was often a subject of ridicule even within the extended family. Fairer cousins were considered more attractive. When young, I have liberally used various fairness creams in an attempt to whiten my skin. Keralites are arguably one of the biggest consumers of such creams even today. These days many brands are marketed as Ayurvedic or herbal medicines claiming to have no side effects. The only side effect seems to be loss of money. What other results can we expect? I thought. In a land of the scorching sun, it is but natural that melanin remains the persistent villain.

This infatuation for fair skin is only matched by

the adoration for gold. Many women waiting for their buses were wearing several pieces of gold jewellery. The Malayali woman's love for 22k gold jewellery and silk saris are stuff of lore.

Auto rickshaws, cars and motor cycles zipped past. Most scooter and motorcycle riders were not wearing helmets. Despite constant attempts by the traffic police to enforce its use, helmets are universally abhorred here. The lame excuses are many. Some complain of the heat and others about hair loss. They never understood the logic that it was better to have a bald head than not have one at all.

I had to cut my rebellion short as my stomach declared war. I called the reception and the person at the desk, in an unusually cheerful voice, informed me that I had missed the complimentary breakfast. It seemed to me that he was secretly enjoying denying me what he thought was a rare experience, as it might be for a lot of the 'ordinary' travellers. Presumptuous idiot, I thought. He had no clue that I was a globe-trotter. With a smirk on my face, I simply ordered a Spanish omelette and toast. I think I was able to convey the order rather rudely.

I was famished as I had not had a proper meal since lunch yesterday. On top of the two drinks that I had at the Dubai International Airport, I had also gracefully accepted two large pegs of single malt the airhostess had served in the business class. The alcohol overdose had lulled me into deep sleep and I missed the sumptuous dinner served in the sky.

Though I wasn't a big drinker, I did enjoy my tipple on the weekends. Lakshmi had an alcohol phobia as one of her close cousins had died due to alcoholism. On weekends, to discourage me from visiting friends and risk getting drunk, she permitted me to drink at home. The rule was that she fixed the drinks. Her leniency did not extend beyond two small pegs. She would dutifully measure the whisky and turn a deaf ear to my complaints that the drink contained more ice and soda than scotch. My frequent travels abroad gave me the opportunity to breach the liquor limits. More than the alcohol, it was the mutiny that gave me a high.

While waiting for breakfast to arrive, I started unpacking my favourite leather duffel. Lakshmi's packing unravelled itself. I knew exactly where each item was. Though I was the frequent flyer, she was always the one who planned and packed my bags. I had one less complicated task to do.

Among the multiple roles she donned, packing was a prominent one. Each of the roles would come to the forefront based on circumstances. I would often taunt her saying that she had a multiple personality disorder. She hated that. If she missed packing something, it was still my fault. Didn't the great man Darwin once say, "It is not the strongest of the species, nor the most intelligent that survives but it is the one that is most adaptable to change?" So, I adapted. I learnt to praise all her skills, including that of packing.

Despite my protests that good hotels always provide fresh towels and toiletries, Lakshmi insisted on packing them along with spare clothes, as part of her imaginary contingency plan. Inevitably, I always ended up lugging heavy luggage across airports. Like an undesired continuum, Lakshmi seemed to have shades of my mother in her. She seemed to have the very attributes that I hated in my mother.

meeting lakshmi

Lakshmi was the only daughter of a very successful businessman. A former expatriate, the old man had earned his fortune by working in various cities in the Middle East. He had been in the region at the right time – the time of the oil boom. The Nairs were an old, well-known and prosperous family who had lived in Thiruvananthapuram for many generations.

In comparison, *achhan* was a military officer. I grew up in a salaried household and it was only after moving to Dubai that I saw serious money. Apart from the financial polarity, Lakshmi also belonged to a caste higher than mine. Overall, the social differences between us were vast and could have been intimidating.

It was *achhan*'s closest friend, uncle Murali, who had broached the subject of an alliance with the Nair family. *Achhan* was worried about the dynamics of marriage with a family which belonged to a higher caste and was extremely rich. Uncle Murali knew the Nair family well and tried to allay his fears. He said that time had ironed out the wrinkles of the caste system, especially among the upwardly mobile families. He also thought that though we were a step below the Nairs in the caste hierarchy, we had an aristocratic background to boast of. Uncle Murali was very confident that the Nairs would find my professional status acceptable. It was *amma* who finally convinced *achhan*. Uncle Murali sent my profile to the Nairs who in turn invited us for a formal visit.

When *amma* spoke to me about Lakshmi over the phone, I was not keen at all. I was not ready to settle down. Not yet, anyway. Nevertheless, she was trying hard to sell me the idea. As part of her sales pitch, *amma* told me that the girl was a very socially active person, a member of many prestigious clubs and that she was an acclaimed performer of the classical dance of Bharathanatyam.

Despite my reluctance, I agreed to meet the Nair family out of sheer curiosity. I had never met a prospective bride before and I thought it would be fun. Since I did not take this visit seriously, I hadn't even bothered to ask for a photograph of the woman. Despite no intentions of marrying, there was a sense of curiosity building inside me to meet the woman who could potentially be my bride. This meeting had a seductive umbra to it. I did nevertheless mentally prepare the script of a small talk designed to overwhelm the person. Sometimes I think like a typical male chauvinistic pig! I wanted to see adoration on that person's face.

I told my friends about this meeting and they goaded me to approach this little more seriously. After all, what if I ended up liking the girl?

"I have seen really beautiful women and none of them could trigger thoughts of marriage in me. At least not yet." I had poured water on their hopes that I would, like most of them, finally settle down. They didn't seem to like me enjoying my bachelor life. Only Ajay was excited beyond any plausible reason. He was the only one who wanted to accompany me.

As per the custom in Kerala, we went to the Nairs' house to meet the prospective bride and her family. We had started quite early from Kochi to reach Thiruvananthapuram at around 9 a.m. As we drove into the courtyard of the mansion, I saw many high-end luxury cars parked neatly. The portico was brimming with well-dressed people. The large house was situated in the midst of a property spread over almost two hectares.

The garden in front was neatly manicured. Flowers of many hues danced gently in the breeze, as if welcoming us. The house was perhaps a century old and had been extensively renovated, retaining the core Keralite architectural features. The old roof tiles that seemed to spread over a large area amplified its grandeur. Several members of the Nair joint family had grown up here. The current patriarch of the family, Mr Nair, Lakshmi's father, had inherited the house along with its memories and legacy. It was indeed an inspiring monumental structure.

As we alighted from the car, the parents of the 'girl' walked down to receive us. They looked good together. Mr Nair was a tall, rotund man, about 65 years old, with a large belly and a little white hair on his otherwise bald pate. His hair looked like well-manicured shrubs to me. He had intelligent eyes and appeared affluent. Sporting a wide smile, he shook hands with *achhan* first and then me. His grip was firm and warm. His thick gold framed spectacles gave him the look of an academician. One couldn't miss the gold Rolex on his wrist.

Mrs Nair was a short and portly woman, about 55 years old. Her hair was dyed jet black. The thin frame of her spectacles were also made of gold and her watch was the identical, women's version of her husband's Rolex. The antique necklace that adorned her neck, a couple of diamond studded bangles on her left hands and the diamond earrings whispered gently of elegance. She wore an expensive silk saree, of a subdued yellow, that seemed to have been custom-made. She also wore high heels that made her look taller. They appeared to be a sophisticated couple used to high society who didn't have to put much effort to project their wealth and prominence. As she greeted *amma*, she put on her carefully cultivated sophisticated smile.

We were escorted inside. Once seated, the elders began unabashedly shooting questions at me about my job, salary and career prospects. I felt as if I was being grilled for a senior position in a large firm. I could gather from the conversation that most of these men had returned home after long stints abroad. They had all made fortunes and lived well here. Lakshmi was the youngest unmarried girl of her generation in the family. Most of her cousins, though younger, than her had been married to expatriates and lived abroad. I noticed the women, both young and old, peering at me from the room inside. They seemed to be assessing my 'worthiness'. I felt very conscious of being the centre of so much attention. A strong urge to run away was building inside me.

As the conversation got more serious, a few young girls trooped in giggling. They were carrying plates stacked with sweets and savouries. They were placed on a large, carved, teak coffee table before us. In a minute or so, Lakshmi walked in with a tray of tea served in finely crafted cups and saucers. She was wearing a bright red silk sari, some jewellery, and lots of jasmine flowers on her hair. She extended the tray to my family first and everyone took their cups. When my chance came, I saw her gazing directly at me. She didn't appear bashful. I turned my gaze away as I picked my cup.

There was something about her that was very attractive. Something stirred in me and suddenly I was not averse to marriage anymore. She stood for a minute or two and then returned inside. Ajay was sitting beside me and ogling at the women. Before giving in to his insistence of accompanying me, I had warned him exactly to not do that. I should have known. He came closer to me and whispered, "She's an attractive girl." I felt like shouting back at him as I had started feeling the same about Lakshmi.

The elders suggested that we spend some time in private to get to 'know' each other. A little girl escorted me to Lakshmi's room on the first floor. As we passed the drawing room, the interiors caught my eye. They were embellished with massive elephant tusks that had yellowed with age and sported fine cracks. Mounted on the walls were horns of wild buffalos and large antlers. In the centre was a mounted double barrel gun. The echoes of a glorious past resonated all over the house. This building reeked of old money, aristocratic wealth, and social influence.

Lakshmi's room was large and it was obvious that her father had spared no money to create a customised bedroom for his only daughter. The large cot, chairs and table were hand-carved from Burma teak. The bed was covered in a silk bedcover and the colourful pillows were neatly laid out. There was a shelf containing all the trophies and medals that she had perhaps won in various competitions. A collage of her photographs was mounted on the wall. The room smelled of perfume. There was nobody in the room.

I could see the greenery outside the window. Many fruit-bearing trees such as jackfruit, mango, guava, sapodilla, custard apple and papaya swayed gently with pride. The quintessential coconut trees were many in number. It was a beautifully tended orchard - like some secret garden!

Lakshmi walked in gently and sat on the bed. Her thick hair was a rich shade of mahogany with interrupting golden streaks. Full lips and a slightly long nose complimented her round face. The eyebrows were well crafted and she wore minimal make-up. She was a little on the plumper side and of average height. She had a wheat-ish complexion and clear skin. But it was her eyes that caught my attention – the expressive large black eyes lined with kohl seemed to hide more than they revealed. Though not a stunner, there was something magnetic about her. She came across to me as part-siren, part-enchantress.

When I didn't say anything for a minute or so, she asked me, "Haven't you ever spoken to a woman before?" She was playfully taunting me. "I work with many women. But none of them are my prospective brides," I said.

"You seem to be very shy," she exclaimed.

I realised that Lakshmi was not the person who will be impressed by the content of the pitch that I had prepared. She didn't seem to be the kind who could be easily impressed. I felt tongue-tied. So, this brief yet splendid isolation with her did not turn out the way I thought it would.

I mumbled back. "I take time to open up." I got that awful shrinking feeling. It made me a little defensive as I couldn't improvise on my script to suit these changed circumstances. I couldn't adapt quick enough.

After about 30 seconds, she again took the initiative and asked me, with a smile. "So, do you want to ask me something?" It was a good ice-breaker but I was still tongue-tied. Evidently the victim of performance anxiety, I just shook my head. She looked at me straight in the eyes as if assessing me. I didn't respond. There was a smile playing on her lips. She said, "Okay, then let's go." It had a tone of finality. Then it dawned on me that this meeting had been an utter disaster.

As we went out, I desperately wished for a second chance. A strong desire for her was slowly building inside me. Lakshmi wasn't the average woman and seemed clear about what she wanted. I thought she had rejected me without giving me a fair chance. She appeared to have taken this meeting casually. Or at least that is how she made me feel. I did not know if it was her casual confidence or her good looks that drew me to her. Just like I had felt few days ago, Lakshmi too didn't seem keen to get married. A kind of role-reversal. It was at that moment I decided that I did not want to visit the house of another eligible girl.

However, I had lost the game. It hurt hard because this was the second time my lack of confidence had come in the way of love. Radha. After many years, my thoughts went back in time.

I walked back dejected. Ajay was chatting away with the elders. He looked at me in a quizzical manner. The look was meant to ask, "How did the meeting go? Hope you did not fall for her and decide to get married?" I didn't oblige him as I was ashamed of my performance. Knowing that he was dying to know what transpired in that room, I kept him waiting deliberately.

After sometime, the women joined us. Lakshmi and her mother were among them. *Amma* was in a particularly chatty mood. Lakshmi intently listened to her and laughed at her light-hearted remarks. She didn't forget to playfully warn Lakshmi that I was a particularly difficult man to handle. She advised her to make a decision after careful consideration. We all laughed. Lakshmi kept throwing glances at me. Her smile still perplexed me. Her face didn't reveal much. After further pleasantries, we took leave. While Lakshmi stayed back, her parents escorted us out and bid us goodbye. Her parents seemed happy about the alliance but it was also clear that the ultimate decision-maker was their daughter. I hoped against hope.

As soon as our car entered the main road, *amma* asked me if I liked the girl. I thought a bit and said softly, "Kind of." She sounded worried and asked, "Why, what happened?" I just said, "Nothing. Let's wait for their response." Convinced that I would be rejected, I was frantically searching for a face-saving reply for Ajay and other friends. We had been at Lakshmi's house for barely an hour and yet it seemed to me that the impact would last a lifetime.

Being a Sunday, the national highway had thin traffic. The driver treated the road like a racing track. We reached home around 2 p.m. After reaching home, Ajay insisted that we go out for lunch. Reluctantly I got into his car. Rejection, my biggest fear, began to haunt me and Ajay generously let me wallow in my sorrow. He drove the car in utter silence except when he screamed obscenities at other drivers who got in his way slowing his journey.

Ajay stopped at a hotel, a 19th century boatyard, whose building sported a combination of Victorian and traditional Keralite architecture. An unusually large anchor, strategically placed on its lawns to impress people, served as a reminder of its colonial past. The view of the sea from the restaurant was stunning.

I was not aware that Ajay had called some of our old classmates for lunch. As we walked in, I saw Unni, Suraj and Basil waiting for us. I stared at Ajay. I realised that he had planned this well in advance. "Rascal," I muttered, shaking my head slightly in resignation. I could anticipate how this meeting would go.

As the only one in the group who worked abroad, I had to bankroll get-togethers at expensive restaurants. My friends had their excuse ready; "For you, is money a problem? Don't you earn in foreign currency? That too without paying taxes." I would tell them, "Wish all that money grew on date palms and I could just gather what I wanted. I have to earn every dirham."

As we settled down, Ajay couldn't contain his curiosity anymore. He asked me, "So, what did she say?" My embarrassment returned in full force. I wanted to weave a fantastic story but I couldn't come up with a believable one in such a short time. The image of Lakshmi walking out wouldn't leave my mind. Ever since we left her house, I desperately wanted to make amends.

Despite choosing my words carefully, I ended up telling them the truth. Perhaps they were waiting to hear something like this, as they all burst out laughing once I finished. The patrons of the hotel, both the locals and the foreigners, turned and looked at us. They must have thought that we were rowdies from well-to-do families. Despite the provocation, I refrained from reacting.

"Can we order some beer?" Ajay stopped laughing and asked me. Without waiting for an affirmative reaction, he waved to the waiter. After ordering beer and some expensive appetisers, he asked me once more, "So, you didn't utter a word?" He started laughing again. That hurt and I shot back, "What would you have done?"

He said, "She is indeed beautiful. I would have introduced myself, asked her to say something about herself and then told her impressive tales. Then gently hold her hands, looked into her eyes, and complimented her looks. Women love flattery." Though he was mocking me, he was also conveying his superior ability to connect with women.

"What makes you think that she would have let you hold her hands?" I asked. As I visualised Ajay's description, I became angry. "C'mon, buddy. You know me. I am irresistible and a natural charmer. There is no woman who can say no to me." He looked at me intently as if he was searching for something. Then he said, "If I were in your place, I would not have let gone of this opportunity." He continued, "Now that you have screwed it up, I will reach out to her. I know where she works. I hope you don't have a problem with that."

There was a sense of relief in his voice. He had a knack of reaching out to women. This conversation made me uneasy. Actually, I was a little afraid. I had noticed him looking at Lakshmi with interest as she served us tea. Ajay and I were the same age. He was one of my oldest and trusted friends but today he was driving me into panic and insecurity. Sometimes he didn't know where to draw the line. Tension was slowly building up.

The bearer came with two large pitchers of ice-cold beer. He was dressed in colonial uniform like his counterparts from many decades ago when the British still ruled the country. Behaving like what he believed an English butler would, he poured the beer into large mugs in a studious manner. His mannerisms were as exaggerated as his walrus moustache. He served us lightly spiced fried cashew nuts in a small ceramic bowl that was much older than him.

All of us raised a toast to our enduring friendship and sipped the full-bodied beer. Ajay finished his beer bottoms-up as though he had not touched alcohol in a long time. I felt disgusted. Everything he did today was irritating me.

It was Basil who changed the subject. He talked about the wedding of one of our old schoolmates, Veni, recently.

Veni was the fairest and smartest girl in our class. Every boy in class was secretly in love with her. She knew it but never acknowledged that. She didn't speak much to us boys but when she spoke to any of us, it was regarding academics. The boy with whom she spoke would end up besotted and the others would feel deceived. She knew how to play her cards and to enjoy mass adulation.

Among all the boys, Unni was the one who adored her the most. He almost worshipped her but couldn't gather enough courage to convey his love to her. He always harboured an inferiority complex due to his lower middle class background. He would often discuss his desire to marry her and raise a family with her, in graphic detail. He would tell us confidently that someday he would become very rich and then propose to her. Somehow he was fixated with the idea that pretty girls always seek only those who are very rich.

Once school was over, most of us joined colleges in different places. Unni couldn't continue his studies as his father passed away. He had to manage his father's pharmacy. As his friends studied, he struggled in a shop full of medicines finding no remedy for his predicament. Many years passed and Unni still remained within the confines of his shop.

It was purely by chance that he met Veni at a friend's wedding. This was last year. She had completed MBBS and trying for post-graduation. It was she who had initiated a conversation. He was pleasantly surprised that she was still single. They kept in touch and, over a period of time, he finally managed to convey his love to her. She surprised him by reciprocating his feelings. After a few months of courtship, they decided to take the relationship to the next level.

Veni's father strongly opposed the marriage proposal. He wanted her to settle down with a well-qualified professional from the medical domain. She had managed to get a seat for Masters in a medical college located in Bangalore. Her relationship with Unni prompted her father to start seeking 'suitable' alliances. He wanted her to get married while continuing her studies. He wasn't willing to wait. Time was not on the side of the lovers.

Veni conveyed her desperation to Unni who didn't know what to do. She suggested that they get married secretly. Once the marriage was officially registered, her father would have no choice but accept Unni as his son-in-law. Unni wasn't ready for that as he felt that there was stigma to marriages like these.

He had a younger sister and was worried that such an act would affect her marriage prospects adversely. He was clearly caught between the proverbial devil and the sea. He had to choose one and time was clearly running out. Unni could not take a decision in favour of marrying the woman he had longed for all his life. Veni was very upset and cursed him. "Why did you reveal your love to me if you didn't have the spine to marry me against my father's wishes? Like your sister, am I not a woman? What about me?" She stopped short of spitting on his face.

Last month, she got married to a diamond merchant and relocated to Amsterdam. Unni was also invited to the wedding. He actually attended it, thus becoming the subject of ridicule among his friends and accomplices.

At this point, Unni's eyes turned moist. The others hugged and consoled him and, at my expense, ordered more beer and food to celebrate his continued bachelorhood. I was the only one who was still angry with him for not marrying Veni.

I already knew what it was to lose the person whom one loved dearly. I remembered Radha and my almost obsessive love for her. Didn't I behave like Unni then? And now Lakshmi, whom I lost as I couldn't even talk to her properly. Despite Unni being a good friend of mine, my sympathies lay with Veni rather than him. I couldn't understand Unni's decision of not marrying a woman who was willing to go to extremes just to be his wife. How would him marrying Veni against her father's wishes affect the chances of his sister's marriage? It didn't make sense to me.

Friends of mine didn't give me any time to think over this. They prompted me to drink more beer and my anger was slowly diluted by alcohol.

We made a lot of noise as we discussed our school days. It was almost 5 p.m. by the time we finished. As expected, I paid the hefty bill. All of them were thoroughly drunk. I took a taxi and returned home.

I was surprised to see that Uncle Murali was at home sipping tea. After greeting everybody, I walked towards my room quietly as I was drunk. I also wanted to avoid hearing the news that I had been rejected by Lakshmi. It was *amma* who called me from behind and said, "By the way, they liked you. We are meeting the astrologer to choose an auspicious day for the engagement." I didn't stop though my heart seemed to skip a beat. I pretended that I had not heard her. They all laughed.

They knew.

My room was my greatest sanctuary. As the news sunk in, I jumped up and down like a boy. It felt like I finally accomplished something I could be proud of;

it meant something, it felt real. It felt like the balm I was desperately seeking for the seething pain that I had hidden in the corner of my heart. Radha's marriage was something that I had not completely reconciled with, until now.

Once I settled down, my insecurities took over. Was I good enough for a person like Lakshmi? Would I be able to live up to her expectations? Did she really like me? She seemed quite ambitious. Her eyes…they were hauntingly beautiful and heavy with expectations. What drove her decision to agree to marry me? Was it because she actually liked me or was it her ambition to settle abroad like her cousins?

She was an extrovert and liked to socialise. I was the opposite. I had grown up in a middle class family whereas she was born with a silver spoon in her mouth. My inferiority complex raised its hood and struck me repeatedly. Its sharp fangs dug deep. The venom of inadequacy can indeed cause long-term damage. My mind became a battleground of powerful, contradictory forces.

A strange longing for Lakshmi started building up. This feeling was not just sensuous in nature but it was something far more cavernous. It was like an intuitive feeling of predestination. Was it destiny that we meet and live together? I badly wanted to talk to her.

I continued to sit in the room fighting my mental demons when *amma* called out for me. It was time for dinner. As I went out she complained, "Why are you behaving like a heartbroken girl? What were you doing in the room alone?" I didn't answer her question but gently asked her, "*Amma*, I need to talk to Lakshmi. Can you get me her number?" She looked at me with a steady gaze for a second or two and then walked back into the kitchen. She didn't respond.

I sat on the dining table where *achhan* was having his customary drink. I heard my mother talk on her phone but I couldn't hear her clearly. After we finished dinner, *achhan* went to the veranda for his regular stroll.

Achhan was a disciplinarian and an old school soldier who frowned upon any exhibition of emotions. While my parents went everywhere together, rarely have I seen delicate moments between them. He loved both of us dearly but refrained from letting us know that.

Amma had had romantic notions about marrying a soldier. She was a die-hard romantic but *achhan* never responded in that way. Though he never shouted at us or hit us, his word was the final one. He never asked or consulted *amma* for her opinion. Frustrated with dealing with a seemingly unfeeling man, *amma* suffered from mood swings. Though she was a very affectionate woman, at times she would get very angry and beat me or shout at me. She could be unpredictable.

Despite all this, I was very close to *amma* and she found an emotional anchor in me. For a child who did not make friends easily, she became my friend, confidante and protector. I thought she could do anything. She was the only superwoman I knew.

When I grew up, I took the responsibility of driving her to temples, her friend's home, weddings and other social functions. Once when I was stricken with chicken pox, she stayed close to me for days together despite the risk of infection. She was afraid of losing me. When I began making friends, she encouraged me to spend time with my friends but I was always around when she was unwell or needed me. I was her son, brother and friend all rolled into one. She never realised that I had grown up and become independent. She always believed that I needed somebody like her to look after me. According to her, I was an extremely dependent person. When I relocated to Dubai, she was heartbroken. But she never discouraged me and I made it a point to call her regularly and come home twice a year on short vacations.

As he aged, *achhan* became a milder man. He spoke to both of us and sought *amma*'s opinion on anything and everything. There was increasing intimacy between the two. They would talk to each other for hours at end. As *achhan* rightfully took over the role of being her emotional crutch, my absence hurt her less. But she remained possessive about me. Ours was an old bond and she was on an emotional rollercoaster today. Though she was the one who wanted me to get married, deep inside she thought that I would resist the idea and reject the girl. Contrary to her expectations, her son had found somebody other than her to share his affection with. Probably, *amma* didn't expect such a quick turnaround from me.

She could gauge the intensity of my longing for Lakshmi. Her face was unusually taut. She was also battling conflicting feelings. Though every mother knows that this is inevitable, when it happens not many are prepared. She certainly wasn't.

Her idea of emotional continuity was to get me married to a girl within the larger family. In our custom, marriage between certain cousins is allowed, especially with the paternal aunt's daughter who is designated as one's *murapennu*. As I didn't have one, she found excuses to take me to the houses of distant relatives so that I could meet pretty and educated girls. What she didn't understand was that I needed someone who would be able to seamlessly move into my upwardly mobile social circle. However, the real reason had been that I couldn't find anybody like Radha.

radha

Never has a woman captured my imagination like Radha.

She was the daughter of *achhan*'s distant cousin. She and her family lived in Palakkad, close to my paternal ancestral home. Her father, uncle Venu, and *achhan*, were childhood friends and had gone to school and college together.

While *achhan* joined the Indian Army as an officer and moved away, Radha's father inherited a large tea estate in the picturesque Nelliampathy hills. He married the daughter of a business magnate from the neighbouring district and settled down in Palakkad.

Radha was two years elder to me. The only girl child among many cousins, everybody adored her. Her uncles, some of them settled abroad, would shower her with expensive toys and gifts when they came home for vacations. She was indeed a pampered and snooty child. Whenever we visited Palakkad, we spent a substantial amount of time at each other's houses. She made it a point to show off her toys and would not share anything till her mother, aunty Shilpa, ordered her to do so. Whatever game we played, she had to be the winner. We fought and argued with each other a lot.

She was a very fair and pretty girl. Despite her adamant attitude, there was something about Radha that always attracted me. I liked to be with her. She seemed to be a natural seductress who could get her way without much effort.

While we were still small children, uncle Venu once invited us to his tea estate. He sent his prized Willy's jeep to pick us up. I sat near *achhan* in the front seat. He was very proud to be a Palakkadan and took the opportunity to pass on his local knowledge to me. As we entered the protected forest, he said, "Nearly 80 per cent of Nelliampathy is a natural evergreen forest and the rest are plantations. Portions of it are tiger reserves."

The mention of tigers sent a shiver down my spine. "Will we encounter them on the road?" I asked fearfully. *Achhan* laughed loudly and then said, "Except monkeys and an occasional mongoose, you might not find any other animal on the road during the day. The tigers, elephants, leopards, and wild buffaloes live in the deep forests. They do not come out on these steep winding roads." The driver skilfully maneuvered the jeep and climbed the steep hairpin roads. There were tall thick trees everywhere. I had never seen a real forest before.

On the way, the driver stopped the jeep and showed me the Pothundy reservoir. From that height, it looked like a shimmering small blue wet dot. *Achhan* said, "That dam was built with just mud. They used no cement nor concrete. It stands as an ode to the skills of some of the finest engineers." I couldn't agree more.

It took us about an hour to reach the estate. As we entered its large gates, thousands of tea shrubs spread out like an amazing, living carpet. It was late evening and the workers were winding up for the day. It was getting cold. Uncle Venu came out to receive us and took us inside the medium-sized house. Radha and I had fresh hot milk and biscuits. Uncle Venu called out to his servants and asked them to start preparing the barbeque pit outside, while he and *achhan* sat down for a drink of scotch. After sometime, we all went out to watch the servants pit-roasting a wild boar.

It was considerably cold and the mist had descended. Both Radha and I started shivering. Radha's mother brought out a large coarse blanket and covered us both. We sat there enjoying each other's warmth. *Amma* brought a small plate full of roasted boar. It tasted hard and rubbery. Neither of us ate it.

As the adults were immersed in deep conversation, Radha said softly, "Look." She stuck out her tongue and said, "Touch and see." I touched it with my finger. She was cross. "No, with your tongue," she almost hissed. I hesitated but gave in to her wish. It tasted slightly slimy and salty but it generated a strong sensation that I could not comprehend. She asked me, "Did you like it?" I nodded my head like a fool. She said, "I saw my parents doing that yesterday night." We sat there in silence for some time. I didn't know what to make out of it. I am not sure if I could call that my first kiss. Aunty Shilpa then ushered us in and put us to sleep in her bedroom, while the elders continued talking, Radha and I lay hugging each other. She went to sleep quickly. For some time, I lay there looking at her. I could hear her soft snores till sleep overtook my admiration. Till the morning we slept, remaining in a tight embrace.

Since he was handling a sensitive assignment, *achhan* could not get his annual leave for two consecutive years. He was noticeably upset about not being able to meet his parents. He had never missed his annual visits. He asked us to go to Palakkad but *amma* was adamant that she wouldn't go without him. It was apparent that she was intimidated by her mother-in-law.

It was just after I had given my 12th grade exams that *achhan* got a call informing him that grandpa was terribly ill. Though they were never really close, that was the first time I saw him on the brink of tears. We were surprised as he had always presented a tough façade.

It was also the first time that I travelled in an aircraft. Throughout the journey, *achhan* was lost in thoughts. The possibility of losing someone dear can indeed be frightful since death has an irreversible nature.

The ancestral home consisted of two buildings. The grand old house built in traditional manner where my grandparents lived and the small new building built for my youngest uncle.

Many people had gathered around the old house. *Achhan*'s brothers who lived in faraway cities had also arrived. This was bad news. Grandpa seemed to be on his death bed.

Grandpa was a tall, lean and visibly strong man. Ruggedly good looking, he had a thick mane even in his old age. Every day in the morning, the local barber would come to give him a shave. He was a dashing man and I always thought that he had an Indiana Jones kind of look. He exuded a sense of authority that was intimidating.

While *achhan* and *amma* went to the room where my grandpa lay, Kamala took me to the new house. The young people weren't allowed to see him as he was emaciated and in the last stages of colon cancer.

Kamala was my youngest aunt, married to the 13th and youngest uncle. We had attended their wedding two years ago. Grandpa began to fall sick after this marriage. She was being kept away from grandfather. That room had turned into the sanctum sanctorum buzzing with political activity. Many relatives believed that it was she who brought bad luck to the family. She was called a bad omen. It was easy to blame a defenceless woman for all misfortunes even if it was a medical one. Not surprisingly, the ones who seemed to have taken the lead were other women in the family. The men must have just fallen in line. They all had found their scapegoat.

She was just about 22 years old. Uncle was close to 35; he was literally grandma's pet. She didn't want him to get married and was often heard saying, "He is still young. Let him grow up." The truth was that the old people wanted somebody around to look after them. They didn't want him to migrate outside Palakkad like the other children had.

Uncle grew up to be a lazy person and, unlike his brothers, he stopped studying after matriculation. He never bothered finding work and looked after the extensive family properties. Though he never picked up a spade or did any work that could break a sweat, he loved bossing over the workers. He was an immature person who mostly behaved childishly. He hated taking responsibilities and loved the easy life.

The elder brothers dominated him and were now making him run around getting things organised. He didn't like it but was afraid to say no.

He was so different from Kamala. She was from a lower middle class family and was brought up by her father. Her mother had passed away when she was young. They were farmers and she was used to hard work in the fields. A very slim woman, she sported a lean, muscular body with a flat stomach. My uncle was a podgy man with a big belly. His chest was loose and resembled mammaries. The only saving grace was his thick mane that he had genetically inherited. Grandma wanted a bride who wouldn't rebel so Kamala fit the profile.

Despite the gloom, uncle made it a point to take Kamala for a 'siesta' in the afternoons, which would typically last no more than 10-15 minutes. As they came out, she had a bored look on her face. Her blouse would be full of sweat patches. She seemed to want to be among us cousins. The family didn't get together quite often. She wanted to make the most of it.

Kamala found it easier to relate to me than her husband. We were like friends. Once I had told her that her lean body could make her a model on the ramps sporting classy outfits. She had seemingly dismissed my comments but my words would have made her secretly happy. I was surprised that she had never been to a large city. Palakkad was her world. Despite the presence of many servants, grandma made her do most of the household work. She seemed to be taking revenge on Kamala for marrying her pet son.

The next day morning, we cousins got together at the orchard in the compound. With nobody to admonish us, we started throwing sticks and stones at the guava tree to bring down the ripe fruits hanging on the high branches. I was the leader among them.

After a while, uncle Venu's black ambassador car came through the gate and screeched to a halt. He quickly got out of the driver's seat and opened the door for the old doctor who had arrived to examine grandpa. He was the family doctor and we all knew him for years. Uncle Venu reverently carried the doctor's battered black leather bag and escorted him inside. People who were gathered outside quietly made way for the two men.

Aunty Shilpa stepped out of the car and opened the boot to take out their luggage. Radha followed and exited the car with an exaggerated grace. Though her sense of pomp was not much to my liking, I did not fail to notice that she had become more beautiful. "She has the glamour of a budding film star," I thought.

I stood still and looked at her. She had a soft clear face with rounded cheekbones. Though slim and tall, she had ample bosoms and a wide hip. Always dressing to the occasion, she wore a short sleeved, white cotton blouse that stopped at the hip and a knee-length black skirt. Two large bangles and a gold watch adorned her hands. Gold anklets complimented her thin beautiful legs. Her thick long hair was tied in a long plait. She walked towards the house with deliberate elegance. The younger cousins were still labouring to bring down the fruits as I sat near the corner munching on guavas, thinking of ways to get close to her.

Till Kamala came looking for us, we remained in the orchard. It was time for lunch. As per the unbreakable rule set by grandpa, the kids always ate first in the household. Due to the rush of people it was difficult to use the dining room. Just behind the house, a shed had been built as a temporary dining room. Long benches and makeshift dining tables were hired to accommodate a large number of visitors. We had already started eating the food served on plantain leaves when Radha arrived; fashionably late.

She acknowledged us with a gentle nod of her head and a half smile. She sat across the table and asked me, "When did you come?" It was as if the pampered princess had finally condescended to speak to the shirtless common people.

I gave my best smile and said, "Yesterday. When did you come?" I pretended I hadn't seen her arrive on the scene.

She said dryly, "When you guys were bringing down the guavas." That stung. She had seen us. No wonder she was extra conscious.

A plantain leaf was laid and food was served by Kamala. I felt that Kamala had chosen a better leaf that had no tears for the princess. She was sitting right in front of me. She looked at the food and ate the spicy mango pickle first. Her dark black eyes were accentuated by kohl and complimented by her neatly shaped eyebrows. They were thicker in the middle tapering into thin lines towards the end. The dimples on her cheek were deep and perhaps it was the pickle that turned her full lips redder than usual. Small earrings dangled from her ears as she ate slowly displaying deliberate finesse as if she was in a fine dining restaurant. She looked up and asked, "You didn't like the food?" as though she hadn't noticed me staring at her.

As we finished eating, grandma was escorted into the dining table. She hadn't eaten since the previous day. All her children were persuading her to eat something. They were just vying for her attention. They wanted to impress upon her how much they cared. It was assumed that the property would be divided after grandpa's demise. With so much property scattered all over Palakkad in the form of orchards, farmlands, houses and shops, everybody wanted to make sure that they got prime properties. They were all preparing for hard negotiations.

Radha walked back to uncle's house with us. Summers were oppressively hot in Palakkad. The younger ones played cricket indoors with a rubber ball and plastic bat. The young ones were oblivious of the emotional environment and made a lot of noise.

She sat on a chair in the drawing room and crossed her legs just like the elder women of the family. I went into the room, picked up the recent bestseller I had carried, and sat on a chair beside her. "Have you read this?" I asked her. I knew that she was a voracious reader.

"No," she said. I handed the book to her.

"Keep it. I will take it from you when I leave."

She looked at me with disinterest but took the book and leafed through it. A half-smile played on her lips. Or was it a smirk? Deciphering girls was always a difficult task for me. But I think she knew that I was trying to impress her. Since she did not say anything further, we sat in silence. She just sat looking outside.

Kamala and uncle came to the room after the customary 'siesta'. She looked surprised at our presence. I didn't know when they had gone in the bedroom.

She smelled of sweat. She seemed a little embarrassed. "Why are you guys so quiet?" she asked us. I think she just wanted to deflect attention.

"Shall we play cards? It is only when you people visit that I get to have some fun. Let's make the most of it. Sometimes I fear dying of boredom," said Kamala. She brought out a set of cards. The three of us sat on the ground to play.

The modus operandi I adopted ensured that Radha wouldn't lose. Kamala stopped playing in between and asked me angrily, "You are playing to win or lose? There is no fun playing like this." I protested weakly. That made her angrier. "You are helping her win, Krish. Are you both lovers or something?" I was startled at her statement and looked at Radha. She was blushing and immediately made an excuse to step out of the room.

I don't think Kamala meant anything when she said that. She was upset at the reaction her statement had evoked. Kamala looked at me and asked, "What's cooking between the two of you?" Pretending to protest I said, "Nothing. But why do you ask?" I asked.

"I have been noticing the change in you since Radha stepped in," said Kamala. She paused. "You have been looking at her all the time. Watching her every move. There is deep admiration in your eyes."

I thought about a suitable response and then said, "Well, what do you think?"

"Well, I am not sure. I think you like her," she said stoically. "I like you too. That doesn't mean anything, Kamala," I tried to change the subject.

"Don't try to fool me. Don't forget, girls always know," she said with supreme confidence.

I was not sure of trusting Kamala with my innermost secret. "Does she know?" she persisted.

"Nope," I responded

"Are you serious?" she seemed to be brimming with curiosity. She behaved as if she was on the brink of making a major discovery.

"I have been in love with her since I was very young,

Kamala. I think there is no other girl like her," I told her in a brittle voice.

Kamala looked at me. She understood. There was a tinge of sadness in her eyes. She said softly, "You are two years younger than her. Once she finishes graduation, her parents will begin seeking marriage alliances for her. When will you be financially ready?"

The steely reality in her voice hit me like a hammer. I had never thought about those practicalities till this point.

"I don't know, Kamala. I wish I knew the answers," I mumbled. Truth struck home. The unfolding melodrama was having an effect on Kamala who was trapped in a loveless relationship. For her, there was no escape.

"Are you sure about your feelings?" she asked again. I just looked at her with desperation. Subconsciously I was manipulating her and knew this was the greatest opportunity to convey my love to Radha without any apparent risks. There was always the tool of denial that I could use. Just in case.

Kamala got up and walked away without saying anything.

I went and stood in front of the large dressing mirror inside the second bedroom. All I saw was a thin, dark boy-man with a slight moustache who was definitely not growing up into a good-looking person.

There were so many contrasts between us, Radha and me.

She was very beautiful and already behaved like a lady. Why would she desire a person like me? Angry with myself, I shouted at the boy in the mirror, "Shouldn't one desire what one deserves?" I plunged into self-loathing and slapped myself hard again and again. I cried. I was perhaps initiating a relationship that was doomed from the beginning.

As my rage waned, a new fear propped up its head. What if Kamala told *amma* or *achhan*? What if Radha complained about me to her parents? How would they react? It would not take much time for the others in the family to know. The idea of being punished in front of all the relatives was unbearable. Worried, I curled up in a corner of the bed and fell asleep.

Amma shook me awake. "Why are you sleeping at dusk? I have been looking for you everywhere." I looked at her in fear, thinking she already knew. My hands instinctively went up to defend any blows. But she looked concerned. "Do you have fever?" She gently touched my forehead. The fear started subsiding.

"Get up," she ordered. "Let me get you a hot cup of tea."

I followed her to the kitchen. A few uncles were gathered around the table discussing something intently. I saw Radha and Kamala. They were cutting vegetables. My first instinct was to flee. But I couldn't. Mustering enough courage, I sat at the dining table without looking at their direction

"Did you see a ghost or something?" It was Kamala. Radha and Kamala looked at each other and started giggling. Girls, they always have their secrets, don't they? They never reveal anything and are always thick as thieves when it comes to safeguarding each other's secrets. Every man wants access to this inner world, I thought. But the doors to these chambers are mostly closed for losers like me.

I took the mug from *amma* and walked back to the new building. On the way, I saw another group of men including *achhan* and uncle Venu huddled together. They would have identified, divided, and sold the property already in their minds. I felt disgusted.

It was dark when I went to the veranda adjacent to our room to have a quick smoke. It was a new habit I had picked up from my friend Ajay. He never revealed his source but regularly brought cigarettes to school. Though I resisted initially, I gave in to his persuasions. Smoking became a new habit. As I stood smoking, I heard the door creak. Afraid that it was one of the younger cousins, I hid in the corner. The last thing I wanted was to be caught with a cigarette in my hand. If a young one saw me smoking, it would take very little time before the news spread.

It was Kamala. I came out of hiding. She looked at me with horror and asked, "Gosh, you smoke?" Like a veteran, I took a puff and exhaled through the nose to impress her. I was not afraid of Kamala anymore. I trusted her.

She said, "I like the smell of cigarette smoke just like many people like the smell of petrol." She kept looking at the glow of the cigarette. I think I gained some respect from her. What my sparse moustache couldn't do, the smoking did.

"I like men who smoke and drink occasionally," she said. "Look at your uncle. He is always behind his mother like a puppy!" She hit my shoulders and said, "I like bad boys." Then she laughed.

I was dying to ask her if she had mentioned our conversation to Radha, without appearing desperate. It seemed that Kamala wanted me to ask her about it. I threw the cigarette and looked at her. It was getting dark and I couldn't read the expression on her face.

"Hmm, so what do you think, Krish?" she initiated the topic "Think of what, Kamala?" I feigned ignorance, though it wasn't difficult to understand what she was hinting at.

Her tone changed. She asked in an authoritative manner. "So what do you think Radha's reaction would be if you professed your undying love to her?" She had obviously spoken to her and was bearing her reply. I didn't respond. It was she who had to give the message.

She made me wait for a few seconds and said triumphantly, "I told her, Krish." My stomach churned in excitement. She sounded positive, still I wanted to be sure.

"And?"

"And what? She does like you." Kamala smiled happily. "What? Tell me again." I pleaded with her.

"Are you deaf? Didn't you hear what I said? She likes you too," she exhibited faux anger.

My happiness knew no bounds and my first reaction

was to hold both her hands and kiss them. I felt as if I always knew that Radha loved me. That was my way of coping with immensely positive news.

"Let me hug you, Kamala."

She came near me and I held her gently. She hugged me back tightly. We stood there for a few moments It was rather awkward but an unexpected intimacy seemed to creep into the act. Her breasts pressed against my chest and I felt her heartbeat. This was the first time a woman outside the immediate family had hugged me.

She wasn't wearing any perfume but the smell of coconut oil on her hair and talcum powder was prominent. The darkness and guilt presented a strange yet strong allure. As we stood there in each other's arms, sinful pleasure started to affect our bodies. I had this compelling urge to kiss her. She gently pulled away and said, "I have done my bit. Now you will have to take it from here." As she walked away she said, "You will have to tell her what you feel for her. Till then nothing will change."

She left me confused. I couldn't interpret what was on Kamala's mind. She had never before come across as somebody who sought intimacy, physical or otherwise. Maybe my admission of love for Radha triggered something in her. To be stuck in a loveless relationship can be cruel.

There was a lot of commotion building around the old house. As I stood pondering what had transpired, Radha walked into the house followed by *amma*.

She had been crying. When she saw me, *amma* said, "There was a scare. We thought that he passed away." She paused and whispered, "He will not go with *Yama* that easily. He is an adamant person," she sighed.

Amma sat with us for some time. She said, "The doctor says that he will not outlast the night."

She then looked at both of us and said, "It is your responsibility to look after the younger ones. Take care of them." We knew that the terrible event was going to happen tonight. *Amma* returned to the old house.

Radha had a sombre expression on her face. I sat near her but she didn't move away. The children who were playing outside were shooed in. Suddenly I felt as though we were parents looking after a bunch of unruly children. A smile broke out on my face when I thought this scene could be enacted in the near future. I gazed at Radha. She looked at me expectantly. I should have told her then but didn't. I procrastinated.

She sat with her hands wrapped around her legs. Her bosom looked more prominent. I could see the blue shadows of her veins on her pale skin. Though she didn't look at me, she became conscious of my unwelcome attention. She pulled up her blouse but sat where she was. I think we both wanted to talk but each of us waited for the other to initiate conversation.

Around 8.30 p.m., Malu came and called us for dinner. The children shouted in excitement and she told them firmly to be quiet. I have seen Malu since my childhood. Malu was from the lower caste potter community but was never treated like that. She understood her limits. Her husband was grandpa's trusted henchman. The couple stayed in a small hut inside the compound. She always wore a loose, faded blouse and a *lungi*. She looked the same even now, except her hair that had turned pure white. Despite being the servant, she had an air of subtle authority. None of us children dared defy her instructions. She was also grandma's trusted assistant.

I walked alongside Radha as we went to the makeshift dining area. Our hands brushed against each other. I fought the urge to hold her hands. We sat next to each other at the dining table and ate quietly. As we herded the young ones back to the house after dinner, the adults waited impatiently. It is as if they were worried that grandpa would die before they ate. They looked like hyenas to me.

Radha was busy putting the children to sleep. She handled them very well. I think she was deliberately displaying maternal abilities, as though we were engaged in some kind of a family role play. She lay next to the youngest child.

She betrayed nothing to indicate that Kamala had conveyed my message of love to her. Yet, something had changed in her. I wanted to confess my love for her.

As she lay there with her eyes half-closed, I hesitated. Then I switched off the light so that everyone could sleep peacefully. Lying on the sofa, I tried to catch some sleep but couldn't. So I decided to go out for a smoke.

Radha didn't know that I had started smoking. I lit a cigarette and walked into the veranda behind the bedroom. I felt like a man. A married man.

It was a bright night, in contrast to the impending darkness of death. The full moon looked as if it was soaked in honey. The numerous stars shimmered like sprinkled sugar on a sponge cake. The gentle breeze made the leaves sway rhythmically like the hips of a woman dancing gently. Like a *Mohiniyattom* dancer. The shadows under the trees appeared darker than usual. The night was unusually silent.

The calm was disrupted by the sudden loud howling of grandpa's dogs. He had always loved big, ferocious dogs from his days as a forest range officer. Deep in the jungles where many wild animals roamed in their own kingdoms, it was the man who was the intruder. Killing trespassers was the animals' primal instinct. It was grandpa's dogs that had saved him many times from death. He always said, "Dogs are more loyal and affectionate than one's own children." Based on the unravelling greed of his children, I think he was right.

In Kerala, it is believed that dogs could see supernatural beings, including *Yama*, the God of Death, arriving to reap a soul. Whether this was true or not, in about five to ten minutes, there was loud wailing from the house. The sounds of grief came from both men and women. The inevitable had happened. The sorrow was deep and profound. A titan had passed away, never to return.

I went back to the room. The sound of the air-conditioner insulated any noise from outside. Radha and the children slept peacefully. Despite the setting sadness, I couldn't help but admire her beauty as she slept. Her chest heaved up and down lightly. I stood looking at her for a few minutes and then softly called out to her. "Radha, Radha, wake up." She was deep in sleep. I gently shook her. As she opened her eyes, she knew why I had woken her. There was angst in her eyes. Her face was clouded as if it would rain tears. For the first time, I saw the soft side of Radha. That made me love her more. We closed the door gently behind us and walked out. As the cries grew louder, she ran towards the old house. I followed her into it and saw my grandpa's body was being prepared for the customary final bath.

The corpse was dressed in white and then brought out into the hall and placed on a bed of plantain leaves. It was indeed distressing to see a dynamic man lying absolutely still. The smell of incense and tuberose flowers hung in the room strongly. It was the smell of death.

He had shrunk and was just a pale shadow of his imposing former self. The emaciated body looked like his cane. There was barely any flesh on it. He resembled a skeleton. The doctor had bound his jaws tightly with a strip of cloth, closed his eyes, and stuffed cotton in his ears and nostrils. His face looked as though he was furious at his fate.

He had never believed he was growing old and frail, never accepted his age. The sudden stillness was stunning. Though his death had been impending, no one really believed that he would actually die. The last time I saw him, there was no indication that this would be his fate. Cancer won, where wild animals had failed!

A glaze came over my eyes. I lost my composure and tears rolled out uncontrollably. Radha was sitting near her mother sobbing. Though we never loved him in the conventional way, he had been the masculine symbol for all the men in the family, who tried to emulate him unsuccessfully. There would be only one like him and he had gone away, forever. My tears were an outcome of genuine grief.

Despite it being only 3.30 a.m., one of the elders sat beside the phone calling up people and informing them about grandpa's demise.

The men were busy discussing the details of the cremation while the women were wailing. But grandmother was calm and composed. She was instructing her sons on the rituals. As dawn broke, the high and mighty of Palakkad started walking in to pay their respects. Grandfather had many friends and admirers.

He was an atheist and wanted to be cremated in an electric crematorium. He didn't want any religious rituals of death to be conducted. But the family members took a contrarian stand. It was decided that the body would be cremated by fire and his remains would be buried in a corner of the property. It was easy defying him when he was dead. In a way, his children rebelled. Finally!

It was my favourite mango tree that became the victim of this petty rebellion. It was cut down to fuel the pyre. As the fire burned, I noticed Radha standing some distance away. Tears were rolling down her cheek. I moved closer to her. We stood shoulder to shoulder and watched the fire consume the patriarch with vengeance. In my mind, we were one. Already.

After around 30 minutes, when the men returned after lighting the pyre, the gravity of her loss dawned on grandma. She broke down. The old doctor was worried about her frail health and administered sedatives.

Despite the liberal use of fuel, it took a few hours for the body to burn completely. The bones that had resisted the fatal, amorous advances of the flames were collected in an urn. By noon, everything was back to normal. The fire in the kitchen was lit and simple lunch was served to everybody. Grandfather's children stood in groups, openly discussing the division of property. It seemed like a congregation of crows to me, salivating at rotten food. Their conversation sounded like 'caw', 'caw' and made little sense to me. I was wondering how easily they had forgotten their father and focused on money. If it had been the mother who had passed away first, these 'children' would not have been so bold. Grandmother had lost all her authority as her 'masculine' half was no more.

I didn't see Radha throughout the afternoon. As the harshness of the sun started waning, I found her in the portico with the other women. She was lying down, resting her head on *amma*'s lap. Though she was always fond of my parents, she had never done this before. Over the next couple of days, she was always around *amma*. She seemed to have built a warm bond with *amma,* as if she had decided to become her daughter-in-law.

Considering the ill health of their mother the doctor strongly advised the men not to talk about property division now. They, reluctantly agreed. But they would be back soon. As each of her children left, grandma, who was otherwise a terror to her daughters-in-law, seemed to disintegrate. The lion had left the den. The hyenas would now divide the spoils that the lion had hunted. Grandma didn't seem to matter much anymore.

We were the last family among grandma's dispersed children to return home. As we prepared to leave, Radha seemed sad but she barely acknowledged my presence. I told her casually, "We will see you again soon. In the meantime, I will call you regularly and write letters to you."

She snapped back, "Do you even know my address?"

"I will take it from your mother."

She gave me a stare which made me back off. I guess I should have asked her for it.

As I was packing my rucksack, the son of the servant came looking for me. He said, "This is for you. Don't tell anybody." He was holding a small bar of chocolate in one hand and a piece of paper in another. The address of Radha's college was written neatly on the piece of paper. The choice of address meant she was not yet ready to let her parents know. I still have that piece of paper with me.

As we bid goodbye, Radha hugged *amma*. Her eyes were red as she had been crying. I didn't dare say goodbye to her and walked towards the car. As we settled down in the plane, *amma* said, "I don't know what happened to Radha. She has become very close to me." I just shrugged my shoulders as if I was least bothered.

I started writing my first letter to her the same day we reached home. Completing it took me almost a week after changing the draft many times. The final letter was bland, risk-free, and devoid of any affection. She didn't reply for the next few weeks.

By then I had started college. Radha's possible reply became one of my biggest worries. What if *amma* received it? She might not read it but what if she hands it over to *achhan*? He would literally skin me. He was keen that I join the military as an officer and follow his footsteps. He had an aversion towards the private sector, while I didn't fancy a secure government job. I considered it boring. This was a sour point in our relationship. If he knew that his son was harbouring desires of marrying his best friend's daughter, he would explode. Every day I walked home in trepidation.

Almost a month passed by since my letter to her and I lost any hope of receiving a reply. But one day, as I returned from college and sat on the sofa to remove my shoes, I saw a letter placed on top of the coffee table. My name and address were written neatly in large letters. I knew it was *amma* who had kept it in such a dramatic position. Despite the fear, I definitely experienced an adrenalin rush.

Though dying to open it, I left it there. *Amma* was in the kitchen. I wanted to remove the letter from the table before *achhan* came home. *Amma* was making tea as she said, "Radha sent you a letter." Her tone was flat.

"Hmm," I said, betraying no emotion either.

She had a dead pan expression on her face as she gave me my mug of tea. "When did you get her address?" she asked. "I asked her," I mumbled.

After this, I felt the awkwardness fade away. I took the letter and read it. *Amma* didn't enquire further about the letter. Maybe she had her doubts.

Radha's letter was equally bland. It barely had ten sentences. It took me another two weeks to carefully draft a reply. She never wrote back.

One day as I was having a quick breakfast before leaving for college, *amma* asked, "Did you stop writing to Radha?"

"Yes. There isn't much to write anyways," I said as if I didn't care about her.

She said, "I spoke to Kamala."

I had a bad feeling about where this was going. "Good. How is she?" I asked casually.

"She told me everything," said *amma*, throwing a meaningful look. There was something in her voice that made me uncomfortable.

"Told what, *amma*?" I asked innocently. These women are always united. While they don't share any of their secrets with us men, they keep no secrets among themselves, I told myself. I was angry at Kamala. I felt she had betrayed my trust.

She confronted me. "You and Radha aren't children anymore."

I think *amma* was hurt at the first cracks that began to appear in her perfect world. A world in which her son never took a decision without her concurrence.

"So you want to marry her?" The question embarrassed me and I remained quiet. It was too sudden. She didn't seem shocked at Kamala's revelation. The pieces were falling together.

"She is two years older than you. You know what that means, don't you? It will take you many years before you are ready to propose marriage to her. Her father is in a rush to get her married and is waiting for her to complete her graduation." Hadn't I heard this before from Kamala?

"*Achhan* and uncle Venu are childhood friends. If you were elder to her, I am sure they would have been happy to entertain this. But in this case, they may not even give it a second thought." Her words seared.

Finally she hit the nail on the head. "How long do you think both of you can wait?" Her question shook my confidence.

"I will find a job quickly," I said defensively.

"You are in your first year of graduation. The only way to secure a job without completing graduation is to join the Naval Defence Academy. But then you don't want to work for the government. What is the guarantee that you will clear the exams and interview for the academy? Even if you do, are you sure that Radha or her family will approve of your choice of profession? Are you willing to burn your ambitions for her? You have to finish your MBA before finding a well-paying job. You know how Radha was bought up? If you can't fulfil her basic aspirations, the initial romance will soon fade. I am saying this is from experience." She spoke like my professors. "The odds seem to be heavily stacked against you, son."

"I understand, *amma*. But I can't live without her. She has been in my mind for a long time." She looked at me as if I had betrayed her. The truth that I had another woman in my mind all this while and that she didn't know hit her hard. I had taken a critical decision without her consent. That hurt.

As a mother, she possibly understood my dilemma. She said, "Let me have a word with her. I need to know what is on her mind. By the way, I hope you have conveyed your feelings to her directly."

I remained silent. I didn't have to say anything. Mothers know.

"How long can you convey your feelings through others?" She scolded me.

Amma spoke to aunty Shilpa who informed that Radha had gone to college. Radha didn't return the call that day. I slept fitfully that night.

When I returned from college the next day, *amma* said, "Radha called. I spoke to her at length. She said she was willing to wait as long as she could."

Amma looked worried. She said, "But how long can she hold on? She and her mother don't have much say in decision-making in that household. Anyway, please call and talk to her directly." She knew that both of us were serious about this relationship but its impracticality was bothering her. The only positive thing she saw in this relationship was that her daughter-in-law could come from within the extended family. She wouldn't challenge her authority nor take-away her son from her.

I should have called and spoken to her but instead of calling her, I started writing to Radha again. For every two bland, non-committal letters I wrote, I received one. It seemed she was hoping that I would be explicit about my feelings to her in my letters. In hindsight, I think she was tired of my letters that were too general in nature. Her replies stopped. Gradually, I started losing any hope in the relationship. *Amma*'s questions seared many apertures in my love for Radha. However, the dreamer that I was, I continued to harbour a strong love for her. I planned to call and talk to her many times, but I was not sure what to say. I continued waiting for the right time. The coward in me was confident that eventually things would turn all right. It was nothing but wishful thinking.

It was when I was into my second year of college that I heard *achhan* tell *amma*, "Radha is getting marriage proposals. Her family is considering one of them. The prospective groom is completing his PhD. His family owns a small rubber plantation. He works with an MNC."

Amma asked, "Has she approved?"

"Not yet. She wanted some more time," *achhan* said.

Amma threw a glance at me. I interpreted that look as a sign that either I speak to her or I had to brace myself for the inevitable. Pushed to the corner, I called and spoke to Radha a couple of times. Yet, something prevented me from telling her explicitly that I loved her. She sounded neutral and was never warm. Though this could have been my imagination. She was hoping against hope that I would confess my love and begin a fight for the relationship. I think she would have waited but I didn't ask.

I asked *amma* for help and pleaded with her to talk to *achhan* so that we could find a way out of this. But she was afraid of talking to *achhan* about this. I don't think she had much hope right from the beginning.

I spent the next few days fretting and fuming. I told *amma* that I was willing to apply to the Naval Academy. She advised me to let it go. Then onwards, I nursed a grouse that she had ditched me when I needed her the most. My only choice was to gather enough courage to talk to *achhan* myself. If he spoke to uncle Venu, there was a real chance. But fear overcame my desires. I spent the next few days blaming everyone and everything for my fate except myself. It never occurred to me that my admission of love to her could have opened the doors to a different logical culmination. Hindsight can sometimes be cruel.

A few days later, uncle Venu called to convey that Radha's marriage had been fixed. He wanted *achhan* and *amma* to be present for the engagement.

When I heard about it, I felt numb. If Radha had been willing, she could have delayed this a little longer. She was not exactly growing old and knew that I loved her very much. I blamed her for this predicament. Deep inside, I knew that this had been the fate of my 'relationship' right from the beginning. Denial can sometimes be the panacea for weaklings. Today as I reminisce, I ask myself many a times, "Was this relationship really doomed from the beginning? Was it not practical?" and I answer myself, "It was not really doomed. A two-year gap meant a longer wait. That's it. Possibly uncle Venu would have been happy that his beloved daughter would join the household of his best friend."

But then I had to trigger that chain of events. I wasn't much of a risk taker. At least then.

That evening I went to meet Ajay. He laughed at me. "There are so many impracticalities in this relationship. But if you cannot overcome your fear and speak to your father, how can you hope to be married to Radha? You haven't even told her directly. The writing is clear on the wall."

"She could have waited," I grumbled.

"On what basis? And for how long? What assurance have you given her?"

The muscles on Ajay's face twitched. He was visibly angry now. He sat quiet for some time and said coldly, "You don't deserve her, Krish. You don't. Let her live her life. You are expecting her to argue with her father for you. Why would she wait for someone who doesn't even have the courage to tell her that he loves her? " He spoke like a sage who had attained nirvana. Ajay concluded softly, "You should desire what you deserve." He then walked away.

I feigned sickness to avoid attending Radha's engagement. It was late in the evening when my parents returned from the engagement. Radha's mother had sent me food. I didn't touch it.

My father didn't seem particularly happy with the engagement. His facial expression betrayed his anger. I gathered courage and asked him, "*Achhan*, what happened? Did something untoward happen during the engagement?"

It was *amma* who volunteered with the answer. "He is very lean and dark. Totally unpresentable groom. His family has a lower social status than ours. They own a small patch of rubber plantation that they tend to themselves." There was spite in her voice.

"Then why? What was the rush?" I was perplexed. "Because he holds a PhD from a reputed university and is a manager in a corporate organisation. He is expected to travel abroad frequently or even relocate. Radha can see the world. She will also not have to live with her in-laws. Uncle Venu thinks that the prospective groom has a bright future," said *amma*.

"Why didn't she say no? There would be other equally well- placed grooms?" I was secretly happy.

"Apart from his education and career, uncle Venu thinks that because of his low family status, the groom would remain humble and loyal to Radha's family. Uncle Venu cannot let go complete control over the well-being of his daughter. She is 23 years old now and almost all her friends are married. By the way, that guy seemed to adore her," she continued.

"The marriage is fixed for two months from now," *achhan* said with a tone of finality.

I had mixed feelings. Was Radha expressing her anger at me? Having known the depth of my feelings, was she extracting her revenge? Did she choose this man deliberately to make me jealous and feel inadequate? If I had gathered courage to tell *achhan* about my love for her, things could have been different. Even if *achhan* had resisted the idea, Radha could have had a reason to tell her mother. It was not an impossible relationship. I strongly believed she would have weathered all opposition and waited for me. *Amma* always used to say, "Women respond better to love than fear. We can gauge feelings much better than you men." I was the weakling. Did I deserve her? Probably not!

Radha possibly dreamt about living with me. Had she appeared a little more responsive, a bit warmer, I would have gathered the courage to tell her that I truly loved her. Somehow, her beauty and seemingly insensitive nature intimidated me and she knew that. All my life, I would never forget losing her. I think she internalised her anger and took terrible revenge on herself. Women can be complicated beings.

I spent my days in anger as it was my refuge from uncomfortable emotions. I tried to flush all her memories from my mind but the more I tried the harder they became ingrained in my mind. I turned reclusive and focused only on my studies. As the wedding day came closer, *achhan* decided to set aside his reservations about the groom and support uncle Venu wholeheartedly. The day Radha and her family visited Kochi to shop for her trousseau and jewellery, I went to college early and returned late.

Achhan insisted that we go to uncle Venu's house a few days in advance to assist him in the wedding preparations. When I protested saying that my exams were nearing, he thundered, "The entire family should participate during functions like these. Family is primary."

Amma played the peacemaker. She spoke to me. "Don't make a fuss now. Whatever happens, happens for the best. There is another woman equally beautiful waiting for you. There is a long life ahead of you." She spoke like a philosopher.

It was easy for *amma* to say so. It was not just Radha's beauty that attracted me but also her supreme confidence. The look in her eyes had a certain potency– like a predator preparing for the hunt. While she wanted to be admired and worshiped, she also wanted to be possessed. She knew what she wanted, yet made it clear that she was not easily obtainable. She made me feel that we were intertwined in many ways. My craving for her almost bordered on the psychotic.

Despite the agony of being forced to attend her wedding, I did want to meet the person she had chosen over me. As the date neared, I spent sleepless nights thinking about the only man who would get to know her intimately. I couldn't imagine anybody other than me to disrobe her on her wedding night and enjoy the sensualities that she had to offer. I tried to pacify myself that she was a prude icy woman who would never really enjoy erotic encounters. My mind conjured up these 'realities' and derived a crude sense of happiness. This was the only way I could cope up with the terrible reality that was unfolding.

My parents left for Radha's home three days before the wedding. Uncle Venu was tensed and needed *achhan's* support for anything and everything.

On the D-day, I got out early to take the train. I was wearing the ceremonial outfit that *amma* had carefully laid out. I chose to go to the venue directly rather than to Radha's house. The hustle bustle of the rituals would have prolonged my torture.

I ate the bland breakfast served in the train as I was not sure if I would stay for the wedding feast. Throughout the three- hour journey, my mind was preparing for war. To see her being married to another man was difficult to handle. The scars would never heal, I knew that.

The venue was the most prominent temple in town, where most of the relatives, including my parents, had been married. *Achhan* was standing among the elders and other prominent men. I felt like a complete outsider. Couldn't this have been my wedding? I found a quiet corner and lit a cigarette. It was difficult to cope with the rising tension.

While I was desperately dragging on the cigarette, a premium SUV and a series of premium cars entered the gates of the temple. The bride had arrived.

The white vehicle in which the bride was travelling was tastefully decorated with red roses. On its rear window was written 'Radha weds Anil' in thermocol. One of our cousins opened the door and the bride stepped out slowly, with a familiar exaggerated grace.

She wasn't wearing any footwear; the intricate deep-orange designs of the henna made her feet look lovely. She was draped in a blood-red *Kanjeevaram* silk sari and decked in gold ornaments. Many large necklaces, thick gold bangles, and a waist band adorned her body. She stooped slightly due to the weight of the ornaments. Her long hair was completely covered with jasmine flowers. The beautician had done a good job. Radha wore moderate make-up and the light pink lipstick complimented her fair complexion. The mascara made her eyes look large and deep. She looked like a Goddess. Well, almost. She was the Aphrodite of my dreams!

As she gently moved towards the *mandapam* where the groom would formally tie the *thaali* to signal the culmination of the wedding, I noticed the groom who was sitting on a low plank.

Amma found me in the crowd; she pulled me by my hand and said, "Where were you till now? Sit here with us." The front row was reserved for the women of the household. Young and old, they were all decked in jasmine flowers and gold jewellery.

Radha sat near the groom. There was neither joy nor sadness on her face, it was blank. Her eyes were searching the crowd and then she saw me. Something happened to her. I think I saw a sudden glint in her eyes. She rolled up her eyes slightly and slowly smiled. It was more like a smirk mixed with equal parts anger and disgust. She had found her target. I felt as though I had been spat upon.

Then on, she enthusiastically participated in the ceremonies. She knew I would remain a helpless witness throughout. She could afford to ignore me completely. The intoxicating sounds from the *nadhaswaram* reached a crescendo as the groom tied the *thaali* around her neck. As he applied a pinch of red vermillion on the parting of her hair, some of it fell on her forehead. Mixed with beads of sweat, they made her look more alluring.

Adrenalin pumped hard into my bloodstream and my heart beat faster than ever. The other ceremonies took hardly ten minutes. Both the bride and the groom stood up to receive blessings from the elders.

The groom was a tall, lean, dark complexioned man who sported the typical Malayali bush-moustache. Attired in a ceremonial *mundu*, he wore a thick gold chain around his neck complimented by a thick bracelet and a gold watch. His deep yellow silk shirt accentuated his dark tone. Radha too behaved as if she was truly married to a blue-blooded prince.

Relatives jostled with each other to hand over gifts to the newly-weds and pose for the customary photographs with them. I didn't want to go near the couple but *achhan* called for both me and *amma*.

It was a predicament I desperately wanted to escape from. I got up. *Amma* held my hands. I looked at her feebly. "*Achhan* would be very cross. Everything is destiny," she murmured.

Radha introduced my parents as her dearest uncle and aunt. Then she looked at me and said, "This is Krishnan. Remember, I told you about the interesting character?" She emphasised 'interesting'. She coyly held Anil's hand as if to indicate that everything was over and irreversible. Ad finem!

"Oh, yeah. Krishnan," said Anil. There was a mocking look on his face! Bastard, I thought.

I shook his hands and stood for the picture. I felt like a lamb ready to be slaughtered. He emphasised my name. Krishnan, the much loved God, known to be a playboy. And what a contrast I was to my namesake. I felt smaller and smaller.

As I moved away, Anil said, "See you again, Krishnan!" He winked meaningfully. My distraught mind read it as his way of saying, "Veni, vidi, vici." He behaved like a victor!

Though I didn't want to stay any longer, *amma*

was adamant. She took me to the hall where the feast was being served. The strong smell of curries was overwhelming.

Though I loved the typical Malayali *sadhya* or feast, today I wanted to finish the food quickly and leave the venue. It was then that the newly-wed couple chose to sit right across us. The photographers were buzzing around them for prime shots. One of them asked Anil to feed Radha in a symbolic gesture. As he did that, she threw a glance at me. I cringed. I knew the game of insults was not over. It seemed they had planned this to the last detail.

I refused dessert. As I walked towards our car, my mind screamed, "It will be done. Tonight the consummation will happen."

Radha moved to Chennai to live with her 'prince'. To me, it seemed like she had extracted a terrible revenge. She seemed to be punishing me for being spineless and a non-risk taker. I don't think she really liked her husband but she knew that this marriage would hurt me badly. In a way, she hurt herself only to leave me with enduring pain.

In the initial few months, I was curious about any news of her marital life. Then the interest ebbed. I returned to my studies. I could never forget her rebuttal. This failure served as a fuel and triggered my desire for success and money.

marrying lakshmi

As I started towards my room, *amma* handed me a crumpled piece of paper and said, "Here, your girl's number." There was a subtle emphasis on 'your girl'. She smiled. That smile carried a million meanings. Deciphering them was not an easy task.

Visibly, *amma* seemed happy that I was finally overcoming the deep psychological scars caused by my failed relationship with Radha. Having ignored my transition into a man, she seemed to harbour deep doubts if her little one was mentally prepared for marriage. Indeed, it was a classic irony!

Was she ready to let me off the emotional hooks? It was not too difficult to gauge that her role was shrinking in my world. Her opinion would still matter but not as much as before. I hoped she wouldn't see a rival in Lakshmi but an ally who would take care of her son like she did. Yes, I also wanted her to understand that my new family would be the core of my life. She would have to wean herself away from her possessiveness and tendency to micromanage my life. I would have new perspectives apart from hers and I was indeed prepared to accept a new woman in my life.

"How did you get her number?" I was curious.

"Why? You don't have confidence in your mother now?

She was cross.

"No ma. That's not what I meant."

She let it go and said, "I spoke to her mother."

I looked at the 10-digit number scribbled on the piece of yellow paper and thought how mobile phones had made communication far more personal and easier; unlike when I was trying to talk to Radha.

It was already 10.30 p.m. and excitement began to build up slowly like the crescendo of drumbeats. Over phone, I decided to make up for my shyness in the morning. As I dialled her number, my heart beat harder. Her voice on the other side triggered instant panic and I cut the call.

Like a weakling, I hoped she would call back. After waiting for a few minutes, I had no choice but dial again. She answered. "Krish?" I was tongue-tied as always. All I could manage was a murmur. "Yes."

It was Lakshmi who put me at ease and I let her take the lead. She spoke flawless English with a neutral accent acquired at her convent school. What I initially thought would be a five-minute conversation went on till dawn. I couldn't go to sleep after the call. The experience of talking to a girl throughout the night was exhilarating.

We continued speaking to each other the following nights. We frantically exchanged messages during the day and reserved conversations for the nights. I desperately waited for darkness to descend. There was something alluring about the nights. As the world slept, indulging in intimate conversations with one's to-be fiancée had a provocative feel that was unbeatable. As I spoke, I imagined her facial expressions. It was absolute madness.

The more I spoke to her, the more I wanted to meet her. After the third day, like an addict who needed a bigger fix to gain a high, I asked her if I could meet her.

She said, "Sure, why don't you come home?" Meeting her at home in the company of her parents was not what I had in mind. I told her, "I want to meet you alone." My voice sounded more like a whine to me.

She understood my eagerness and suggested, "Why don't you come to my office? We will meet for lunch?" For me, this was a small victory. "What time?" I asked impatiently.

"12.30 p.m. Today looks good to me." She said it as though she was checking her calendar to make an official appointment.

Lakshmi didn't seem concerned that she lived almost 200 kilometres away in Thiruvananthapuram. It would take me nearly four hours to reach there by car. She signed off saying, "I look forward to seeing you at lunch."

It was already 6.30 a.m. Heavy traffic would soon choke National Highway 47, creating bottlenecks.

Achhan and *amma* were having their customary early morning tea. She poured some tea for me and asked, "How come the prince woke up so early?"

We heard the tinkle of the newspaper boy's cycle bell. *Achhan* got up and went to the veranda to pick up the newspaper. I told *amma*, "I am going to meet Lakshmi."

"When?"

"Today for lunch."

"Is she coming to Kochi?"

"No, I am going to Thiruvananthapuram."

Amma just looked at me without saying anything.

"I am driving there. Planning to leave in another half an hour. Can you tell *achhan* about it?"

"You sure?" She almost stared

"100 per cent," I ignored the look and murmured

"I will quickly make some breakfast for you."

"I will have it on the way." Breakfast was the last thing on my mind

"Have breakfast before you leave," she said firmly. There was disguised anger and frustration in her voice. It was an order. I hadn't heard that tone in so many years. She wasn't pleased but I was determined not to miss my date.

I finished my shower quickly and came out dressed in my favourite blue jeans, white shirt and boots. She was waiting for me at the dining table. *Amma* asked sarcastically, "Did you shower in perfume?" Adding, "Come, have breakfast."

As I quickly gulped down the tea, omelette and a couple of slices of bread, *amma* watched me intently, astonished at the transformation in my behaviour.

"Drive carefully. There is no need to rush. She will always be there for you," she advised me. She sounded as if she wanted me to miss the meeting. I suspected that there was a tinge of envy in her voice.

I was aware of what *amma* was going through but I wasn't too affected by it today. An invisible curtain had descended between us. I still loved her, but my feelings for Lakshmi were stronger.

"I am a bit concerned about your long conversations in the night. Anyway she is yours. Why are you in a hurry? Doesn't she have to go to office? If she can't sleep, how will she work?"

Besotted with my victory, I had not thought about that. *Amma* interjected, "Remember, if you truly love somebody, then do what is good for them and not what is good for you." This hurt me. I think she was playing for both sides in a desperate attempt to slow down my journey towards emotional independence.

Was she eavesdropping? How did she know that I was on the phone all night? I guess mothers always knew.

It was almost 7.15 a.m. as I rushed towards the car. This was one of the rare times that I had not asked discussed an important issue with or asked permission from *amma*. *Achhan* was sitting at the veranda engrossed in the newspaper. He looked at me but did not ask anything. I knew he would check with *amma* as to where I was rushing.

As I drove the car, I furiously planned the day ahead to the minutest detail. The traffic on the road to the highway was heavy. Cars, buses and other vehicles drove bumper to bumper. The engines sputtered and black fumes belched out of the exhaust pipes. It was like a funeral procession. There was no room for escape and this made me tense. I was cursing anything and everything.

Luckily, the highway was relatively free of heavy traffic but *achhan's* old car allowed me the luxury of driving only between 80 and 100 kilometres per hour. It didn't have enough horse power to gallop at a higher speed. Fortunately, I didn't have to enter the city of Thiruvananthapuram as Lakshmi's office was at a tech park on the outskirts, where most IT companies were located.

As I came closer to her office, I drove into a premium hotel to pick up a bouquet of red roses and a box of gourmet chocolates. This visit had to be memorable. As always, I had prepared a script for the date with Lakshmi. I practiced the opening lines that I would use to impress her during the meeting.

It was close to 12.30 p.m. by the time I got the visitor's pass to enter Lakshmi's office. Many young people passed by as I waited at the plush reception. The girls looked at me and giggled at each other. Though I did let her know about my arrival, Lakshmi made me wait for almost half an hour.

Finally she came, accompanied by a group of young women.

Lakshmi was dressed in casuals – a pastel pink T-shirt, dark blue jeans, and sneakers. A bright Kipling bag hung loosely on her shoulders. She wore light make-up and no jewellery apart from an Omega constellation that dangled on her hand. She didn't seem dressed up for the occasion. The long conversations through the night made me feel as though I had known her for years but in person she looked like a stranger to me.

The group came towards me and I stepped forward to present the flowers and chocolates to Lakshmi. The girls screamed, "How romantic!" She accepted the gifts and we stood near the reception. She left the bouquet casually on the table, opened the box of chocolates, and offered them to her colleagues. They were gone in no time. I didn't feel good about this. The chocolates were meant only for her and she was sharing it with her friends. Eating, to me, always had a certain intimacy attached to it.

We stood there for about ten minutes with the women chatting among themselves. I felt like an exotic exhibit and just wanted to become invisible. After deciding that they had had their share of fun, the women left us alone. Lakshmi suggested that we go to the food court for lunch. As we walked down the stairs, I was quiet. This was not what I had expected.

At the food court, many young and seemingly well-paid employees were enjoying their lunch at leisure.

"Beneficiaries of the information technology outsourcing boom?" I asked Lakshmi.

"Hmm…And look at those European and American clients. They are here to meet their 'offshore' team-mates. Collateral outcome of globalisation!" Lakshmi spoke like a business honcho.

"And why do they need a psychologist like you here?" I asked.

"There is a lot of work pressure and expectations." She sounded almost guilty saying that. She then said, "Let me get you some lunch." She found us a table. "Wait here."

"Let me help you," I offered chivalrously

"This is my territory, sir! Please be my guest." She had clearly misunderstood me.

"Hold the seats or we will have to stand while having lunch," she warned.

Lakshmi was right. The crowd was swelling by the minute. I always felt suffocated in crowds.

Minutes later, Lakshmi walked in with a large tray full of food. She left it on the table.

As we settled down for lunch, she said, "See, Kerala is becoming as advanced as your Dubai and we too work in a professional environment." She sounded slightly defensive.

I simply nodded.

The food on the tray was an eclectic spread – lemongrass chicken rolls, fried chicken, kababs, tacos, French fries, wok-seared egg noodles and Greek salad. Lakshmi handed me a glass and said, "Strawberry-mint soda for you and mango juice for me. I am sure you will like the food." Her confidence surprised me.

We began eating. In an attempt to break the ice, I said, "People in the campus are dressed fashionably."

"Dubai is not the only upmarket location, sir! Many of these people travel frequently abroad." Sensing the combative mood she was in, I decided not to argue.

We barely had a proper conversation. Lakshmi didn't seem excited that I had driven many miles just to have lunch with her. The romantic in me was disappointed.

"Maybe I should not have rushed. She is taking me for granted. I should kill my over-eagerness," I told myself.

As we finished the food, she asked, "What happened to you? Why are you so quiet?"

I didn't reply.

"You speak so much on the phone." She prompted me again.

I was suddenly upset and angry.

"What is there to speak?" I snapped back.

Lakshmi sensed that the meeting was not going according to my expectations. She leaned across the table slightly and whispered, "Will you always be shy like this?" A naughty smile spread across her face. My anger began to melt away. She started a conversation. Her teasing persona was back. But I wasn't really convinced. There was barely any romance and that would be her characteristic throughout our married life. Sometimes she gave me the impression of being an unfeeling person. Nothing seem to touch her heart. She called herself a pragmatic, almost as an excuse for her remoteness.

She was always talkative in the company of other people but when we were alone, she barely had anything to talk. The little conversations that we had would always revolve around her family, her college life, and her ambitions. She seemed to be wedded to her past.

Lakshmi was smart enough to notice that I was getting bored. She asked, "We have to plan for our engagement. Don't we?"

"Sure," I replied. I had lost interest by then. All I wanted was to leave as soon as possible.

I told her, "It's probably time for you to get back to work. I better start now before peak traffic."

"Work? I am on leave this week. Do you think I can work after talking to you till the wee hours of the morning?" she said as a matter of fact. She had never mentioned she was on leave during our phone conversations.

"So, why did you suggest this food court for meeting? There are many restaurants where we could have met."

She looked at me and said, "Krish, we are not even engaged. My father has friends all over Thiruvananthapuram. What if somebody saw us?"

I wanted to say "So, what? Wouldn't that little risk add to the fun of the meeting?" but then I was learning not to expect romantic overtures from Lakshmi. I kept thinking that I should not have asked for this meeting. The telephone conversations would have helped maintain the fantasy of romance. It was as though she had a split personality. One over the phone and the other in person.

Lakshmi displayed shades of Radha. Rarely romantic, predominantly pragmatic. Craved attention but never acknowledged its need. Never took the initiative to build the soft bridges of romance or intimacy.

She spoke at length about our engagement, marriage, and finding a job in Dubai. It seemed I was just a catalyst for her ambitions rather than a life partner. She was a complex personality.

I thought about the flowers she had left at the reception table. Most probably it would end up in the garbage or one of the cleaners would take it home. I never bought a bouquet for her ever again.

As I drove home, I felt low. It was quite late when I reached home. Surprisingly, *amma* had not called me during the entire day. She asked me, "How did your lunch go?"

I put on a mask of excitement and said, "It went well." I didn't want my mother to get concerned. This is when masks come in handy. They help conceal one's internal turmoil.

That night I decided to take a break from calling Lakshmi. I texted her – 'Tired. Need to catch up on sleep'. She responded – 'Yes. You were looking tired today. Please sleep early'.

I don't think she realised the extent of the hurt I was nursing. I turned off my mobile phone and drifted to sleep.

The next two days, I chose to spend time with *amma*, visiting relatives and informing them about my impending engagement with Lakshmi. *Amma* was eloquent describing Lakshmi and her family. She was proud of the alliance.

I did not call Lakshmi the next night nor did I respond to her messages. Eventually, she called and asked, "Are you angry with me? What did I do?" She sounded hurt.

"I am leaving in a couple of days, so I have certain commitments. That's why late night calls are a bit difficult for me," I lied.

She didn't seem convinced but reacted by turning on a romantic and sensual persona. I wasn't happy about her switch-on, switch-off style, nevertheless she managed to hold my attention. She toyed with my mind; she could be charming whenever she chose to. We spoke for around an hour that night.

Meeting her at her office was kind of an anti-climax for me. Sometimes I had doubts if Lakshmi was the person with whom I wanted to spend the rest of my life. Though these thoughts gnawed me, I was strangely enamoured by her.

My short vacation reached its end. As I reached the airport, I was surprised to see Lakshmi and her mother there. "She fought with her father for permission to see you off at the airport," Lakshmi's mother said. "Sending off a person with whom you are not formally engaged is considered improper."

I was indeed happy to see Lakshmi. She sported a completely different personality and appeared coy, like a would-be bride.

"Why didn't you let me know?" I asked

"Just wanted to give you a surprise," she mumbled.

"You drove four hours to see me off?" She never ceased to surprise me. She just nodded

"Did you wait too long?"

"Not really." It was Mrs Nair who answered.

"If you had informed me, I would have come a little early." Lakshmi just smiled.

We spoke for some time. Both Lakshmi and her mother laughed at my jokes.

It was time to board the plane. We exchanged goodbyes. I saw her eyes welling up and she ended up crying. I didn't look back as I walked into the airport. I was more confused than ever. Here was a woman who had difficulty expressing her intimacy in person yet she was a very emotional person. Which was the dominant personality? Who was she as an individual? Whoever she was, I loved her more than before. It felt great to be loved and longed for. Albeit occasionally.

Why do I have this tendency of getting close to those who express their disdain for me? Didn't *amma* take me for granted? Hadn't Radha too treated me like that? Wasn't Lakshmi's behaviour at the food court insensitive? Or was I expecting too much from them? The more I thought about it, the more confused I became. The human mind, I thought, is a mirror of complexities that reflects multiple, distorted images. Yet again, I failed to decipher women and their thought processes.

I slept through the flight to Dubai. As requested by her, I called up Lakshmi to let her know that I had reached Dubai safely. Though I had the excuse of being far away, I did call her at night. But I learned to hold back my emotions and let her do the talking. There were days that I deliberately didn't call her. The power structure slowly tilted a bit in my favour. Now, it was she who craved for my phone calls. I listened to her patiently, as she described the preparations for the engagement ceremony in microscopic detail.

Despite my parents' request to come for at least a week, I only took three days of leave for the engagement.

I lied to everybody that I was in the middle of a large consulting pitch.

The choreographed ceremony was a simple yet elegant affair. Attired in a custom made Kerala sari and simple jewellery, Lakshmi looked beautiful. Most of her relatives were present in all their ceremonial finery.

It barely took five minutes to complete the ring ceremony. Despite protests from her family, I had insisted that I would purchase the rings from Dubai. I wanted to make an important statement.

I had chosen a B.ZERO 13-band ring in 18k yellow gold for her. The admiring looks from the women from the family made Lakshmi happy. It was worth the investment.

The photographers were an intruding lot. Like mosquitoes in Kochi, they were all over us, barely giving us breathing space. They requested us to strike various poses in the garden outside. Though I felt embarrassed, Lakshmi seemed to enjoy the photo session. She stood so close to me that I could smell her perfume. Every time I held Lakshmi close to me, I felt waves of excitement in me.

But very soon I got bored and told Lakshmi, "It's hot and humid. Let's go inside." We were sweating profusely and the air-conditioning inside came as a welcome relief. I soon regretted my decision to go inside. Now that the ceremony was over and I was formally part of the family, everybody wanted to talk to me. I hated being the centre of so much attention.

I had not invited Ajay for the engagement. It was a private affair and I didn't want him to ogle at the women of the Nair household. It felt great to be part of the aristocratic Nair clan. Ajay wouldn't fit into the crowd.

There was no turning back now. After a sumptuous lunch, we returned home.

The Nairs did not want to delay the marriage and the date was fixed for two months from then. Lakshmi and I continued to talk to each other over phone. She was planning the wedding to the minutest detail. This was one of the biggest events in her life and it had to be carefully choreographed for maximum effect. For Mr Nair, this was an occasion to invite his close friends and business associates. He wanted to make a big statement and boost his prestige among family, friends and business associates. He behaved like the Roman emperor who wanted to organise a spectacular chariot race at the Circus Maximus.

Though my parents were part of some of the arrangements, the Nairs took complete control over the wedding planning and execution. One of the biggest banquet halls in the finest hotel was booked, many cars were rented, and hundreds of invitations were sent out to the prominent denizens of Thiruvananthapuram and other parts of Kerala. He threw money to buy the best available products and services.

Lakshmi resigned from her job to plan and shop for the wedding. Her saris and jewellery were custom-made at some of the oldest and most famous establishments. I was invited to be part of the shopping but I chose to stay away from the nitty-gritties. Though I would have loved to shop with her, I didn't cherish the idea of going out with many relatives in tow. Familiarity breeds contempt, I told *amma*, justifying my absence.

The wedding was indeed an elaborate affair. The entire Nair clan was present in full force. Many had flown from distant countries to attend this function. It was like the convocation of the rich and mighty.

The Nairs, being ardent devotees of Lord *Krishna*, insisted that the wedding be conducted at the famous Guruvayur temple. It is one of the oldest temples in the country. Though there are no historical records to establish, legends date it to 5000 years. The devotees seem to have chosen to believe the legend, unbothered about the lack of historical proof. Despite this, the temple should be at least many centuries old, thereby being a true specimen of ancient architecture. It is indeed one of the most important places of worship for Hindus, considered the holy abode of Vishnu, the God of all Gods. I was told that the doors and the roof of the sanctum sanctorum or *garbhagriha* where the main idol is placed are covered in gold as are other articles used for worship. The temple, richly adorned by detailed mural paintings, was generously funded by devotees.

It is said that more than 200 weddings are conducted here on peak days. There were many weddings scheduled for that day too. The actual ceremony barely lasted five minutes inside a small gazebo built right outside the main temple structure. Many brides and grooms were patiently standing in anticipation for their names to be called out. It was hot and humid.

I could barely catch a glimpse of Lakshmi in the crowd. There was cacophony all around. There have even been some instances where the bride and groom had been mixed up in the melee and the wrong people ended up marrying each other. Some corrected the mistake but many chose to live with the partners chosen erroneously. They believed that it was the will of God which they didn't want to change.

As was custom, I stood there without my shirt but a thin white linen towel wrapped around my shoulders. I was sweating profusely while awaiting our turn. Finally when our names were called out, I saw Lakshmi being escorted by her father and other Nair elders to the gazebo. She was adorned in heavy antique jewellery. Some of that must have been part of the heirloom. She was attired in a bright red Kanjeevaram sari and her hair was full of jasmine flowers. She walked through the crowd quickly. The opulence of her family made them stand out even in such a crowd.

As we entered the *mandapam*, the priest fervently uttered Mantras, that I didn't understand, and the wedding ceremony began. Lakshmi's father took her hands and placed them in mine. This is called *kanyadhaanam*. That was perhaps the last time I saw a coy Lakshmi. We exchanged garlands; I applied red vermillion on her forehead and handed her a Kerala *kasavu settu-mundu* on a tray as a symbol of accepting her as my legally wedded wife. The ceremony was formally over. We were asked to pray to the powerful and much loved Lord *Guruvayoorappan*. She seemed lost in prayers. I just stood there with folded hands thinking about the long day that lay ahead. Sweat had spread the vermillion over her forehead like blood. She looked really beautiful. My true Aphrodite, I thought. We were led to the temple office to sign the marriage register.

As we walked out of the temple office, *achhan* handed me my shirt. That was a great relief for me. We were surrounded by relatives from both the families. Everybody wanted to have a good look at us. I felt like a celebrity. We were escorted to the small dining hall where a typical Malayali *sadhya* was served on fresh green plantain leaves. My shirt was already soaked in sweat. With no air- conditioning, the heat and humidity was hard to bear. I saw the same group of photographers from the engagement ceremony here too. They were trying to film every moment. Though I was irritated seeing them, I heeded to their requests as I didn't want to spoil the festive mood.

After the feast, many relatives came to meet us and hand over wedding gifts. Mrs Nair stood next to us, ensuring that the exquisitely wrapped packets were collected and placed in the waiting cars. I was pleasantly surprised to see a Mercedes S-Class sedan, decorated with expensive orchids, arrive to pick us up. This was Lakshmi's father's gift to her. Most of my relatives maintained a safe distance. They were in shock and awe at the grandeur. Except for a few people like us, not many even owned a vehicle in my family. My parents and elders in the family who stood nearby didn't seem happy that the Nair clan was running the whole show. They also wisely realised that the role of the rich and powerful Nairs would increase in my life as time went by. I had literally moved on and became a remote figure for them. No longer the boy they were used to teasing.

Radha's parents had come for the wedding but Radha didn't.

As per custom, we went to my house where Lakshmi was welcomed home in a traditional manner. *Amma* handed Lakshmi a lit bronze lamp called *villakku*. She stepped into the house putting forward her right leg first. The women of the household ululated loudly. The long, wavering, high-pitched sound made by many women together sounded like a war-cry.

We were taken to the master bedroom and *amma* gave me a small glass of milk. I sipped a little and passed it on to my bride. We then shared a banana. This ritual denoted the initiation of a formal, shared life between the couple.

The house was full of relatives and neighbours. Everyone seemed to jostle just to have a look. After the ritual, *amma* escorted us to my room for some privacy. Lakshmi wanted to have a shower and change her clothes but people kept coming in to meet the bride, mostly without knocking. It would have been rude to lock the door. We barely managed to snatch a few minutes of conversation. Privacy was rare. However, Lakshmi seemed to enjoy the attention and compliments that were being showered on her. She was clearly the very rich bride in a society of middle class people.

Achhan and I had arranged a grand reception that evening at the newest luxury hotel in Kochi. This was for those who weren't invited for the wedding. The Nair clan stayed in the same hotel. It must have cost Mr Nair a lot of money, but it didn't matter to him. He refused my offer to pay for the accommodation. It was his only daughter's wedding. He had invited many of his friends and business partners to the reception. Air conditioned buses were arranged for people to come from Thiruvananthapuram and other distant areas.

Time seemed to race and *amma* constantly reminded us about leaving for the reception. It was she who finally persuaded people to leave us alone in our room. I wore a bespoke suit and a Dormeuil tie gifted to me by my colleagues. Though many female relatives wanted to help Lakshmi dress up, Lakshmi didn't trust their sense of style. Despite murmurs from the relatives who were deprived of their right to dress the bride, only her beautician was allowed in. Those who managed entry into the room after arguments were to remain mute onlookers. *Amma* made sure of that.

I sat in the drawing room entertaining relatives, neighbours and acquaintances. Ajay, along with a bunch of my old friends, walked in, all of them wearing suits just as I had instructed. The married friends had bought along their families. The wives wore their finest silk saris and gold jewellery. Even the children were decked in gold ornaments, especially around their necks and wrists. I preferred my friends to be at the reception rather than the hot and crowded environs of the Guruvayur temple. Their arrival came as a relief to me.

The elders were busy running around, shouting orders, and generally being impatient. The women were busy in the kitchen preparing tea. The servants kept coming in and out of the kitchen serving tea, soft drinks and savouries. The house resembled an Indian railway station during peak hours.

Achhan walked in. He was agitated and said, "Aren't you guys ready yet? It's time to leave." He still managed to frighten me. I pointed to the bedroom where Lakshmi was getting ready. He called *amma* and whispered instructions to her. An excited *amma* barged into the room and ordered all the relatives to leave the room immediately. Her presence added a sense of urgency and the beautician accelerated her job. In 20 minutes, the three women walked out of the room.

Lakshmi wore a heavily embroidered, light pink Kanjeevaram silk sari. While she had worn gold jewellery in the morning, she chose diamonds for the reception, which included a wide choker, drooping ear rings, and bangles. Her hair was styled in a Princess French braid. Light make-up and lipstick with shades of plum made her look gorgeous. Like a princess, I thought.

The intricate designs of the henna on her hands seemed to have turned brighter. The only excess was the number of rings she wore. The heavily embroidered, hand-made, pink sandals were designed to match her overall attire. My heart missed a beat. She looked like Venus, the Goddess of Beauty and Lust. "Isn't this the potent combination that has dictated the fate of many men?" I thought.

This was the second time the women I loved the most were in a bridal attire. Comparisons between Radha and Lakshmi was inevitable. Despite the commonality of affluence, Lakshmi's was an upmarket and well-travelled family. The tastes varied considerably. There was a difference in the way the functions were planned, choreographed and executed. The class of people who attended the soirée also differed.

As we got out of the house in the company of my suited friends, *amma* stockpiled all gifts received in our room and locked it.

The Mercedes was ready. The chauffeur himself was attired in a *mundu* with gold stripes and a white cotton shirt gifted by his employers, to look presentable. *Amma* sat on the front seat and we both occupied the back. *Achhan* followed in his car with a group of elders. Other cars came in a line from their parking places to pick up those who were joining us at the reception. There was a scramble among the less fortunate relatives to get into the larger cars. As the convoy moved silently, led by the Mercedes, those neighbours who hadn't been invited stood staring from outside their houses or terraces. I whispered to Lakshmi, "Looks like we transformed this lane into Circus Maximus." She just raised her brows and I said, "This is a middle class neighbourhood, such flamboyant weddings are very rare here." She nodded her head delicately.

I squeezed her hand to indicate my appreciation of her beauty. She pointed towards *amma*'s seat and smiled. She could keep me waiting as long as she wished. The power structure was now shifting in Lakshmi's favour.

As the convoy reached the hotel gates, we saw many of the guests waiting for us. It wasn't difficult to predict that the evening would be hectic. As we alighted from the car, my in-laws received us and took us to the stage where we were to stand, like exhibits. They, and Lakshmi, introduced me to a steady stream of invitees. I had to smile, shake hands, and mumble greetings to strangers. Lakshmi received the gifts and handed them over to her mother who carefully stored them for cataloguing. It was their obligation to return equally valuable gifts when the time came.

Posing for the mandatory photographs with the guests taxed me the most. After an hour or so, my mouth hurt due to the constant and forceful smiling. My legs started aching and I desperately wanted to sit on the chair. Lakshmi seemed to love the limelight. She had an endless number of friends, colleagues and cousins. They stood around us and regaled her with marital jokes.

There was a commotion as *achhan's* colleagues walked in with their full military regalia. These officers came together and caught everybody's attention. They walked in upright and formally met both of us. Those who personally knew me as a child squeezed me in a tight embrace. The back-slaps and firm handshakes hurt too. *Achhan* made it a point to introduce his colleagues to the prominent members of the Nair family who seemed to be immensely impressed to meet many war heroes. A separate section was arranged for the group to enjoy their Scotch and food.

Boredom started to settle in. Smiling became an arduous task and my legs started becoming wobbly. I finally sat down despite Lakshmi's disapproval. I desperately wanted to have a drink. As I wallowed in my agony, I saw *amma* escorting a couple to meet us. It was Radha and Anil!

I hadn't expected them to come and the sight almost electrified me. I had been waiting for this rendezvous for years. This would be the raison d'être of the day. Subconsciously, Lakshmi was an integral part of my poetic retribution.

I had told Lakshmi about *l'affaire* Radha. Though I hadn't shown her any pictures, Lakshmi had no trouble recognising Radha. Her face froze as she confronted my first love. She had a wry smile as *amma* introduced her to Radha and Anil. Though overtly cordial to each other, there was palpable tension in their interaction.

My parents had already disseminated information about the wealth and political prominence of Lakshmi's family. I guess Radha was curious to meet my princess and had come attired in her finery. Bedecked in her heaviest jewellery, she possibly wore her most expensive silk sari. Anil was wearing a red shirt, white *mundu,* thick jewellery around his neck and wrists, along with the archetypal golden Rado Diastar watch. He was at his garish best.

Honestly, the sight of Radha sent my heart racing. Lakshmi didn't like me shaking Radha's hand. She greeted both Radha and Anil with folded hands. I introduced Radha's father and mother as close relatives and Radha as their daughter. I ignored Anil. It was left to Radha to introduce him as her spouse. Though the conversation appeared warm, the intent was cold. After photographs, they moved on.

I told *amma*, "Ma, I would like to have dinner with Radha and Anil. Choose a large table where we all can sit together. You, *achhan*, Lakshmi's parents, us and them." *Amma* looked at me and said, "Let bygones be bygones." I knew that she wouldn't oblige as she didn't want any trouble in her paradise.

We had been standing for nearly three hours. I indicated to Mrs Nair that I was tired and would like to have dinner. She nodded in acknowledgement. Just then Lakshmi said, "Mummy, can you call that couple who we just met to dine with us?"

"I do not know them," said Mrs Nair. "Radha," whispered Lakshmi.

Mrs Nair's eyes twinkled. She shrewdly went towards Radha's family and invited them for dinner at a large table that was reserved for the Nair family. Once they were seated, she went to Mr Nair and asked him to join us.

As we congregated around the table, Lakshmi and I sat across the rival couple. *Achhan* formally introduced Radha's parents to the Nairs. The conversation between the elders was full of bonhomie. They interacted as if they had known each other for quite some time. There was a lot of laughter at the table.

Radha was drawn into the conversation by *amma* but Anil was largely left out. Lakshmi and her mother played the game very shrewdly. They managed to subtly convey their superior status without being vocal about it. Mrs Nair asked Anil when they would be settling abroad. It was Radha who replied, "Nothing has materialised yet, aunty."

Mrs Nair went on to inform them that we were going on our honeymoon to Europe the next week and then fly to Dubai where we would be residing. Anil seemed hurt. I don't think the other elders noticed the machinations being played out at the table. Lakshmi looked at me. Though there were no emotions displayed, I knew that she was indicating to me that the war was on. She had taken up the cudgels on my behalf.

Mrs Nair ordered tenderloin sizzlers for all of us. I watched Anil's discomfort using the steak knife and fork intently. To add to it, I asked him, "Have you not had steak before?" He just smiled. This was my veni, vidi, vici moment. He quickly gulped some beer, as if to overcome the embarrassment.

The couple had no choice but endure the insults till dinner was over. The 30-45 minutes seemed like a lifetime to me. It was like a theatre of subtle jibes.

Post dinner, Lakshmi's relatives wanted to spend more time with us. In the privacy of family, there was a lot of dancing, singing and drinking.

Finally, as we sat in the car, I couldn't forget what had transpired during the meeting with Radha. What was I trying to do? Attempting to show off my new wife and her upmarket prosperous family? Did I want to tell her that I had married a socially forward woman? Was there an inevitable comparison being drawn? It was perhaps a mixture of everything. The truth was I was still trying to impress Radha. Despite my best efforts, it was a struggle to forget her completely. Her memories and a longing desire for her would remain like a stain forever in my mind.

Both Lakshmi and I were too tired by the time we reached the privacy of our bedroom. We changed into our night dress, hugged each other and slept soundly. Consummation would have to wait for the next day!

vishnu

The phone rang again. It was Lakshmi. I decided to let it ring. She called again. Reluctantly, I picked up the call and asked with a little irritation in my voice, "What happened? We just spoke some time ago?"

She didn't like the tone but said, "Hey, I called to say that Meenu and I are going out for breakfast at the mall on Sheikh Zayed Road. We plan to watch a movie and pick up groceries after that." She loved details. Her itinerary and its nitty-gritties were the last thing I wanted to know, especially when I was on a holiday.

"Sure, go ahead," I said, after a few seconds of silence. "I am in the middle of planning and organising the trip. Will call you later." I was not in the mood for a regular conversation. She would have felt slighted, I could visualise her face tighten. She cut the call.

Meenu was a replica of her mother not only in looks but also attitude. Both hated sitting at home on the weekends or holidays and loved eating out. Given a chance, they would start the day with breakfast and end it with a late night dessert at various restaurants. As a frequent traveller, I spent most of my time in hotels. For me spending time at home and eating home-cooked food was a rarity. It was an unfair battle that I always lost – one man versus two adamant women. They always dictated the agenda. "Mall rats!" I muttered.

The clock showed 12.30 p.m. I decided to walk down to the bar for a beer. It was crowded with people in formal attire. I guessed they had come for a conference and were taking a break. Alcohol was the big draw in Kerala. It was a joke that the only place where the Malayalis would display civic sense or stand in a queue without getting frustrated and angry was at the government-owned outlets that sold liquor.

Sipping the cold brew, I browsed through the messages on my phone. There was one from Vishnu. It said, "Hope you are enjoying Kochi." He was after all, the instigator of this whole idea.

This was one trip that almost didn't happen. During a visit to Bahrain for a project, I happened to read an article on the *Bhaghawathis* or Mother Goddesses of Kerala written by a Vishnu. He turned out to be my counterpart for that project. That weekend, he invited me for a drink. I was keen to know more about the article. I was not disappointed as he spoke with excitement and passion. His article centred on the annual *Bharani* festival held at the *Bhaghawathi* temple at Kodungallur.

"Isn't that the festival where the devotees hurl the choicest of abuses at the Goddess?" I asked. "Along with songs loaded with sexual innuendos," Vishnu added.

"Why abuse a Goddess?" I was curious.

"The *Bhaghawathi* is supposed to like it. Isn't this kind of worship unique?" He lifted his eyebrows and looked at me as if gauging my interest.

Vishnu continued, "The *Bharani* festival lasts for around a month and peaks with the practice of *kaavu-theendal* or the 'ritual pollution' of the temple. During the *kaavu-theendal*, the peasants and people from the lower castes congregate, dressed in bright red robes. The drunk men and women hold sabre-curved swords and wear anklets. They smote their foreheads with these sabres while singing expletive songs. They describe sexual acts and organs in an explicit and vulgar manner to the Goddess. Their sweaty faces and bodies are covered with a mixture of turmeric, vermillion, blood and blind faith. The atmosphere is electric. It is an interplay between the sacred and the profane. It is one of the oldest festivals to honour the fierce Goddess Bhadhrakali."

Vishnu spoke with a certain intensity. I think he loved my interest in the subject.

"This was one of the very few temples that allowed entry to members of the lowest castes many decades ago. There are many stories regarding the construction of the temple. One of it says that it was a king who built it in order to appease Kannagi, the tragic heroine of the Tamil epic Silappadhikaram, estimated to have been written between 100-300 CE.

"Kannagi's story is a powerful one. In short, she was married to a merchant called Kovalan who was enamoured by a courtesan called Madhavi. Despite his marriage to Kannagi, he spent most of his time with Madhavi. After losing all his wealth in pursuit of his illegitimate love, Kovalan, in repentance, returns to Kannagi. She not only accepts him but also gives him her anklet to sell and raise money to restart his business. He goes to the Madurai market to sell it and raise funds.

"Unfortunately, the queen's anklet had also been reported stolen. Kovalan becomes a suspect. He is arrested and taken to the court where the king orders him to be beheaded. Kannagi hears this and rushes to the court in anger. She breaks her other anklet (from the pair) with so much force that the rubies in it scatter all over the floor. The queen's anklet was filled with pearls. Thus, Kovalan's innocence was proven.

"The king's repentance does not calm Kannagi's rage. She rips her breast and throws it at the city cursing that it would burn. She was still a virgin as their marriage had remained unconsummated. It is this power of virgin chastity that burns the city of Madurai. She withdraws the curse only when the Goddess of Madurai pleads with her. After recalling her curse, she goes to Kerala and attains *samadhi* or ritual death. Legend says that her mortal remains are entombed in this temple," finished Vishnu.

I asked, "But she is supposed to be the heroine of a mythical story, isn't she? How can there be a body to be buried?"

I had touched a raw chord. He asked, "That is the challenge, isn't it?"

"Sometimes fragments of truth can be ingrained in myths," he said after a short pause.

"There have been allegations about the presence of a secret granite vault in the recesses of the temple. We do not know if it has the remains of Kannagi or any other woman whose bold defiance of authority could have become the basis for the character of Kannagi. Euhemerism amplified her myth. Beliefs can be so powerful that even mythical characters seem real." Vishnu nodded with a big smile.

"Have you seen the place where she is allegedly buried?" My heart began to pound with excitement at the mystery.

"No, I haven't. The temple authorities don't allow research or scientific explorations. The mystery will persist and the riddle will remain unsolved. Destructive power has been assigned to her due to her chastity as not only a faithful wife but also for accepting her philandering husband."

"She is regarded a Goddess for forgiving adultery? What if it was she who had erred?" I was upset at the depiction. Vishnu chose silence over an argument.

"Stories suggest that after the destruction of Madurai, Kannagi, en route to the Kodungallur temple, stopped at the Attukal temple in Thiruvananthapuram. She appeared before an old man in the form of a little girl and asked him to help her cross the Killi river. She vanished after that and reappeared in the man's dreams in full regalia and requested him to build a temple for her. The old man followed her instructions. She is depicted as an awe-inspiring figure with four hands. She bears weapons such as the sword, spear, and shield and holds a human skull menacingly.

"The *Bhaghawathi* of Attukal is the patron Goddess of women. She is attributed with a dual personality who is predominantly benevolent but retains the latent ability to be violently aggressive. During *Pongala* festival, women from all over the globe come here to participate. They wait in the sun for hours for the priest to come and bless their utensils before starting to cook jaggery-rice as an offering to the Goddess. Naturally, only women are allowed to participate. This has entered the Guinness Book of World Records as the largest congregation of women in the world."

After ordering another round of drinks, Vishnu continued, "There is another interesting temple called the *Chottanikkara Bhaghawathi* temple. It is located in Kochi. Here, the same *Bhaghawathi* is worshipped in three different forms. In the morning as *Saraswathi*, the goddess of knowledge, in the noon as *Lakshmi*, the goddess of wealth, and in the evening as *Durga*, the fiery form. Many people who are 'possessed' are brought here for exorcism.

"Every night, the priests conduct the great sacrifice to propitiate *Durga*. Twelve large vessels are filled with a liquid prepared from a mixture of lime and turmeric. This mixture is symbolic of blood. The senior priest offers this *guruthi'* to *Durga* or *Bhadhrakali* by sprinkling and pouring it around the temple in a symbolic enactment of blood-sacrifice.

"This is when those who are possessed are brought in. It is believed that the Goddess, roused by the blood, purges the evil spirits from the body of their victims. The women tremble and shake violently as the malevolent beings apparently resist the Goddess before the ultimate surrender. After the exorcism, the person is made to hit a metal nail into a *pala* tree with their heads. They bleed profusely. It is not an easy spectacle to watch. I couldn't see the ceremony but the numerous nails struck on the tree remain mute witnesses.

"Kerala is a fascinating world. Like a series of intertwined cobwebs, this is an astonishing psychological world of ancient and medieval beliefs. There is much to learn and unravel."

Vishnu was indeed a compelling narrator. "Krish," he said softly. "I have found my calling. In a couple of years, I plan to relocate to Kerala. I want to write a few books on its ancient mysteries."

"What will you do there? Especially after you write a couple of books? How much scope does Kerala present to you professionally?" I played the doubting Thomas. "Leaving behind the kind of tax-free money you make here…"

But Vishnu seemed to have made up his mind. "Kerala's ancient and medieval religious beliefs, the famed practice of black magic and spirit worship have much to offer to an inquisitive mind. There's enough to keep a bright researcher busy for a lifetime. After all, there is only one life. How much of it will you devote to making money?" He turned philosophical. "With the drop in oil prices, I am not sure how long we will be able to earn these fat, tax-free packages."

That discussion left a deep impression on me. Vishnu seemed to share my interest for the mysterious. After returning to the hotel, I pondered over the discussion.

Once I returned to Dubai, I broached the idea with Lakshmi. I told her that, in the near future, I would like to settle down in Kerala. As a prelude, I wanted to take a short vacation and tour Kerala. Though she pretended to be empathetic, she was horrified at the prospect of leaving foreign shores and returning home on a permanent basis. She dismissed my thoughts, saying that I suffered from the 'return-of-the-prodigal' complex. She expected my enthusiasm to fade away with time.

Life went back to being a discordant harmony of routines. Subconsciously, the thoughts of returning to Kerala gathered strength in me. I started dreaming about becoming a celebrity thinker who would be respected for his structured and well-presented thoughts. The idea was very seductive. I built and lived in an inner world that was not accessible to Lakshmi. It was safe that way.

I devised a plan. I focused all my energies on work, travelled more frequently, and spent most of the time in office. I kept aloof at home, exhibited a reduced appetite, insomnia and occasionally feigned headache and chest pain. I stopped my regular five-mile runs. I became increasingly irritable and angry outbursts at home became normal. Lakshmi began to worry that I was on the brink of a burnout. I refused any treatment despite her constant persuasion.

She insisted that I take a break from the stress at office. I initially refused. I knew Lakshmi would insist on a vacation or a break as I had desired. Sometimes, I felt I was a mean person. Behind her rigidities and insensitive facade, Lakshmi hid a large heart. She was not too difficult to manipulate.

I let her worry by herself. Finally she told me, "Krish, you want a short vacation, right? Maybe this is the right time for that." I chose not to respond. This was going my way.

Lakshmi kept broaching the subject for the next few days. Finally on a weekend, as I was sipping whisky, she sat near me and said, "Honey, I am getting concerned about your health. Why don't you take a short break and travel around Kerala for the next two weeks? You can gather enough experiences to publish a book. I will help you prepare the first draft of a manuscript." She appeared to be genuinely worried. For a change, she was the one who was desperate to send me to Kerala. I responded, "That's a good idea. Let the project I am currently working on stabilise." This was a tactical retreat for me. I didn't want to win the battle so easy.

A couple of evenings later, she told me, "I was talking to Ambika, my best friend. Her family is conducting a Theyyam performance at their *tharawad* in the next couple weeks. She was describing it as a unique religious experience. Why don't you visit her house in Kannur? It could help you craft a compelling story."

I didn't want her to dictate the nuances of my trip. "I want to visit very specific places in Kerala. I don't want to go and stay with people I don't know. Watching Theyyam is not on my agenda now." She was visibly hurt but didn't react. She continued to try and sell me the dreams of being an instant author. Finally, I relented to the trip.

Listing out the places to visit, I decided to begin and end the trip at Kochi. She took over from there and started fretting and fuming over the minute details. She chose the clothes and suggested what to wear and when. I didn't interfere. I wanted her to be deeply responsible for this trip so that at a later period she wouldn't accuse me of wasting time on a holiday. I also wanted to avoid visiting her home.

Thiruvananthapuram was not on the itinerary.

She wasn't happy about Kochi. She told me, "Do not meet that rascal Ajay. He is a wayward character. I don't like the way he looks at me or other women. I despise him."

J ust then the hotel phone rang loudly bringing me back to the present. It was from the reception. "Sir, there is a guest to meet you. Can we send him to your room? His name is Ajay."

Think of the devil and there he is, I thought. "Please do send him."

Of all my old friends, it was with Ajay that I was in touch regularly. I had met him during high school. Our friendship was the talk of the school.

But it all started with a big fight in the school bus one day. Due to a misunderstanding, we ended up calling each other nasty names. A couple of days after that incident, his mother came home and complained to *amma* that I had called her son a bastard. *Amma* beat me badly that day. A few days later, during an inter school football match, Ajay and I found ourselves seated beside each other. We ignored each other at first but as the match started turning in our school team's favour, we cheered enthusiastically together. Rivalry softened with that thrilling victory. As days went by we started talking to each other and Ajay apologised to me for lying to his mother. This led to the solid foundation of our friendship. But my dislike for his mother continued for a long time.

Ajay was sort of a rebel in class. Though I was not good at academics, his marks used to make mine look really good. His academic performance warranted undue attention from the teachers. His mother had to come to school to meet our class teacher regularly.

She was a very refined and attractive woman. She came to school with light make up, lipstick and sunglasses, driving her own car. Most of our mothers weren't like that. After her meeting with the class teacher, Ajay would get some respite. Ajay had inherited her looks. I used to tell him, "The class teacher is infatuated with your mother; that is why he keeps summoning her. As long as you don't score great marks, he must be happy." We used to laugh at that. His mother had worked abroad as a nurse. She was very possessive about him.

One day, on the way back from school, Ajay looked unusually sullen. He responded to my persistent questions mumbling, "My father is home." We boys all had only seen his mother at school. We had assumed that his father had passed away when he was young. So in order to not hurt him, none of us enquired about his father.

I asked him, "Oh, where is he working?" Ajay replied in a sarcastic tone, "Gulf." As this upset him, I didn't pursue the subject any further. During the short period that his father stayed, he went home on time.

Ajay had shades of an anti-hero. He was the one who brought a packet of cigarettes to school and showed us how to exhale smoke through the nose. Ajay was also the one who brought a packet of condoms to school. That was the first time many of us knew what a condom looked like. Each one of us had boasted that it was far too small to fit us. When he laid his hands on an X-rated magazine from his uncle's collection, Ajay let us feast our eyes on the models. He was large-hearted enough to tear the book into half and give one part to me. When *achhan* discovered it, he gave me a sound thrashing and a parting advice, "If you are not clever enough to hide these things, then you are not mature enough to read them." *Amma* looked at me as if she had lost her innocent son forever. She could be over-dramatic at times.

Ajay's good looks and his unusually fair complexion always earned him the attention of the girls in school. He was the recipient of many love-letters, which were left anonymously inside his desk. He never seemed to care about the 'love' the girls expressed for him. Being a diehard romantic, I was always jealous of him. It hurt that none of these girls ever looked at me like that and I didn't get any love-lorn scribblings.

Everybody knew that Ajay and I were best friends. As we moved into the senior classes, some of these girls handed me the letters and chocolates meant for Ajay. Occasionally, I took some of these letters home and read them over and over again. I wondered when a girl would write something like this for me. I dreamt about romancing the prettiest girls in my school. But they remained just that - dreams.

He rarely read the contents of these letters. All he wanted to know was the name of the sender to whom he would reach out. I have seen him with many girls in various corners of the school. It was always afterhours when the building would be almost empty. He used to tell me that he had kissed all of them. Some of these girls were under the impression that they would marry him. He was indeed a girl-magnet. He told me that he needed only the letters and not the chocolates. I unsuccessfully tried to use these chocolates to win the hearts of other girls. They were happy to eat the chocolates but I got nothing in return except 'sweet' smiles. In desperation, I used to plead with him to give me some of his girlfriends. He would laugh and say, "Girls can't be 'made' to love anyone, Krish!" I didn't believe him. But that was then.

From the beginning, I was always the marrying type. Marriage-junkie, Ajay used to call me. He had something against marriage that I never fully understood. Women still fell for him regularly. But true to his stand, he has remained a bachelor. We school friends were jealous of his single but 'active' status.

While I kept falling in love regularly with some girl or the other, Ajay was focused on finding out how many girls in class had reached puberty. He said that if they had hair on their armpits, then they had started menstruating. While talking to girls, he would try to take a peek through the sleeves of their loose school shirts. Once, while playing football after school, we stumbled upon a used sanitary napkin. Ajay used a stick to examine it. He claimed to know a lot about the female reproductive system. He explained to us how and why a sanitary napkin was used, in intimate detail. He became a bigger hero in our eyes.

Ajay seemed to detest long-term relationships. Whenever I told him about my desire to marry some girl or the other, he would laugh saying that marriage was not for him. All he wanted to do was hug girls, feel them, and kiss them.

Ajay always seemed to have money with him. If I asked him about the source, he used to snap at me, "Why are you bothered? Let's spend it in the canteen." Despite his obvious flaws, I found him to be a warm, generous person and I genuinely liked him. I saw in him a man's man. A sort of big brother. He was there for me whenever I needed him. He was my saviour from many bullies.

Ajay used to come home frequently during vacations or on weekends on his bicycle. During one of our long vacations, he dropped by my house and invited me for a movie at a cinema close by. The movie was adult-rated and, despite my keenness to watch it, I was mortified of being caught. If somebody who knew my parents saw me, I would have to suffer a couple of rounds of beatings. Ajay didn't understand my hesitation or the fear of my father. However, he didn't force me and went to watch it alone.

He came back to my house to brag about it. We went to a nearby shop where he bought cigarettes. As we smoked, he explained to me in detail what he saw on the big screen. I suspected that he was exaggerating. However, his descriptions were fairly captivating. I do not know how he was allowed to enter the movie hall. More than the movie, it was the excitement of breaking the law that he seemed to enjoy. The rascal liked to make me jealous with his feats and I admired him for his audacity.

The shopkeeper faithfully reported the cigarette-buying incident to *amma* who surprisingly chose to punish me with a long lecture than the cane. I preferred to be beaten than to be lectured at. She forbade me from interacting with Ajay.

After I completed school, *achhan* requested for a transfer and relocated to Delhi. He felt that it would give me better educational opportunities. I was not happy being away from Ajay, but I suspect it didn't affect him too much. He could sometimes be detached. I wrote letters to him, but gradually I stopped as I never got a reply. We never met for a long time after that.

After my professional education, I was hired by a company based out of Dubai. My family relocated to Kochi after *achhan's* retirement. I wanted to spend a couple of weeks with my parents before I moved to the Middle East.

I decided to meet Ajay during this time. He wasn't home and I met his mother. She looked much older than her age. She looked at me like a stranger and I had to re-introduce myself. She invited me in and started crying.

She kept lamenting how Ajay hadn't settled down yet. He had apparently dropped out of college and had joined a travel course at a local institute. He now worked in a travel agency. She was worried that, unlike others, her son had still not found a focus in life. I left my number with her.

When Ajay called, he sounded happy that I was back. He insisted that we meet that very evening. He came on his motor bike and we drove to the nearby restaurant. I mentioned my conversation with his mother. He just waved his hands in dismissal.

I asked him, "Why did you drop out of college? Without a degree, what are you going to do?"

He stared outside for some time and said, "I am not a conventional man. Have I had a normal life like all of you guys?" I didn't answer.

"What about your father?" I was curious.

"Haven't met that bastard in the last few years! That woman is mad. She still pines for him," he spoke dispassionately about his parents. His disgust for his mother was quite evident. He could be detached when he wanted to, very detached.

We ended the conversation there. I tried to change the topic. Naturally, it turned to his favourite subject - women.

Ajay held the belief that women liked bad boys. He used to say that while they would like to settle down with people like me, they fantasised and often pursued people like him to satisfy their 'carnal cravings'. This was the difference between angels and demons. He liked to call himself the spawn of the devil. He had a very conflicted mind and belief system.

"Oh, c'mon. Married women do not go looking for people like you, Ajay," I argued. In reality, I wanted hear more about his encounters.

He just raised his eyebrows as if you ask, "Why?"

"If they get caught, they run a higher risk. Don't they?" I spoke like the classic idiot.

"Women are smarter than you think, Krish. And they are trustworthy. Better than us men." He seemed keen not to pursue the conversation further.

His mother was worn out by him. Ajay found joy in tormenting her. Lack of empathy and ego-centricity defined his character. A master of subtle manipulation, Ajay exhibited a lack of remorse and adamantly chased his objectives. Sometimes, I felt that he was Janus-faced. When he wanted, he could switch on a compassionate and charming facade to get his way. Though he hated his father, he subconsciously wanted to be like him. His activities sometimes bordered on the criminal. Infamy seemed to be his objective. Albeit temporarily, he wanted to 'own' his women and hold them enthralled.

"You can't own people," I would protest and his standard reply was, "Win their minds and the bodies will follow."

He believed what he said. For him, life was a constant combat that needed frequent victories.

Ajay was somebody I wanted to be; partly. He was not afraid and embraced his dark side. Whereas I was a conformist.

The constant ringing of the doorbell indicated that Ajay had come. It was 4.00 p.m. Ajay rushed in and embraced me. He seemed very happy. He was dressed in a black suit and a striped tie. "Uniform?" I asked.

For a man who was a rebel, to be attired in any kind of uniform seemed odd to me. "Contradictions of life," he said, shaking his head.

"But conformity?" I asked

"It feels like being in captivity," he removed and threw the jacket on the bed and aggressively pulled out the tie.

"Feel better, now?" he asked as if he had done me a big favour.

It had been sometime since we met, there was much to catch up on. He didn't seem to have changed much.

When I asked him if he would like tea or coffee, he seemed to hesitate for a moment and then asked, "Do you expect me to have coffee with you? That too today? After we meet after such a long time" This was pure theatre.

I understood. "Do you want to drink so early?" He winked shamelessly.

I took out the bottle of scotch and handed it over to him and ordered a pot of tea for myself. He quickly opened the bottle and poured a stiff one for himself. He didn't even dilute it with water.

He finished his first drink and was in a hurry to update me on the local gossip. When I thought I had heard enough and before he ran out of stories, I decided to go for a shower. When I returned, half the bottle was over.

Ajay said, "We should leave now. I want to see the sunset at the Kochi beach." He took the bottle again with the intention of a refill.

"Don't drink yourself to death. You need to live a long life, buddy!" I took away the bottle and closed it before returning it to him.

He looked at me and said, "I am in the throes of taking an important decision. Sometimes, I think of settling down. I am tired of living a nomad's life."

"You? And settling down? With one woman? It must be the whisky talking." I didn't take him seriously.

He seemed to slip into what looked like disappointed contemplation. He said, "I think I have had my share of fun. May be it would be fun to live with just one woman. These days, loyalty seems to appeal to me. Tell me, Krish. How is married life? Does Lakshmi listen to you?"

I didn't want to tell him everything about my life. "Why would she listen to me?"

"Does she obey you?" he asked, hesitating a little.

"Obey me? Am I her lord and master? She is an individual with her own mind. We don't live in the medieval world where the wife's primary job was to let her husband have sex with her, bear his children and look after them all. If that's your expectation, don't even think about marriage."

He looked hurt as if there was a revelation that turned his world upside down. "Let's go and watch the sunset."

I walked towards the door. I didn't want to continue this conversation. It looked like Ajay had a new car. I asked him, "When did you buy this?"

"Buy? This is a gift from one of my girlfriends. Her husband bought her a new car, so she gave this to me."

"Husband? Your girlfriend is married?" My old adoration for him was back in full force.

"Yeah. He works in the United States and she runs a small travel business here. She didn't want to stay away from Kochi. So, she returned from the States a couple years ago. I am her mentor." He laughed out loud.

"Oh! And?" I probed.

"She often feels lonely and needs male company."

"So the car is in return for a favour?"

"No, you idiot! It is an additional bonus."

"She tells me that her husband can't drive her into a sexual frenzy the way I do. Apparently, I make her feel like an insatiable sexual creature," he boasted.

"And what did she tell her husband? I mean about this car?" "She said that she sold it. What else?" he asked me.

"Did you pay her?"

"Of course. In kind." Ajay didn't look at me. "Gracy thinks that she is the only one. But I spend 'quality' time with other women too." He searched my face for signs of envy. "I feel like a Sultan with a harem!"

"So, what happens when her husband comes on holiday?" "Then she turns into an epitome of loyalty and love. Lucky for me, his trips never last more than a week. But I make it a point to visit their house for a cup of tea while he is there. I feel like a victor. For me, her house is a symbolic crime site." He chuckled. "So tell me, Krish. How's your love life? There must be many beautiful women with whom you could sleep. Paid or otherwise?" He seemed to be taunting my masculinity.

"Only if I had remained a bachelor like you, lucky devil!" I felt envious but I wanted to avoid the topic as it always ended up with me feeling small.

"Even if you were…" He left the sentence incomplete.

"You are a narcissist, Ajay. It is time for you to see a psychiatrist," I suggested. Ajay seemed lost in thought. After a minute or so asked, "Do you remember Devi?"

"Yes," I replied.

"She got married to a software engineer and has two little girls. They were abroad for a few years and are back in Kerala now. Do you want to pass by her home?"

"What for?" I asked.

"Let's say hello to her and meet that lucky rascal. I saw her at a mall last week. She is still voluptuous." He sounded just like the lusty school boy that he once was.

"Do you always have women in your mind? Aren't you satisfied yet?" I asked him.

"Women are women. They are like intoxicants. The more you have, the more you need. I can't even dream of spending my entire life with a single woman. Don't you get bored living with the same woman? Doesn't the routine get boring?" he asked. Was he the same person who told me that he was considering marriage some time ago? I wondered.

Since I didn't respond, he said, "I like the hunt. It gives me a high like nothing else can. It is better than the kill. That is why I get bored with all women soon."

"Where do you find so many women to seduce?"

"Most of my women are those who come to the agency to book tickets."

"Book tickets at a travel agency? Can't they book online?" I was surprised.

"Not all are net-savvy like you. Many still prefer booking tickets the old fashioned way. I gauge them and mark out those I am interested in. Their contact details are easy to get from the booking system. Initiating a call is relatively easy but getting them to sleep with me is not. I like spending considerable time seducing them but once they fall prey to my charms, I lose interest quickly. I enjoy my conquests for a short period of time. I love it when they plead with me not to break the relationship. Those moments are what I live for. It's a high!" He spoke as if these women were nothing more than a commodity or prey. A complex amalgam of contradictory feelings - envy and revulsion - rushed through my mind.

Woman at the Shack

Ajay suddenly hit the brakes hard. He started shouting profanities. "Look at those young fools on their bikes? These days, money seems to grow on trees. Every boy who has a shadow for a moustache wants a bike. During our younger days, getting a bike was a near impossibility. There is no dearth of money in Kochi now." Ajay was fuming.

"Even if a biker hits a car, the crowd that gathers around quickly and takes the side of that fool. The person in the car is obviously richer, so the anger of the mob turns against him. The verdict is passed quickly. If one were to protest innocence for too long, the crowd could turn rowdy. One has to shell out a substantial amount of money to the 'victim', who just has to feign extreme pain. Everybody here seems to have become a communist. They love the victory of the poor over the rich. It's all a fantasy people love to indulge in."

He put his head out of the window and spat on the road. "Though communism has died in its countries of origin, many Malayalis still believe in its outdated doctrines and treat the Communist Manifesto and Das Kapital almost as religious scriptures. Look at those walls, defaced with pictures of Karl Marx, Friedrich Engels, Vladimir Lenin, Fidel Castro, Che Guevara and even Josef Stalin." He pointed his fingers at the walls of a public office.

"Many of these local communist champions haven't stepped out of Kerala and they glorify the 'revolutions' that happened in faraway countries. Do these balladeers of revolution know the real stories behind their heroes? The gulags, the genocides, the famines etc.?" He was fuming now. His face had turned red. "These powerful ballads of revolution are still used to intoxicate the rank and file. Thoo!" He spat out loud.

"Don't be angry at everything, Ajay. There have been many honest communists here also who genuinely worked for the cause of the downtrodden." I wanted him to cool down.

"Of course. Most of them died in penury leaving their families in the care of the party." Fortunately, he left it at that.

We reached fort Kochi beach before the sun set. Ajay's anger and irritation had by then tapered down. We ran like children towards the beach to see the red sun being swallowed by the hungry sea. Unaware of the predicament of the sun, a large ship moved painfully slowly, cutting through the thick sea weeds. The salty wind blew on our faces.

Men, clad in faded *lungies* and torn vests, were busy operating the Chinese nets, trying hard for fresh catch. The white sands of the beach had become dirty with litter that included plastic bags, covers and bottles.

The hawker selling groundnuts kept beating his semi-rusted metal frying pan to attract the attention of the customers. He was dry-roasting the nuts in hot sand, which was constantly being heated by a kerosene stove. He packed the groundnuts in old newspaper strips rolled into a cone.

Fishermen in small dugout boats were returning to their abode. The muted splash of their 'rows' were rhythmic. We sat at the beach munching on the groundnuts silently watching the world go by.

Around 7 p.m., Ajay suggested that we get a drink. We walked towards a nearby restaurant. "This part of Kochi is trying to become genteel. Many heritage buildings are being turned into restaurants, bars or art galleries. One can get fancy cocktails here. Some foreign tourists have taught the locals how to mix a good drink." Ajay played the guide.

There was an extensive range of cocktails on the menu but we settled for whisky.

"This was once an old go-down where spices were packed and stored for export. When the original owners migrated to the United Kingdom, they sold it to this young lady. The smart woman renovated and transformed the crumbling building into this beautiful restaurant. She spent a lot of money and effort to collect artefacts from all over Kochi to keep its ethnicity intact. This building, thus, has a 'spicy' history," said Ajay, laughing.

The waiter was a very thin man with a large, salt and pepper, handlebar moustache dressed in jeans and a white shirt. His black bowtie made him look like a joker from an outdated circus company. His shoes weren't polished and looked as old as him. From my mannerisms, he probably guessed that I lived abroad. He treated me with a little extra respect. I felt like a foreigner in my own backyard. It felt good.

We had our drinks at a leisurely pace. Ajay lamented the rapid transition and modernisation of Kochi. He was also angry that the young people were able to find well-paying jobs. He strongly felt that money was destroying the original social fabric. "I feel like an outsider now!"

I was getting irritated with his constant complaining. "Why don't you relocate to another country, then?"

He looked at me as if he had not understood my question. Then he smiled. A knowing smile. But he did not say anything.

We sat there for a couple of hours. Ajay suggested that we have dinner. Both of us were reasonably drunk. When I suggested that we have dinner at the same restaurant, he protested, "These places are designed for tourists, not us natives. Let's have a good Malayali meal from the shacks nearby. They serve excellent seafood. Let me buy you dinner." He was unusually pushy and generous. I went by his decision.

The shacks were small stalls built in a row near the beach, run by young men. The fragrance of frying fish emanated strongly from the small, open kitchens. Makeshift tables covered with rexine and plastic chairs made me uncomfortable. The only light was from the small wicker lamps placed on the tables. The owners, who waited on the tables themselves, spoke reasonably good English. Ajay spoke authoritatively to the 'chef', demanding fresh catch. He wanted to inspect the fish before it was cooked.

Chef Babu rushed into the kitchen and brought out two large plates filled with *karimeen*, prawns and lobsters. He put up a great show and presented it as if he had reserved the fish for us or the fish were caught from deep sea only for our consumption. Ajay listened to the chef's descriptions intently and touched the fish with a finger to check for freshness. The size of fish that Babu displayed wasn't up to his satisfaction. He ordered fried rice, prawn curry and fried *karimeen* but insisted on the large ones. This would be my first authentic Malayali dinner after landing in Kochi.

Babu warned us that we would have to wait for some time so he could get fish according to our order. This meant that our meal would be delayed. Ajay was constantly messaging on his phone. He seemed to be getting impatient.

The customers were mainly tourists, both domestic and foreign. A large Bengali family sat beside our table and chatted loudly. Bored, I unsuccessfully tried to make sense of what they were telling each other.

Hunger pangs hit me. Seated close to the kitchen, I was far more sensitive to the sizzle of frying fish and the smell of curries. The whisky in my stomach seemed to have amplified my hunger.

The chefs were talking to each other animatedly and the manager was shouting orders to the waiters. It was very hot and humid. There was cacophony all around. Ajay was watching me closely. He seemed to be worried that I would leave the restaurant in frustration. He got a bottle of cola from Babu and walked towards the car. Returning in five minutes, he gave me the cola bottle and said, "Go ahead, take a sip."

He had mixed some Scotch in it. Mixing whisky and coke was sacrilege as far as I was concerned. I didn't like the taste but I decided to adapt. Ajay stepped out of the shack and started talking on the phone animatedly. I could make out that he was agitated.

The alcohol and the heat from the kitchen made me sweat profusely. Soon, my clothes were drenched. The waiter came out of the kitchen balancing a few plates expertly, like an artist. I looked at him in anticipation but these large plates of white rice, fish curry and fried fish were for the Bengali family. Watching them dig into the delectable fare made me ravenous. Babu smiled at me sheepishly and signalled that my food would be ready in no time. They clearly needed more people in the kitchen.

As I sipped from the cola bottle impatiently, a young tourist walked into the shack. She was of average height but her slender frame made her look taller. A cloth bag with the picture of *Ganesha* hung loosely on her bony shoulders. She wore a loose, sleeveless, cotton maxi dress printed with large blue and white flowers. She chose a table across ours. A faded, red bandana kept her unruly, curly blonde hair in place. Her sunglasses were large and hung in the front of her dress. Her skin was tanned. She must have spent a lot of time on the beach. The lady would have been in her late twenties or early thirties.

The waiter lit the small wicker lamp on the table. Though I couldn't hear what she ordered, I thought she was asking what the specials were. She seemed to be a regular here. After a short conversation, Babu shook his head vigorously, scribbled on a notepad, and went back to the kitchen. She took out a small bottle of mineral water and a book from the cloth bag. She flipped through the pages and started reading it.

She became conscious of my attention and looked straight at me. In the flickering light of the lantern, her deep blue eyes looked strikingly beautiful. Like miniscule oceans. I shifted my gaze and looked elsewhere. Ajay was busy sending a message or an email on his Blackberry. I disliked people who were always on the phone. At that moment I couldn't resist stealing another glance at the tourist. She had thick eyebrows and wore no make-up. She was busy texting somebody on her phone. She wasn't strikingly beautiful but there was something about her that was attractive. Something that made me want to look at her again and again. I didn't know what that 'something' was.

Ajay finally walked in. He saw the woman and winked at me. Instead of sitting across the table, he sat beside me so that he could have a good look at her. She was reading, oblivious to the surroundings. Ajay kept staring at her. I prodded Ajay and said, "Don't you stare like that. It is awkward."

"She is provocative, isn't she? I can't take my eyes of her." He seemed smitten by her.

I said, "There is something about her. Agreed."

"Look at her boobs. They are small and just a handful." Ajay went on to describe what he would do to her if he could get her in bed.

"Sleazy rascal!" I said and hit him on his shoulders. We laughed like school boys. He reached for the bottle and took a swig.

Babu came out half walking, half running. There was a plate of steaming rice and a large bowl on his tray. He rushed towards her and placed them on the table.

I looked at Babu and asked him in Malayalam, "Didn't I order before her, Babu? You give her priority because I am a native and she is a foreigner?"

That comment hurt him. He said, "Sir, since you had insisted on having large *karimeens*, we had to ask for a fresh delivery. That is why your order is getting delayed. Your fish is on the frying pan. She had asked for shrimp curry and white rice which was readily available."

The conversation attracted her attention. She looked at me with a half-smile. She had possibly guessed that we were upset that she was served first. She went back to reading the book and continued eating. I unsuccessfully tried to read the title. All I could see was the picture of a man whose face was brightly painted in red and black on the cover.

Babu brought our food in a few minutes. The smoke from the plates was pungent with the heavy aroma of spices. Ajay scooped the rice onto his plate as if he had not eaten for three days. I ate slowly and sweated profusely. I looked for the girl but she had left by then.

I told Ajay, "Your beauty finished her meal and left while you were hogging." He didn't seem to care and said absent-mindedly, "We will meet her again." After settling the bill, we started towards the car. He was silent. A slight breeze blew hesitantly.

He dropped me back at the hotel around 10.30 p.m. I was happy to be back in air-conditioned comfort. I removed my jeans and T-shirt and left them on the chair. Then I jumped into bed in just my underwear without taking a shower. I could not have done this at home. As I lay down, I couldn't forget that woman. Why did Ajay say that we would meet again? Was he serious or was it his bravado speaking? I decided to forget about her and waded into deep drunken sleep.

jew street

I woke up early the next day. Despite persistent efforts, going back to sleep again proved impossible. The clock showed 5.30 a.m. Rather than twisting and turning in bed, I decided to go for a run. Due to constant taunts from Lakshmi that I looked older than my age, I had taken up running last year. Though a five-mile run was demanding, the resultant 'runner's high' was thrilling.

The sun was on the brink of victory with the night and Kochi looked beautiful in the first rays. I was beginning my research today and wanted to go through the plan in my mind as I ran. The next three days would cover the socio-cultural history of Kochi. Watching Kathakali and Mohiniattam was high on the agenda.

Kathakali is Kerala's iconic classical dance-drama. The predominantly green facial make-up, beautiful head gear, and elaborate costumes would present great photo opportunities. Skilful make-up transforms Kathakali actors into various characters from the epics like deities or demons. Ironically, male actors performed the roles of female characters too!

Mohiniattam is the dance of the enchantress. Generally performed solo, it is gracefully feminine with wave-like body movements. Delicate themes of love are performed with suggestive gestures, rhythmic footwork, and lyrical music. It would be great to watch and photograph these artists wearing their white or off-white costumes with gold border. This was a dance performed by women.

I thought I could start my story by elaborating and contrasting these two dance forms. As I ran, my mind planned furiously. There was little time to waste.

I stopped at a nearby tea stall and asked for strong tea. The vendor asked me, "With or without?" When I had a confused look, he clarified, "With sugar or without?" My body craved for sugar.

The vendor poured out tea from a large shapeless aluminium saucepan into a glass tumbler. He used an old steel spoon to dig into a jar full of sugar. He then took another tumbler and poured tea into it from a considerable height. This transfer happened three to four times and the tumbler was filled with frothy tea. Just like beer! He did this without spilling a drop. The tea was strong and too sweet, yet it tasted better than the one served at the hotel.

After breakfast at the hotel, I loaded my backpack with my digital camera, a notebook, pen, and other essentials. I wanted to record my experiences the old-fashioned way.

An auto-rickshaw seemed appropriate for the trip, rather than a taxi, for an authentic feel. I stood outside the hotel trying to find a driver who would accompany me to the places I wanted to visit.

I flagged down many vehicles but none of the drivers agreed for a reasonable price. It was getting hotter and I began to lose hope of an auto-rickshaw trip. As I turned back to return to the hotel, an old vehicle came towards me slowly. It screeched to a stop painfully. Driving it was an old man with thick glasses and a tattered khaki shirt. His hair and stubble were white, in contrast to his dark complexion. A short man with a large belly, he took a moment to gauge me.

Haggling with him was not easy and he put up great resistance. He asked for 750 rupees, all-inclusive for the whole day. It wasn't difficult to understand that he was merely trying his luck. The entire trip would consist of just a few kilometres. His old vehicle would barely consume two litres of fuel. It was a windfall for him. I feigned a lack of interest.

He was not willing to lose the opportunity to earn a decent amount of money with relative ease. With a condescending smile he said, "Okay, okay, I will give you a 100 rupees discount. Normally, I don't settle for less." He made it sound like he was doing me a great favour, which was reserved for exceptional circumstances. I didn't fall for it and started walking away slowly towards the hotel.

He got out of the vehicle and walked towards me, obviously in an attempt to strike a deal. "What is the amount you have in mind?"

"500 rupees all inclusive. Let's start at the Mattancherry Palace."

His eyes looked like large old balls through the thick lenses of his spectacles. He displayed a hurt so dramatic as if I wanted to buy his rickety vehicle, which he treated like a racing car, for a paltry amount.

"I might as well take a taxi for the money that you are demanding." I think he got the point. He relented.

The rexine upholstery was worn-out, with most of the sponge missing. The exposed plywood looked partly naked. Old posters of yesteryear actresses adorned the sides, as if to offer some relief. As I sat gingerly in it, he said, "I have been a guide and mentor to many tourists who visit Kochi. You do not look like somebody who lives here. Let me be your guide today." He gave his rehearsed smile. He was trying to upsell his services.

Now that he had assured his earnings for the day, he indulged in what seemed like his passion. Talk! He introduced himself as Anthony and informed me proudly that he had been driving the auto-rickshaw for more than two decades. Without waiting for my response, Anthony continued his conversation as if he was talking to himself.

The rickety contraption moved at the speed of a bicycle and its loud noise made it difficult to converse. Though I missed much of what he said, I gathered that he had a 'small' family of five members. When he said that God had 'blessed' him with three children, two boys and a girl, I had to muffle a laugh.

He said proudly, "Both my sons are in Dubai. They earn a lot of money!" That caught my attention, "What do they do to earn so much money?"

"One is a welder and the other an aluminium fabricator. It is my daughter who didn't study much."

"Why, Anthony?"

"Despite numerous attempts, she failed to clear her matriculation exams." He laughed out loud and didn't seem worried at all.

"Aurlin now helps Celine in the household chores. She watches all the Malayalam soaps on the television dutifully and dreams of a rich husband from the Middle East!"

"Aurlin? Is that your daughter's name?" I asked.

"Yes, Celine is my wife. The names of my sons are Ridson and Rocklin."

"How did you choose these names? These are not typical Malayali names."

"We are not typical Malayalis, sir! We are of Portuguese descent." There was a tremor of pride in his voice. "My full name is Anthony Rozario."

This was interesting.

He slowed down his vehicle to reduce the noise and said, "We are also called *Parangis*." He seemed to giggle.

"Isn't that an insult?" I asked. He behaved as if he didn't hear me.

On the road, numerous vehicles were jostling with each other. Everybody wanted to overtake the other. In a state where fiery speeches on communism or socialism, still stirred hearts, capitalism seemed to be in full swing. Evidence of money and prosperity were hard to miss. The blood red flags of the communists fluttered at the junctions like doctrinal contradictions. Considering the popularity of leftist ideology in Kerala, people seemed to enjoy worshipping Mammon at the altar of communism. The best of both worlds.

The lethargic movement of the vehicle enabled me to observe life unrolling slowly. Anthony gradually brought the vehicle to a halt. We had reached our first stop, the Mattancherry Palace.

Despite being a Kochiite who grew up here, I had never been to this area before. As it was a weekday, the place was nearly deserted. There was a spatter of foreign tourists loitering around. After the palace, I planned to visit the Santa Cruz Basilica and St. Francis Church before ending the trip at the Paradesi synagogue. Ajay had insisted that we meet at the synagogue in the evening.

The palace was smaller than what I had imagined. Despite Anthony's generous offer to be my guide, I wanted an experienced person to take me through the history and significance of the monument. Though dejected, Anthony introduced me to Raghavan.

Raghavan was a tall, dark man who sported a thick moustache and an air of historic importance. He opened the sales pitch, "Our family has been closely associated with the Kochi royal family for long. My forefathers have worked in various capacities at this palace." His story was a little far-fetched. The objective was to convey that his close association with the former royalty made him the best guide. He asked for 400 rupees for his services making it sound like a paltry amount. Anthony slowly shook his head that seemed to indicate "Couldn't I have done the job? It was your choice. Now, you suffer!"

Raghavan didn't know that haggling was a skill I had considerable command over. "I will give you 200 rupees. Not that many tourists seem to be seeking your guidance today. I can always find somebody else or find detailed information online." I tapped on my tablet gently but was careful not to challenge his ego. I moved towards the ticket counter alone.

Raghavan's pride did not allow him to follow me. Anthony played the peacemaker and told me, "Lets close the deal at 250 rupees so that both of you are happy." The extra 50 rupees must have been Anthony's fee for breaking the deadlock. It was a win-win deal. Raghavan seemed secretly relieved that he wouldn't have to go home empty-handed.

The large, well-preserved mural paintings on the walls were breath taking. They depicted scenes from the Hindu mythology in intricate detail using natural dyes. Considering the age of the paintings, photography was not allowed. I tried to soak in as many details as possible. The dexterity and depth of imagination of the painters was admirable.

Raghavan insisted on giving me structured information befitting his status as a palace-insider. "Let me tell you a little bit about the palace before we go on."

"Please do," I encouraged him.

"This was built in 1555 by the Portuguese and gifted to the King of Kochi. They had plundered a temple nearby that had angered the king and his people. This gift was an attempt at redemption. Then the Dutch captured Mattancherry in 1663 and seized it. They made significant alterations to it. From then on, this is known as the Dutch palace. It was wrested by Hyder Ali, the soldier-ruler of Mysore, and then by the East India Company."

"Significant political traction for such a small structure. Impressive."

Raghavan then pointed towards the polished shiny black flooring. "Looks like black marble, eh? This was the traditional Kerala style flooring. It was made from a mix of burnt coconut shells, charcoal, lime, vegetable extracts and egg whites. Like the palace, it has endured," he said with a slight philosophical tone.

We took our time moving through the various sections that showcased palanquins that once transported the royals, their weapons, and hundreds of photographs of the members of the erstwhile royal family. To me, the royals looked like normal people. The princes and princesses weren't extremely beautiful, as described in stories. None of them wore too much jewellery either. My objective wasn't to examine museums. I wanted stories about people. Exciting snippets about ordinary folks who lived and died here. Suddenly, I was not sure if I was doing the right thing.

After exiting the palace, Raghavan took me to the adjacent *Pazhayannur Bhaghawathi* Temple. "This is where the ancestral deity of the Cochin royal family was consecrated."

It was a fairly small temple located within a large compound.

"Goddess? Why not a God?" I posed a casual question.

"Mother-Goddesses were considered very fierce and powerful. In keeping with that spirit, mothers and elderly women were attributed with spiritual power. They were highly respected."

And then his expression changed. "Although a predominantly matrilineal society, very few female members of the royal families enjoyed temporal power. Sometimes, decisions were taken in their name, yet the actual decision-makers were men." He ground his teeth in anger. Was it a practiced performance or a natural reaction? I tried to read his face. Unsuccessfully. In less than an hour, the guided tour was over.

There was something about Raghavan. It occurred to me that he would be able to help me with the human stories I was seeking. The best way to spend more time with him was to buy him tea. As we sipped the hot brew, I probed. "Many women in traditional Nair families owned property and had a strong say in the matters of the household. Isn't it true?"

He stared at the road and said absent-mindedly, "Many owned property and had a say. But that was within the precincts of the house or *tharawad*. It was the men who enjoyed political authority." He was quiet for a few moments, focused on finishing the tea. He consumed the piping hot sea as if it was lukewarm water.

"They were insecure about their women and connived with each other to maintain control over them." He looked at me as if he was measuring my interest.

He continued, "There were a couple of customs that existed in medieval Kerala called *mannapedi* or *pulapedi*. Literally translated, they mean the fear of the lower caste *Mannans* or *Pulayas* respectively. In the time of rigid caste system and untouchability, conceptually, members of these lower castes could defile a Nair or upper caste woman by throwing stones or twigs at them or by touching them. In certain cases, even if they sighted a woman and shouted '*kande, kande*' which means 'I saw, I saw', the woman could be considered polluted. The poor woman was left with no choice but go with the man who defiled her or, alternatively, pursue a life as a mendicant. Also, the woman who lost her caste in this manner could be killed by her relatives or sold as a slave. This was allowed mainly during the month of Ramayana."

"Oh, but how? The Nairs were higher caste warriors who bore arms. How could a member of the lower caste dare 'defile' a Nair woman?" There was disbelief in my voice.

"Fear is the key." He sounded ominous. "An effective way to keep the women in their places. In those days, loss of caste was akin to social suicide. It worked as a deterrent to those women who took matrilineality too seriously and wanted authority," Raghavan winked.

"Eventually a ruler banned this practice and decreed that such pollution could be washed away with a ritual bath. This was offered as an escape route for women who repented and fell in line. Authority through matrilineality." He raised his brows; his voice had a tinge of anger. I had inadvertently pushed his 'activist' button.

"In medieval Kerala, women from the lower castes were not allowed to cover their upper bodies. In case they did, they had to remove it at the sight of an upper caste male or female. There were severe penalties for breaking this rule. Did you know that *mulakkaram* or breast tax was also prevalent in the region? Based on the size and attractiveness of the breast, a certain amount of tax had to be paid. Of course, the officials could ogle the 'assets' for 'valuation'."

A twisted smile played on his lips.

"Humiliating!" I said, feeling disgusted.

"Fighting these customs was not easy, but Nangeli, a low caste woman, decided not to pay the breast tax. When the tax collector came, she cut her breasts and offered them on a plantain leaf to him."

I cringed at that thought.

"Nangeli died due to excessive bleeding. But, she made a powerful political statement that triggered a revolt. This forced the ruler to abrogate the law. Considering the strong caste hierarchy that existed, it would have taken a lot of provocation to revolt. The place where Nangeli lived is called *Mulachi Parambu* or 'The Land of the Lady of the Breasts'.

While the lower caste women could at least move around freely, the high caste *Nambuthiri* women suffered the most. They were subjected to extreme seclusion, confined indoors, and addressed as the *antharjanam* or 'people who lived inside'. Confinement, even in golden cages, can be the biggest punishment. Isn't it?"

"Was there no escape for the women from the oppression of the caste system?" I empathised with the women.

He nodded his head slowly, "Conversion to Christianity offered some immunity. But this was not an option available for most women," Raghavan concluded.

It was close to lunch time and I offered 100 rupees more than the fees I had negotiated. He refused to take anything additional despite my insistence.

Raghavan seemed to have enjoyed my undivided attention. Wanting to hear more, I offered to buy him lunch. I requested Anthony to take us to a good restaurant. This was my way of keeping him happy. He chose his favourite restaurant and it showed. It was a dingy restaurant that apparently served the 'best *biriyani*' in town.

Anthony smartly chose to sit away from us and eat. Despite being a modern professional, I had my reservations sharing the same table with a 'driver'. Raghavan was different. He was the interpreter of local traditions and history. We sat across each other.

Raghavan started again, as we waited for our food, "Child marriage was the norm in medieval Kerala. Societal pressure ensured that a girl was married off before she was ten and lived in the abode of her in-laws. Though consummation would happen only after she attained puberty, she started contributing in the housework from day one. This was the most prevalent practice among the higher castes.

"The caste system did not impose any restrictions on the higher caste man for having sexual relations with a lower caste woman. But the woman could be punished for inappropriate intimacy with the man. The caste system was a mere tool in the hands of men and could be used for subjugation. We men have an innate fear of women, don't we? Most men are insecure around women. Like modern men, medieval men imprisoned their women using taboos and customs." Raghavan nodded slowly.

The waiter, dressed in an old t-shirt that must not have seen detergent for few weeks, and blue faded *lungi*, came in with plates filled with chicken *biriyani*. It was hot but Raghavan started digging into it right away. He seemed very hungry. He said, "Haven't had breakfast."

He finished the meal in no time and returned quickly after washing his hands. When I asked for a spoon to eat the food, the waiter stared at me. He seemed to admonish me with a look that seemed to say, "Nobody eats good *biriyani* with a spoon!" I had no intention of using my hand to eat the oil-soaked spicy food. I also wanted to avoid the wash basin. From where I sat, I could hear people rinsing their mouths and spitting in it. They made a lot of noise and it was revolting for me.

Satiated, Raghavan watched me struggling with the food. He said, "The repulsive sati system was also prevalent in Kerala. The wife was expected to immolate herself in her husband's funeral pyre. This was glorified as *sahagamanam* or accompanying the lord. The Brahman women who did not commit sati lived under severe social restrictions. They were not allowed to participate in social functions, they were allowed just one meal a day, and had to sleep on the ground lest her husband fell from the heavens. Many widows were quite young.

"The Devadasi system ensured that many women were dedicated as the dancing girls of the God. They resided within the temple complex to look after 'his' comforts. They were trained in fine arts such as singing and dancing. However, in reality they eventually ended up as captive sexual mates of the kings and the other powerful elite."

Raghavan was getting angry again. I left the food unfinished. After settling the bill, I dropped him back at the Dutch Palace. I had learnt so much from a humble guide.

It was already 3 p.m. Anthony suggested we skip the rest of the places on the list and move to the Jew Street as entry to the synagogue would close at 5.30 p.m. I didn't mind as I had heard enough stories today about the lives of women in Medieval Kerala. They definitely didn't enjoy lives where they could take their own decisions. That was sad! I hope that the modern Malayali women who have a far different quality of life than their ancestors understand their stories.

Jew Street was a well-preserved old town with narrow alleys lining a quaint road. Life here seemed to revolve around the old synagogue. There were numerous shops selling spices, antiques, handicrafts, clothes and knick-knacks. Though there were not many Jews left, history hung over the place like a heavy curtain. It was as though we were being transported back in time.

We met Paily, a close friend of Anthony. He promised to help me shop at the spice market and bargain for artefacts. He was definitely not driven by altruistic tendencies and looked forward to earning a commission for his efforts. He would possibly buy a bottle of rum for Anthony. It was like a well-oiled symbiotic partnership.

I wanted to pick up a few small gifts for my colleagues and fresh packets of spices for Lakshmi. Paily seemed to know everyone in the street and I ended up with more packets of spices and curios than required. My backpack filled up in no time and I also ended up with additional polythene bags. Paily also insisted on visiting Kochi's famous emporia and warehouse showrooms.

Paily spoke non-stop, like a history enthusiast. Anything old was ancient for Paily and his ilk. The large warehouses were stocked with a variety of artefacts from a different era. The traders in these outlets are famous for selectively entertaining those who they think have money. My backpack, the non-local look and Paily's presence made a huge difference. The salesmen took pains to show me 'antiques'. Indeed, there were authentic items dating from the Portuguese, Dutch or English times, but most of the pieces looked old only due to the many layers of dust over them. It took me a lot of strength to hold back from shopping. Paily could narrate detailed stories behind each of these 'historic-pieces'. Though Paily was no Raghavan, his stories were interesting too. He spoke a lot about life in Medieval Jew Street.

There were many small but cosy coffee shops on top of some of these warehouses. I desperately wanted to have some coffee but Ajay's call reminded me that it was close to 4.30 p.m. He asked me if I was already at the synagogue. When I said no, he was upset. I skipped the idea of having coffee and took a five-minute walk towards the synagogue.

The white-washed building with traditional Kerala roof tiles stood like an authoritative grandmother who had seen it all. There was a large wooden clock with the figure 1760 clearly marked on it. It was a very assuming building.

The entry tickets were quite cheap, at just five rupees. While handing over the ticket to me, the agent firmly said, "No cameras." This was disappointing as I wouldn't be able to 'collate' memories of the monument. Like an obedient school boy, I shook my head in agreement. Anthony gauged my disappointment and just winked at me. As we walked in, he said, "Sir, the rules are for foreigners only. Once you are in, I will look out and you can take a few pictures as long as you don't use the flash." Being the quintessential Indian, I loved the idea of breaking rules.

Anthony was dying to don the role of a guide. He seemed hell-bent on proving to me that he was a better story-teller than Raghavan or Paily.

The synagogue was empty except for the lonely figure of a slender woman looking at the pulpit. She was sitting on the beautiful Chinese blue-and-white tiled floor and sketching furiously.

Anthony began his unsolicited oration. "Traders who started arriving in Kerala bought not just gold, silver and other goods, but their religions too. We Keralites have an open mind towards new beliefs and that helped the rapid conversions."

I looked at that woman and mumbled. "Hmm…"

Despite my disinterested tone, he continued, "Persecuted Jews reached Kerala led by Joseph Rabban in the 8th century. He was welcomed and honoured with the rank of a prince by the then ruler. He initially settled in Cranganore or Kodungallur."

"Kodungallur is the place where the famous *Bhaghawathi* temple is. Isn't it" I remembered Vishnu's narration.

"Yes," Anthony's eyes twinkled. He looked as if he had finally hit the bull's eye after numerous attempts. "The Jews relocated from Kodungallur to Kochi due to political shifts. There were three synagogues here. Many people converted to Judaism. This building was exclusively used by the 'white Jews' or the 'Jerusalem Jews' and another synagogue was built for the 'black Jews' or the 'native Jews'."

This caught my attention. "Racial segregation between the original ones and the native converts?"

Anthony shook his head unsmilingly. Something in the conversation had reminded him of his own social status.

"Why join a group that further discriminates? Was it an escape from the caste system or the desire to be 'foreign' among their own?" I asked.

I didn't hear his answer, as Ajay called just then and the ringing sounded much louder inside the building. Hearing this, the slender woman in the synagogue turned back. She was the same woman we had seen at the shack the day before! I cut his call.

I apologised as she looked annoyed. She was wearing a white cotton skirt and a loose t-shirt. Her hair was swept back in a ponytail and her sunglasses were firmly on her head.

"Sorry! I wasn't expecting a call now," I said.

She smiled. There was a certain warmth in it.

"I think we met yesterday over dinner?" I initiated a conversation.

"And you guys fought with the restaurant manager because he served me first!" she said, laughing.

I felt ashamed and tried defending my behaviour. "Just that we were too hungry and had been waiting for a long time."

"And suitably drunk?" she asked, as she sat on the bench. I smiled sheepishly.

She looked at me, "Are you planning to stand the rest of the day?" I took it as an invitation to sit on the bench.

"So, what brings you to Kerala?" I changed the subject.

"I have been here for the last few days. Kerala has always fascinated me." She smiled and continued, "I am working on a thesis on Theyyam. This trip is to complete it. I don't want to depend on secondary sources alone. I want to experience it myself." There was keenness and enthusiasm in her voice.

I remembered Lakshmi asking me if I wanted to see Theyyam. Though I had dismissed it then, now suddenly I was willing to revisit the idea.

"Are you alone?" I asked.

She smiled and shot back, "Trying to gauge if I am single?" She didn't wait for my answer. "Yes, I am. I prefer travelling alone. That gives me a lot of liberty. Sometimes I feel like a kite cut free from its strings."

"Theyyam is conducted in the Malabar region, isn't it? So why are you in Kochi?" I asked her, dipping into Lakshmi's conversation.

The ticketing assistant walked in and said, "Time to close. It is 5.30 p.m."

I noticed Anthony standing in the corner, eavesdropping on our conversation. We all walked out together.

I asked her, "So, what are your plans now?

"Plan to start working on the thesis. Nothing in

particular today," she said, conveying that she was free for the evening. As we walked slowly through the by lanes, I asked her, "Can I buy you coffee?" I didn't have to be persuasive. She agreed.

I paid Anthony a little extra and promised that I would avail of his services as a 'guide' the next time I visited Kerala. He insisted that I take down his mobile number.

I walked with Maria towards one of the coffee shops located on top of a warehouse.

maria

Large portions of the old Jew Street were visible from the large windows of the coffee shop. People on the streets didn't seem to be in any rush at all, like they were in all in a sedate dream. I ordered coffee for both of us and sat there looking at her not knowing how to start a conversation.

After a few moments of silence, she asked, "So, what brings you to Jew Street?" I guess she understood my dilemma. "Well. Despite being a Kochiite, this is the first time that I have visited this area."

"Really?" She was surprised.

"Well. There is a saying in Malayalam-*Muttaththe mullaiku manamilla*. Literally translated it means that one doesn't appreciate the fragrance of the jasmine that grows in one's own backyard." She looked at me as if she hadn't grasped the true meaning of the saying.

"Do we appreciate anything that is readily available?" I tried my best to convey the meaning.

"Meaning we are conditioned to run behind mirages?" She added a twist.

"Something like that. The place where I grew up is just about an hour or two away. Now, I have come all the way from Dubai to enjoy its heritage."

"Kerala has so much to offer and if its own inhabitants are ignorant about it, it's definitely a shame!"

"Agreed. Many from the new generation do not know how to read or write Malayalam. For some, it is fashionable to speak the language with a deliberately twisted accent."

"Hmm… that's bad! To not be able to speak in one's own language smacks of hypocrisy," she mused, looking unhappy.

As the waiter served us our coffee, she got busy checking her phone. There was a smirk on her face. I was wondering what else to say to impress this incredible woman sitting in front of me. Suddenly, after a couple of minutes she said, "Sorry. I had to answer some urgent messages." She then picked up the mug and took a sip.

"Are you planning to be in Kochi for long?" I asked her.

"I am planning to go to Kannur to attend Theyyam performances."

"Theyyam? My wife was talking about it a few days ago. But I have personally never seen a performance."

"It's a religious ritual conducted in the Malabar region; Kannur being the epicentre."

"Why Theyyam? Any particular reason?" I wanted to know how significant it was for her.

My mobile rang. It was Ajay. I didn't want to take the call, so I put it on silent mode. Ajay was most likely here looking for me. The lecher that he was, I didn't want him to meet Maria. This was my opportunity. He called again. Just then I saw him on the road, walking in the direction of the coffee shop. "How did he know that I was here? Did he guess? Or did he see me through the window? I surely wasn't so recognisable from the window." I was left wondering.

My phone rang again. He looked angry as he walked closer, so I took the call. Starting with expletives he shouted, "Where are you? I have been looking for you for a while now." He sometimes intimidated me with his aggression.

"My phone was on mute. I didn't know that you called." "Why didn't you call me back?" He sounded angry and hurt.

He stood on the road and lit a cigarette. He asked me, "Where are you now?"

"I am having coffee, Ajay."

"Where?" He was getting impatient.

"Look up." He saw me at the window. "So you could see me all this while? Who is that woman sitting with you?" He was almost salivating.

"Come up if you want to." I cut the call. All said and done, he had a knack with women and I was not happy about him meeting Maria. He huffed and puffed as he ran up the staircase.

"Aha!" he said loudly. "No wonder you were hiding from me." Ajay looked at Maria. She seemed startled at his behaviour.

He sat near me. "Where did you find her?" he asked me in Malayalam. I was embarrassed at what I considered boorish behaviour in front of a lady.

I formally introduced Maria to Ajay. Characteristically, he turned on his charm and spoke to her for a few minutes. To my relief, Maria didn't seem keen on having a conversation with him.

"Maria, you were talking about Theyyam?" I returned to the topic.

"Yes, I am working on my thesis. It is titled 'Theyyam: The Dance of the Spirits'. I am planning to attend some of the performances."

"That's a good title."

"Maybe you could help me with some background on Keralite society. I have read extensively about it but I have little context." She had, whether she knew it or not, pulled the right levers. I always loved being a guru.

"Of course. It would be my pleasure. But I am not sure if I have the expertise to help you with a PhD thesis."

"I like your humility. Besides, there would be nobody to guide me in Kannur." She lamented.

Ajay was looking at both of us curiously, feeling terribly left out. "Both of you seem to get along quiet well," he interjected.

I was not sure if he was happy about it or was being sarcastic. "Would you like some coffee, Ajay?" I asked.

"I have been here for some time and it is now that you ask?" He seemed to feel left out.

"Infantile behaviour! If you want coffee, let me know," I admonished him. It was also an opportunity to impress Maria.

"I thought you guys were best friends?" asked Maria. A smile slowly spread across her lips. She knew the battle was for her attention.

"I don't want coffee. A drink would suffice. What say?" He looked at Maria. She remained silent.

"Don't you drink, Maria?" She gently nodded her head and looked at me.

"Let's have a drink? I will buy you dinner after that," I offered. I thought it would be an opportunity to spend more time with her.

She pondered for a few moments "Why not? As long as you are buying me dinner." She laughed out loud and gently slapped my hands.

We didn't wait to finish the coffee. I left some money at the table. I somehow wanted to get rid of Ajay. But with drinks, dinner and Maria on the agenda, it would be nearly impossible to do so. I sighed in desperation.

I didn't object when Maria offered to carry some of my polythene shopping bags.

We walked with Ajay to his car who opened the front door for Maria. She obliged. I wasn't happy sitting behind.

"Shall we go to the bar that we went to yesterday, Ajay?" "Absolutely. I can smell whisky already." He whined.

As I ordered a bottle of red wine, Ajay protested, "Krish, you have to buy me whisky. I find wine a very feminine and weak drink." Maria looked at him. She was clearly displeased. I liked that look on her face. The more she disliked Ajay, the better my chances were.

After ordering whisky for Ajay, Maria and I shared the bottle of wine. I found this very sensual.

Ajay behaved as if Maria and he were long lost friends. His increasing comfort level troubled me but he was the one who kept the conversation going. His bawdy jokes made us laugh out loud. Maria's face grew red as she slowly got drunk.

I wanted to reach out and touch her but hesitated. I was not sure how she would react. It was she who reached out and patted my hands. She asked, "Why are you so silent, Krish?" I liked her warm touch and held her hands for a few seconds.

The wine was over and I wanted to order another bottle but Maria said, "I would rather have dinner now."

Ajay wanted to stay longer but I decided to abide by Maria's wishes. The shack wasn't far away.

Babu saw us walk in. He came running towards us. He shook my hands and asked in Malayalam, with a wry smile, "You guys are together today? How did this happen?"

I chose not to reply. He turned his attention to Maria and Ajay and nodded gently. Babu found us seats in a corner. The glee on his face indicated that he was expecting us to treat Maria to the best seafood. Naturally, the bill would be big. He went to the kitchen and brought out the biggest *karimeen* and the largest prawns for our inspection.

Today, I played the expert. "So Maria, what would you like to have?"

"You are the host, Krish. I will eat anything that you order."

I didn't look at Ajay nor ask his opinion. I ordered fried rice, *karimeen* curry and lots of fried large prawns. I thought that would impress Maria.

I asked her, "What book were you reading yesterday? It had a brightly painted face on the cover, but I couldn't catch its name."

"Gosh, you were spying on me?" She said with mock- seriousness.

"You think I was eyeing you?"

"Of course," she said with certainty.

"Is that my fault?" I asked.

She smiled. "Here. This is the book I was reading." She fished it out of her bag. "Old editions of books on Theyyam are not easy to find. I found a used copy online with great difficulty."

"Can I go through this tonight? I promise to return it in the morning." I was looking for another excuse to meet her tomorrow.

She smiled and told me, "I am quite possessive about my books, but I will make an exception for you."

"How do I contact you to return the book?"

"Will you finish it that soon?" She knew what I was seeking.

"I read pretty fast, Maria." I just wanted to meet her soon.

She scribbled her number on the back of the book. "Is that what you were looking for?" She smiled. I was worried that Ajay would ask for her number too. But he didn't seem bothered about it.

"Who is organising the Theyyam performance for you?" "Nobody. I have a list of temples where it is being held. I will join the crowd." She paused and looked at me. "Who will bother to do something special for somebody like me?"

"Where are you planning to stay?" I was curious.

"I am supposed to stay with a family. Kind of a home-stay. That works cheaper for me." I felt bad for her.

Ajay was silent. I think he was really drunk. I made small talk with Maria. In a strange way, I think I was falling in love with her. She was so different from Radha and Lakshmi. She didn't shy away from the fact that I liked her nor did she remain remote. Without overdoing it, she seemed to be responding to my romantic overtures. Maria came across as a sensitive person.

After dinner, I offered to drop her home. She politely declined saying that she lived close by and needed a stroll to digest the great dinner. Ajay was adamant about driving himself, but I called a taxi as he seemed to be drunk. As we sat in the taxi, Ajay said, "You are totally enamoured by her, buddy. What do you think? Will you be able to bed her? These things take time. I am likelier to get lucky," he taunted me.

I remained silent but he continued throwing the challenge at me. "Gosh, she is very attractive. Man, I won't be able to sleep tonight."

"You are still a bachelor. I am not."

"You think she cares that you are married? Are you so loyal that you would let go of such a golden opportunity? Come on, Krish. Grow up."

"She is not desperate for me. An attractive woman like her would have many suitors even willing to do anything to earn her love."

"Why don't you help her with her Theyyam thesis? That is one thing that would make her obligated to you."

Ajay had a point. What was he doing? Was he setting me up with the woman? Or was he so sure about my failure that he was willing to take a risk? This time, I took it as a challenge and was determined to deny him a victory. After all, opportunity does not knock on one's door many times, I reminded myself. Ajay gave directions to his house clearly. I started to suspect that he was not really drunk. After dropping him, as soon as I returned to my hotel room, I took out the book and smelt it. It still retained the faint smell of her perfume. This was a very special book. As I leaved through the pages, I saw her notes on the edge of the margins. There were many two- tone pictures of various Theyyam performances.

As I lay back on the pillow, I remembered Ajay's words about helping her watch the spectacle. I thought, what if Lakshmi could check with Ambika about the Theyyam performance at her *tharawad*? We could stay with Ambika's family and watch the performances. Maria would be able to document and analyse the performance. I would also be able to collect enough material for my book and also interact with Maria intimately. Won't it be like killing many birds with one stone?

I called Lakshmi. She was surprised. "I thought you wanted privacy and you wouldn't call me till the trip was over?"

Her tone suggested that she knew that I would call her for help. After all, wasn't I dependent on her for anything and everything? She loved her helpless, clueless husband. I was the distressed damsel who she would rescue. Periodically! "As usual, I need your help and advice, Lakshmi." I decided to make her feel good.

"Go ahead, shoot," she said, the confidence in her voice apparent. "Remember you suggested that I watch the Theyyam?"

"Yes, I do. And you had turned it down vociferously."

"I want to watch a Theyyam performance. It would be a great addition to my stories."

There was silence on the other side. "Now what happened? Why this sudden volte-face?"

"Not a volte-face. Can you help me with it?"

"Let me see. I can't promise you anything." She was deliberately non-committal.

"Why are you acting pricey? Do it if you can, otherwise I will find a way myself."

"You suddenly sound desperate? What happened?"

I didn't like the way she questioned my intentions. Lakshmi could help me but her non-committal attitude angered me. She was standing between me and Maria.

"I need to go. Let me know if you can help me here." I cut the call before she could respond. I was getting really desperate. I couldn't sleep well that night. I constantly dreamt about making steamy love to Maria.

The next morning, I woke up early. The first thing I wanted to do was call Maria but hesitated. I didn't want her to think that I was yearning for her. I was too tired to go for a run, so I ordered a cup of tea and asked for the newspaper. Despite my best efforts, I couldn't concentrate on reading.

Having patiently waited till about 8 a.m., I dialled her number. She picked up on the second or third ring.

"Hello," Maria responded in her smooth voice. She didn't know my number but I am sure it would not have been difficult to guess.

"This is Krish."

"Hmm...."

"Hey, your book was captivating. I was thinking about Theyyam the whole night," I lied.

"It is a captivating subject indeed!" She was frugal with her words.

"Maria, do you have anything planned today?" I asked hesitatingly.

"Not really. Why?"

"Can we meet?"

"Hmmm... Sure. Why not?" I felt a rush.

"Where do I pick you up from?"

"You taking me somewhere?" She sounded surprised.

"I was planning to..."

I heard her laugh on the other side.

"Why you laughing?" I was suddenly unsure.

"Nobody has called me out on a date so quickly. You are pretty fast, Krish." She made me feel like a Casanova.

"Does 10.30 a.m. sound good?"

"Okay, I will see you near the shack," she drawled and it sent gentle vibrations through my body.

I couldn't believe my luck. This was panning out like in the movies. A coincidental, brief meeting taking a serious turn. I felt like an adolescent who was meeting the first girl who responded to his overtures. It wasn't really love but a compound of feelings - sexual attraction and physical excitement.

The more I thought about her, the more I wanted her. My body seemed to ache to mate with her. No woman had ever made me feel like this before. The key to intimacy with Maria would be my ability to help her with the thesis. What if Lakshmi decided not to help me? Who do I reach out to? My mind raced. I decided to swallow my pride and check with Lakshmi one more time.

"Oh, there you go. I was expecting your call." That's how she greeted me. There was sarcasm in her voice. "It's difficult to arrange for something so quickly. Ambika is checking with her uncle if the Theyyam performance has concluded at their *tharawad*. She is not too sure. Give me about 30 minutes and I should be able to confirm either way." She set me swaying between hope and despair.

I quickly took a shower and went down for the breakfast. It took another 45 minutes for Lakshmi to call. Knowing her, I am sure that she had made me wait for an extra 10 to 15 minutes. "Okay, I have arranged for you to see the performance at Ambika's *tharawad*. Happy now?" She said triumphantly.

"I owe you one."

"As usual, I am the one who comes to your rescue." She couldn't help take a swipe at me.

"Where is this *tharawad*? How do I get in touch with the people there?" I tried my best not to sound eager.

"It is located in Kannur. It might be difficult to get train tickets at such a short notice."

"Ajay may be able to help me," I blurted out.

"What? Did you get in touch with Ajay?" She lost her temper. "Won't you ever listen to me? He is a bad influence."

"I am not in touch with him. Just thought that he could help me book the tickets as he works in a travel agency. I guess these guys have some sort of a quota…" I managed to mumble.

"Take a taxi if you don't get tickets but don't get in touch with that pervert," she fumed. I never understood why she hated him so much. Yes, Ajay was a wayward character but did he deserve so much contempt? I was not sure. Lakshmi must not have believed me.

"Take down the number of Mr Nambiar who is the patriarch of the *tharawad*. Ambika has already spoken to him. Be very humble when you speak to the elderly man. He is supposed to be short-tempered," Lakshmi warned me.

"Sure. Thanks."

"Keep me posted."

"Will do. Let me speak to him right away." Talking to Mr Nambiar and confirming the trip became the utmost priority for me. I dialled the number that Lakshmi gave and a rough voice answered, "Nambiar." I spoke to him with humility and confidence.

"So, you work in Dubai?"

"Yes, I work as a consulting partner." I hoped he would understand consulting partner as being a business-owner rather than a mere designation. I wanted to ensure that the welcome I received would be commensurate to my socio-economic status. He must not think that I was an average struggler trying to make money abroad.

"By the way Mr Nambiar, one of my American friends who is working on a thesis on Theyyam would be accompanying me. Hope that's fine with you." I kept it deliberately ambiguous. I hoped he wouldn't ask if the friend was male or female. There was silence on the other side.

He didn't ask further details. He must have assumed that married men like me wouldn't have female friends.

"Which university?" the old man asked.

"University of Missouri." As if he knew anything about the world outside Kerala, I thought. "It is a matter of pride for us that a student of a foreign university studies and writes about Theyyam." I tried to hard-sell the idea. There was just a 'hmm…' from the other side.

"So, when is the performance beginning, uncle?"

"In two days. It will go on till the wee hours of the next day."

"Can you give me the location, please? I will take a taxi from the Kannur railway station."

"My car will be there at the station." He was curt and cut the call.

I called Anthony. "Anthony, I need your vehicle for the day. Are you free?"

"Aren't you glad that you took down my mobile number?" I could sense happiness in his voice. "Where to today, sir?"

"The Bolgatty Palace."

"I can drop you at the jetty. You can take a boat to the palace. Why waste money hiring my vehicle for the whole day?" I was surprised at his offer. This was not the Anthony I had bargained with yesterday. I agreed.

Maria was waiting near the shack and instantly recognised Anthony's battered auto rickshaw. She got into the vehicle without a formal invitation and sat beside me. She was wearing black slim-fit capris that outlined her long toned legs, a white short-sleeved peasant top, and multi-coloured cross trainers. Dark wayfarer glasses hid her lovely eyes.

As the old engine dragged forward, I asked Maria, "Don't you want to know where we are going?"

"Should I not trust you?"

"Technically, I am still a stranger."

"Let me indulge in the fantasy of trusting a stranger," she said and laughed.

"Excessive trust can backfire."

"I will take my chances."

"You speak like a gambler."

"I take calculated risks. Do I look naïve to you?" She made faces that made me laugh.

As we reached the Mattancherry pier, or jetty as Anthony called it, he stepped out and bought us two return tickets for the boat. He refused to take money for the tickets. "We will settle the money in the evening." He was being magnanimous in his own way.

There was a wooden boat anchored to the pier that was gently bobbing in the water. There were not too many passengers. The boat started to move so slowly that for the first few minutes it seemed like it was just floating in the water. The backwaters were serene and we had a spectacular view of the Cochin marine drive. The small engine sputtered like Anthony's auto rickshaw and spewed black smoke. We could see small *vanchis* or dugout canoes speeding past, powered by bare chested men, houseboats floating lazily, and ships anchored patiently far away. Surrounded by the backwaters, the picturesque island of Bolgatty oozed an old world charm.

"What's so special about this place?" Maria was holding my hands trying to balance herself on the swaying boat.

"Have you not been to the palace, Maria?" I sounded surprised.

"Nope, tourists like me cannot afford expensive places," Maria said matter-of-factly.

"Built in 1744 by the Dutch traders, the palace is one of the oldest of its kind outside Holland. It is now a hotel run by the Government of Kerala. It is also a honeymooners' paradise." I sounded like an expert. Little did she know that I had gleaned this information just this morning.

"Honeymooners' paradise? Why are you taking me there? What's on your mind?" She exhibited faux alarm.

"I like its romantic ambience, Maria. Where else can I take a gorgeous woman like you?" She looked genuinely flattered.

"Liar," she said softly. Her eyes had a romantic spark. She seemed to love all the attention that was being showered on her.

We walked across the expanse of lush manicured lawns. Many old trees hid young couples, engaged in intimate conversations. Impatient young men looked around before quickly fondling their reluctant, giggling companions. I asked Maria, "Do you want to sit in the restaurant or behind a tree till lunch?"

"I love the breeze. It would be fun sitting here. Look at that grandfather tree."

As we walked towards it, the canoodling couples turned their attention from each other and looked at us. We were indeed an odd couple-a western woman and a Malayali man. I told Maria, "We managed to distract them from their shenanigans."

She giggled hard. "What did we do?"

"They think that I am the lucky devil who has managed to seduce an American woman." I looked at her for a reaction.

"Is that what you did?" she asked provocatively

"Though aspiring to be a lady-killer, I have never been lucky with women, Maria. I just do not know how to read women."

"But then you befriended me so quickly?" she raised her eyebrows. "I think you are a charmer. That is, if and when you want to be one." She reached out and held my hands and slightly pulled me towards the tree. Her hands were bony. "Are you still astonished that you seduced me?" She laughed at her own statement.

"Have I managed to seduce you?"

"Don't put too much pressure on your mind. Sit with me." "This is indeed an aberration."

"Why can't it be fate?" she said.

"I firmly do not believe in fate or destiny. Could be a great coincidence."

"Could be. Why debate now?" She drew the conversation to an end.

We sat under the tree facing the lake. The serenity of the water was being disrupted by the sound of the boats that constantly cut through it.

"I got good news for you," I said. Maria looked at me curiously with her brows arching.

"What's that?" she enquired. "I don't like suspense."

"I have arranged a visit to a *tharawad* where Theyyam

is being performed. You can watch and study the performances peacefully."

"Really?" She almost shouted in disbelief.

"Yes, of course. You wanted something like that, right?" "Oh, I love you." She embraced me tightly. She was very happy and the edges of her eyes were wet. I was overwhelmed by her reaction.

"We leave the day after tomorrow to Kannur."

She nodded like an obedient child. We sat quiet for some time. She seemed to be trying to cope with the good news. "You don't even know anything about me and you do so much?"

"Hmm… nor have you asked anything about me. Technically, we are still strangers, aren't we?"

"Sometimes, ignorance is bliss, isn't it?"

"I would like to know something about you."

Maria sat staring at the darting kingfishers. "What do you want to know?"

"Everything!"

"Everything?" she asked.

"Whatever you want to say."

"I need a cold beer."

We got up and walked towards the hotel. We entered the beer parlour, the Bubble Café.

"I was born in St. Louis in Missouri. My father's family owned one of the oldest breweries. The last man to actively manage it was my grandfather. Towards the end of his life, he sold it and divided a substantial portion of the money among his children. He wanted them to start their own ventures.

"My father was a rolling stone, bitten by wanderlust. He used a portion of his inheritance to travel. For him, journeys were his education. He had dropped out of college since he was seeking practical and not academic education. During his trip to London, he met my mother and fell in love with her. I should say he was besotted with her." Maria smiled.

"It must have been quite romantic for a young woman. She was young and aspiring to go to college. He persuaded her to apply to the University of Missouri. Her quintessential English parents weren't happy with her choice of the man or country. They didn't find him committed enough and weren't sure if he would settle down with her. But she followed her heart. The rest as they say is history."

"They married, had you, and settled down in Missouri?"

"My father wanted to invest in the booming oil industry in the Middle East. He wanted to marry after establishing himself financially. I am their love child."

"Why the Middle East? Oil exploration was big in America too?"

"I think he was still restless and wanted to travel far and wide. Business was his valid excuse. Anyway, he started working in an offshore rig in Saudi Arabia and invested in oil stocks. Mother says he had a knack for business. He was able to make quick turnarounds and substantial profits. Father remitted considerable amounts of money regularly, to mother's account. A true nomad that he was, he moved from country to country within the region. The last time he called my mother, he was in Iran. He seemed to have had enough travel and was planning to return with his fortune."

Suddenly, Maria looked lost. "However, he never returned and 15 years have gone by."

"That must have been tough on the family. What do you think could have happened?"

"Obviously, due to prevailing anti-American sentiments in Iran, we couldn't go to the country. His friends and business associates in the Middle East tried to find him. Despite their best efforts, we could not trace his whereabouts."

"And then?"

"I have only seen him in photographs. He is a terrific looking guy, my father." She wiped the tears that had welled up in her eyes. "My mother still waits for news about him. All she wants is closure."

"So what's your connect with Kerala?" I wondered aloud. "My ancestors from the maternal side were closely associated with the East India Company right from the 18th century. They made their fortune by helping the company expand its spice trade in the Tellicherry or Thalassery region. I grew up listening to their adventures and I have always wanted to visit Malabar.

"Some of my ancestors have lorded over the massive structure of the Tellicherry or Thalassery fort. I want to see that fort. It would be great to walk along the footprints of my ancestors."

"Your ancestors were globe trotters too, eh?"

"I am like my father. I have been travelling since I turned

18. My mother is paranoid about this. She is worried about my solitary trips. But I like it this way. This year, I am in Kerala."

"How do you compare this trip with the rest of your travels?"

"I seem to have a spiritual connect with Kerala, Krish. This land makes me feel as though I am her daughter. I feel very calm and contented here. You know, once during an exhibition in London, I met a Romanian gypsy who said that I was once an Indian princess who had teamed up with the son and the general of the local king and planned a coup. Had the prince won the throne, I would have become a queen. I had played a major role in persuading the general to join the proposed coup. Unfortunately, according to the gypsy, I developed cold feet at the last moment and betrayed all co-conspirators, except the prince. It was a fantastic story but managed to bind me closer to Kerala."

"Wow! A sort of spiritual connection, eh? So, are

you planning to settle down in Kerala?" I asked her casually.

"Not yet. But yes, when the time comes, I would like to be buried in Kerala. Like some of my forefathers."

"You joking?"

"No, I am serious. Though I want to go back to Missouri now, I might return to Kerala when the longing grows stronger."

"But as an educated person, surely you don't believe in past life or reincarnation?"

"Not really. But then it's a romantic notion. Isn't it? To have been a princess? I like conspiracy theories!"

"Do you believe in all these?" She asked me.

"Nope. I have been an atheist since I was 13. I'd like to call myself a die-hard rationalist."

"Why so?"

"I didn't find any divine intervention that made any difference in my life. Especially when I needed it the most. My mother is an ardent believer. She thinks that it is her prayers that have helped me succeed in life!"

"Obviously, you don't believe that?"

"Nope. For me, religion presents a hope that helps in ploughing forward during tough times."

"But religion had existed for thousands of years and millions believe in it. There has to be something about it?"

"Could be. I do not know and I have not had reasons to believe in divinity and celestial beings. However, I like to interpret religion from the psycho-social perspective. How it originated, why it came to be, the way pantheons were constructed, how religion affected its adherents etc. That's a very interesting topic."

Maria listened to me ardently. There was a lot of

interest in her eyes. But I wanted to break the discussion as it was not helping me in my objective of trying to get together with her.

"Aren't you hungry?" I changed the topic of discussion.

"Hmm…yes, but I will settle for something light." We washed down chicken sandwiches with more beer.

"So, we leave the day-after-tomorrow for Kannur?"

"Yes."

"How do we travel?"

"By train!"

"What about the train tickets? That too at such a short notice?" she seemed worried about practicalities.

"Don't worry about all that. Let me use the services of Ajay for this. He should be able to manage a couple of tickets."

After lunch, we went out and sat under the same tree just enjoying the breeze and the silent togetherness. She sat close to me and it felt like I had known her for a long, long time. Her eyes were closed and there was the look of contentment on her face.

I was desperate to restart the conversation. "Do you want me to be your guide to look around Kochi tomorrow?" I asked her gently. I was feeling more confident interacting with her. Hope bobbed in my mind like the red marker buoys far away in the water.

"I have to wind up my stay here. There's a lot to do, I might be busy tomorrow." She almost whispered and then looked at me. Maybe she saw the disappointed look on my face, so she said, "We will be together for the next few days, right?" She pinched my cheek.

"Shall we go now?" asked Maria.

"Sure. It's evening. Do you want to join me for dinner and drinks?" I didn't want to let her go. Not yet.

"We just had a lovely lunch and cans of beer. I need to digest that first before the next consignment goes in." She laughed hard.

"I was planning to spend the day with you."

"There is a lot of time left of dinner. I need to meet the real estate agent to settle my dues with the landlord. So little time and so much to do. Hope you understand."

I just nodded my head. I suddenly felt like I had nothing to do for the rest of the day.

"How can I thank you for all this, Krish?" She stood up, hugged me, and planted a kiss right on my lips. I was aware that many people were watching us. It was embarrassing but I did not want to pull back. The touch of her soft lips turned me on.

She held my hands and said, "Let's go. Looking forward to a wonderful trip to Kannur."

Anthony was waiting for us faithfully at the other end of the pier. I dropped her back near the shack and returned to my hotel. Anthony asked meaningfully, "That madam looks beautiful, eh?" Silently I thrust a few 100 rupee notes in his hands as I gave him a cold look. He knew that I didn't like his comment. He started his rickety vehicle. I guess his destination would be the nearest country bar for a good helping of *arrack*.

I called Ajay. From the noise in the background, I could make out that he was at a party or a night club that started blaring out loud music early. "Hey, where are you?"

"I am with my colleagues, having a drink. What's up?"

"I finally managed to arrange to see a Theyyam performance at one of the oldest *tharawads* in Kannur. I am sure Maria will enjoy it."

"Rascal! All for a woman you met a couple days ago? You are slowly transforming into a lady-killer," he laughed out loud. He seemed to be in a jovial mood.

"Ajay, I need your help. I need train tickets for the journey to Kannur."

"When are you planning to leave?"

"The day-after-tomorrow morning."

"What? Are you crazy? Tickets are difficult to get. It is summer vacation for schools. Everyone is travelling to their native places." He told me as though I was an idiot.

I remained silent.

"I can only try," said Ajay.

"Won't you do this much for your friend?"

He mouthed expletives to describe his love for me and said, "I will have to try hard. Don't thank me. If I get them, I will send over the tickets by tomorrow. I am in the middle of great female company, let me enjoy."

He didn't seem to be paying attention to my plea nor taking my request seriously. I didn't think he was happy to help me with the tickets. He definitely didn't like me travelling with the woman.

"I will try my best, I promise. If not, I will arrange a car for you. Now can I go?" He seemed desperate to get back to the party.

"You're sure you will help me?" I didn't trust him completely.

"You think I don't want you to travel with her? Don't worry, she isn't my type," he tried to assuage my feelings. "But tell me, why do you keep insisting on train tickets?"

"Just try your best, Ajay. I am depending on your contacts." I didn't want to elaborate, but I was relieved that he was not interested in Maria.

I was keen on travelling by train because in the long journey I didn't want to be confined in the small space that a car could offer. I did not want the hassle of an intrusive driver. I hated travelling by public buses. I was also apprehensive about traversing traffic-filled roads.

With nothing to do for the rest of the day, I went down to the restaurant for a cold beer, a lonely dinner, and memories of a soft kiss.

kannur

Ajay did manage to get two tickets in the Ernakulum Kannur Intercity Express train. He kept his word and delivered them at the hotel reception. He did not call to inform me. Neither did I call to thank him. Maria was finally relieved to hear that the tickets had arrived.

Yesterday, I had spent my day in the hotel room itself thinking about the fantastic time ahead. I tried to read up a little on the history of Malabar region in general and Kannur in particular. I wanted enough content to impress Maria.

We reached the Ernakulum railway station at 6.30 a.m. It was a beehive of activity. The food stalls were doing brisk business selling tea, coffee, breakfast, soft drinks and mineral water. Passengers were drinking hot tea, unmindful of the steam emanating from the paper cups. The newspaper vendor had spread his wares on the ground and his regular customers handed over coins and notes in exchange for the day's edition. The newspapers in English sold almost as fast as those in vernacular language. Kerala's high literacy rates ensured that newspapers were consumed fast, just like the hot tea. Stray dogs walked around in gay abandon. Many billboards, advertising soaps that promised 'eternal youth', hung on the walls like old tenants. Small flat-screen television sets blared advertisements hard-selling the local footwear brands. An antiquated sound system made periodic announcements about the arrival and departure of trains. The female announcer's voice over the system sounded bored and monotonous.

Reservation charts were displayed on the walls. A small group of people were standing around the charts, craning their necks to seek their names on them.

The crowd was diverse and included lower rung office goers, families on vacations, and college students. The families lugged heavy luggage as though they were relocating permanently. Finicky men bargained hard with the coolies. Vendors trotted up and down the platform trying to sell their wares. Trains arrived and departed at regular intervals. Habitual latecomers ran behind the departing trains in desperation.

Maria seemed oblivious to the hustle-bustle. She was dressed in blue jeans, a full sleeved top with bright red and yellow floral motifs, and *Kolhapuri chappals*, for a conservative look. Her rucksack hung from her back like an adamant monkey. Many passengers stared at us, assuming that we were a couple. A group of young boys looked at me enviously.

Maria seemed excited and lost in her dream world. She asked, "So in another six hours, we will be in the land of the Theyyam?" I nodded. She reached out for my hands and stood close to me. Though the physical proximity was endearing, I was also worried that somebody would recognise me. After all, I was from Kochi and there were many here who knew my family. Maria stood still resting her head on my shoulder. It was evident from her expression that her mind was already in the mysterious lands of Kannur, visualising the Theyyam. But I was not able to muster courage to ask her to stand away.

Public display of intimacy is considered unacceptable in Kerala. The many stares made me uncomfortable and the staccato announcement about the imminent arrival of our train came as a relief to me.

The hoot of the diesel engine could be heard from a distance. The train chugged and slowed down for its rendezvous with the railway station. There was commotion as passengers huddled towards the platform to enter the train. People rushed for the doors like fleas, as though they would be stranded otherwise. The bogies were full of people and the new entrants jostled with the passengers who were already seated. Some of them pointed at us and smiled suggestively, whispering among each other. It was as if they were expecting us to get intimate in full public view. Maria seemed to disapprove of their behaviour.

We found that our seats were occupied by an elderly couple. They didn't seem to be legitimate ticket-holders. So, I called out our seat numbers aloud. Having got the hint, they vacated the seats. As we settled in, the other passengers looked at us as though we were exotic creatures. The train didn't halt for long at the station and it started moving slowly.

Maria loosened up a bit and smiled at me. People went past the interconnected bogies, opening and closing the door several times.

As the train gathered speed, so did the banter. People were talking loudly. I am sure that most of them had met each other for the first time. Outside the window, numerous coconut palms and lush green paddy farms raced past.

The loud cries of the ubiquitous *chaiwallah* wafted in. He was trying hard to sell the sweet tea in his stainless steel insulated container, "*Chai, chai, garam chai.*" The sound became louder when somebody showed interest in the beverage. He had a large pocket on his shirt filled with coins. As he returned change he seemed to deliberately jingle them. Several other vendors from the train's pantry car, selling *masala dosa, vada, idli* and omelette sandwich, followed suit. They kept coming at frequent intervals. I wondered how they managed to cook in the shaky train.

I asked Maria, "Breakfast?" She nodded like a ravished child.

I hailed the next vendor selling *masala dosa*. He gave us two packets wrapped in aluminium foil. Although I was paying, the vendor handed the packets to her.

Maria was oblivious to all the racket around her. She quickly wolfed down the food and washed it down with generous gulps of mineral water. She was either really hungry or wanted to finish the burdening chore of eating and get on with the journey. She was fidgeting with the water bottle, in obvious impatience to reach Kannur. As she battled with her eagerness, I ate my breakfast slowly. The train stopped at the next station.

She waited for me to finish and then leaned across and asked hesitatingly, "What's the distance that we are covering today?"

"About 282 kilometres to the Kannur railway station. The average speed is 49 kilometres an hour with about 13 halts in between." I elaborated and then paused deliberately. "And about…"

I loved to see the look of anticipation on her face. "Let me think…" She just kept looking at me and I blurted out finally, "About 15 kilometres to Nambiar's house."

"How do you know all this? Aren't you as clueless about this land as me?"

"When will internet come in handy? How else would I satiate your need for information?"

"Hmm…," she murmured. She wasn't amused.

As the train jerked forward to resume its journey, a calm descended on Maria. She took out her e-book reader and was soon engrossed in it. The train chugged along lazily, displaying no obvious rush to reach its destination.

Many of the vendors who passed by slowed down to take a good look at Maria. This was unsettling but there was nothing much I could do. Disgusted, I tried reading news on my tablet. The rhythmic sound of the wheels as they glided over the tracks and the gentle sway of the train drove me into slumber.

Maria shook me awake. Still half-asleep, I asked her anxiously, "What? What happened?" She was astonished at my sharp reaction and said in a low voice, "It's already Thalasseri, we will be in Kannur in another 40 minutes." My watch showed 11.50 a.m.

I needed to use the restroom. It was smelly and dirty and turned the simple task of emptying one's bladder into an ordeal. When I returned to the seat, Maria was busy putting on make-up. She noticed my smirk and asked, "What happened?"

"Nothing," I said dismissively. The bogey was almost empty now.

She leaned towards me. The mascara made her eyes look smoky and mesmerising. Her blue eyes looked agitated, like a raging ocean. She smiled and this lit up her eyes. It would have taken a thousand lights to do that.

Eye make-up make women look hotter! Lakshmi barely used any make-up, though she loved strong perfumes. She justified her plain style saying, "Clear skin is the best make-up."

The little danglers on Maria's ears swayed gently and the lip balm made her lips look wet and supple. The long nails on her slender fingers were painted bright red, resembling blood on spear tips. She looked like a huntress in pursuit of her prey.

She said, "The more I see Kerala, the more I love it. The greenery, the unbridled nature, the cool rains, this train journey..."

"And?" I raised an eyebrow, smiling.

"Some men. Hot like the summer." She was baiting me.

Maria reached out for my hands and gently ran her fingers across my palms. The gentle stir was recasting itself into strong sexual tension. She came closer to me and I could almost smell her lip balm.

"Looks like the succubus is revealing its presence," I said, subtly, sexually.

"Hmm... indeed," she said, smiling.

I wanted to kiss her but just then a group of young women, possibly college students, came walking towards our seat.

I left her hands quickly. The women chose to occupy the empty seats around us. I was angry with them but I could say nothing.

At around 12.15 p.m., Kannan Nambiar called on my mobile to check where we had reached. He was curt and spoke to the point; he also informed me that his driver was already at the station waiting for us.

At around 12.40 p.m., the train finally reached Kannur. We disembarked from the train and looked around for the driver. I hadn't asked Nambiar how I could identify the driver. As we waited, a dark lanky man in jeans, an open shirt, and plastic sandals quickly ran towards us. "Krish sir?"

"Yes."

"My name is Raju. Nambiar sir sent me to pick you up."

It was perhaps Maria's presence that helped him identify us. Raju picked up her rucksack despite Maria's protests. He didn't even glance at my luggage. He led us to a modern SUV. The driver tried to make conversation with Maria as he loaded her luggage in the boot. He left it open so that I could load my bags. Maria sat beside Raju. Either she loved his attention or just wanted to make me jealous.

I was seething with anger and addressed him as 'driver' and not by his name. Maria's decision to sit in the front delighted him. There were too many vehicles attempting to get out of the station all at once. It took us a few minutes to negotiate our way out. The road was teeming with uncontrollable traffic.

They were lined with so many red flags that it felt that the city had been painted in red. Old cars with rusty loudspeakers tied on each side competed with other vehicles. Men inside these cars were speaking into old portable mikes making loud announcements asking for people's mass participation in a meeting that was being organised by the leading communist party in Kerala.

"Is communism so dominant in Kerala?" Maria asked. As the driver began to answer, I cut him short. "Let me answer that," I spoke in Malayalam. Though it hurt his ego, he kept quiet.

"Yes, it has a strong role to play in Kerala. Despite communism having been uprooted in its countries of origin or substantially mutating to resemble capitalism, its doctrines still manage to capture the imagination of the ordinary folk here. The harsh implementation of caste system, rampant exploitation of its peasants and workers and their impoverished state enabled the rise of leftist ideology. Leaders of these movements helped these landless, powerless and socio-politically insignificant people to fight against their powerful tormentors."

"Oh...that's interesting to know," she turned and said.

"In the late 60s and 70s, Kerala was rocked by Marxist extremists. They were also called Naxalites and the movement, Naxalism. Positioned as a people's movement, it fought against landed gentry and for end of peasant exploitation," I elaborated.

"So what happened to Naxalism? Kerala is a peaceful state now. Isn't it?" she queried

"It was suppressed brutally. But it is interesting to know that women played a significant role in the violent movement. The state police that fought against them also became a prominent enemy. Many policemen lost their lives. It is said that the wall of the police station in Pulpally in Wayanad area of north Kerala has a palm imprint in blood."

"Palm imprint in blood? Whose blood?" The mention of blood shocked Maria.

"From what I heard, it is of a leading woman Naxalite who dipped her hand in the blood of a slain policeman."

"Woman Naxalite?" She seemed shocked.

"Why? Aren't women capable of waging battle? Can't they be vengeful?"

Maria did not argue.

As we crawled through the traffic, Maria noticed that the walls of the buildings had large posters with the photo of a young man. She couldn't hold on to her curiosity so she asked, "What is that poster about? There are so many of them. I can't read what is written."

"It is the poster announcing the martyrdom of a young man who was killed by one of the leading political parties," I could read the content as the vehicle was moving very slowly.

"What do you mean martyrdom? That is an old, outdated terminology."

"Since the early 70s two political outfits have been battling for ideological supremacy. This has turned Kannur into a killing field. Political violence seems to be endemic to this region. Rough estimates say that 300 people associated with either of these outfits have been murdered. Tit for tat, brutal political murders have given Kannur a bad name."

By this time, we had reached the end of the road and traffic had thinned. We were all relieved to get out of the congested mess.

The driver took us through sea coastal road. Maria requested him to stop. "Raju, can you stop here for some time? I want to feel the sea breeze." He stopped the vehicle very slowly as if an abrupt halt would have caused discomfort to Maria.

We stood gazing at the sea. There were small strips of white sandy beaches that ran across the sea like a buffer. The sun was at its peak and the seagulls were busy gliding past with their sturdy wings, probably seeking lunch in the deep blue sea. The fierce and large waves ceaselessly hit the shore with steadfast violence. They seemed to be screaming vengeance just like the cadres of the political entities.

Despite the rage below, the clouds floated above like candy floss. The dim silhouette of a ship anchored deep in the sea was visible. Several fishing boats bobbing up and down looked like miniscule toys. The fishermen were trying to set up the nets. The breeze was strong and cool.

She asked the driver, "Raju, is a large part of Kannur covered by the sea?"

He seemed to have been waiting for a query from her. "The sea has been a significant part of the Malabar region." He spoke English with a heavy Malayalam accent. Maria seemed impressed.

He was pleased and threw a glance at me. This was his chance to be her narrator of Kannur's history. Now that he had Maria's complete attention, he continued,

"Kannur was an important port along the Arabian Sea from the early times. Mariners from around the world frequented this place to trade in spices. Even colonial powers such as the Portuguese, Dutch and the English fought among themselves in the seas to set a firm foot in the region. The infighting among the local rulers helped these outsiders."

I looked at the watch. It was already 1.15 p.m. Nambiar would be waiting for lunch. I firmly told the driver that it was time to go. He didn't like my tone but complied.

Maria sat beside him again. Her presence seemed to intoxicate the driver. She kept prodding him for more and he kept weaving stories around historical landmarks such as the Thalasseri Fort and Mappila Bay. He sounded like a balladeer, unravelling an epic, and managed to transport us to another time.

Maria asked, "Raju, one of these days can you take me to the Tellicherry Fort?"

"You mean Thalasseri fort?"

Maria nodded affirmatively.

The SUV started swaying as it entered a small village road. Suddenly, I felt a sense of anxiety overtaking me, it was strong and intense. It was like a choking sensation. Something like this had never happened to me before. Though momentary, it was overpowering. I couldn't understand the reason for my discomfort.

The vehicle entered a huge compound and stopped in front of a two-storied house with large Victorian pillars. The tapered roofs were covered with terracotta tiles that had lost their original colour due to layers of moss. The façade of the building had been freshly whitewashed. Bright mural paintings adorned the sit-out. Understated elegance, I thought.

There was something about the building that was overawing. I felt the same sense of anxiety building back in me. Deep inside, something about that house disturbed me.

Nambiar came out of the house and extended a hand. "Welcome, welcome," he said. "What took you so long?" he enquired. His palms were large and his grip warm and strong. He seemed delighted to see me. He didn't look as strict as he had sounded on the phone. I felt relieved.

"We stopped to admire the sea," I said with new found enthusiasm.

He was a tall and sprightly old man in his late seventies. Clad in a white *mundu*, the modesty of his upper body was covered with a threadbare Turkish towel that barely hid the thick, white, unruly hair on his chest. The sparse hair on his balding head appeared more silver than white. On his wide forehead was smeared a straight line of dried sandalwood paste. His large ears gave him the look of the Buddha. Thick, bushy, white eyebrows stood like a thicket on his clean-shaven face. Deep wrinkles marred an otherwise handsome, chiselled face, complimented by strong jaws. His voice was deep and reassuring. His strong persona reminded me of my grandfather.

When Maria alighted from the car, his smile vanished. "This is the American student?" His eyebrows went up in a questioning curve.

"Yes."

"I thought a man was coming with you."

He didn't seem very pleased. He looked at me accusingly. I was afraid that he would send us back. He looked at Maria for a moment or two. I apologised for the confusion but he didn't seem to hear me and simply instructed the man-servant to show us our rooms.

As we moved into the house, Nambiar said, "Please have a bath and come down quickly. None of us have had lunch." There was a tone of quiet authority in his voice. I thought Maria's arrival was bothering him.

The servant led us upstairs. The old teak staircase creaked as we climbed. The servant left Maria's rucksack in her room and led me to mine. He did not talk to us. The room was large, with an old four-poster bed and a king sized mattress. In contrast to the dreary white of the wall, the bedcover was very colourful.

I quickly unpacked for a shower. The bathroom was small but it had modern amenities including a commode and a shower. Somebody had thoughtfully left a cotton towel and a small bar of herbal soap. As I changed into a white *mundu*, the strong fragrance of food emanated from the kitchen below.

There was a soft knock at the door. "Come in," I said almost intuitively. I had just started wearing my shirt when Maria walked in. She was dressed in a long skirt and a blouse with puffed sleeves.

"You look like a Malayali girl," I commented.

She reached out to button my shirt. When I protested, she hit my hands.

"You seem to have fallen in love with Raju, eh?" I took a jibe at her.

"Is somebody jealous?"

I looked into her eyes. Her strong perfume permeated the room. "His attention was on your anatomy. He must have created a map in his mind." We laughed together. "Attention monger! You love it when men admire you. You like them psychologically prostrating before you. Don't you?" I asked her.

Maria bit her lips. She reacted by pinching me hard on my hands.

"Ouch, that hurt, idiot!"

She cupped my mouth and said, "Let's go. Nambiar would be waiting for us. I don't think he liked me being here."

"We will manage that," I assured her.

She walked in front. Her hips swayed gracefully and deliberately. We quickly got down the stairs.

She said, "Mind the steps; they are old, creaky and narrow. Or else you will fall on me." I took the cue. "That's a position I would prefer." She didn't have the time to reply, as we heard Nambiar's voice from the dining room.

I apologised. "Sorry for keeping you waiting." He ignored me.

The dining room was large and connected to the kitchen by a wooden door. Bright shafts of sunlight peered through the French window. A few women, both young and old, kept peering at us from behind the door curiously. They giggled among themselves.

The wooden table was old, long and rectangular with chairs that looked sturdy despite the delicate hand carvings. It had a cotton cover with a runner dividing it into two on which pickles and other condiments were placed. There was a large glass bowl with small yellow bananas. An old house-help placed plantain leaves in front of us.

Maria sat near me and imitated me by sprinkling drops of water to wipe the leaf clean. The thick glass tumblers were filled with hot, pink water. Maria asked me softly, "Why is the water in the glass pink?"

This was an opportunity to start a conversation. I put the question to Nambiar. "Uncle, Maria wants to know why the water is pink."

The deadpan expression on Nambiar's face did not change. He said, "The water is boiled with a piece of wood called *karingali*. It quenches one's thirst and increases the appetite. Instead of plain water, you would be drinking a herbal concoction that has healing properties too." After a second, he said, "This is purer than the mineral water that you tourists drink!" Though Maria seemed hurt at Nambiar's jibe, she didn't react.

Like a true dominant patriarch, he turned towards the kitchen and nodded. A woman, possibly in her thirties, stepped forward with a large steel bowl full of steaming brown rice. She wore a traditional sari with a large gold border. She was also wearing a gold necklace, many bangles, and *jimikki*, the bell-shaped earring with filigree work. She had a wheat-ish complexion and as she walked I could hear the sound of her *kolussu*, the ankle jewel with beads. She was one of the women who were earlier looking at me and giggling. There was something about her. Her raw sexuality was enticing.

She served Nambiar first and heaped his plantain leaf with rice in just two large scoops. As she came to me, I said, "*Koracchu*." Little.

A naughty smile danced on her large, kohl-lined eyes. "Why? Aren't you hungry?" She spoke as if we knew each other very well. As she bent forward, the loose end of her sari slipped from her shoulder exposing her sizeable bosom. She was wearing a low-cut magenta blouse. The diamond on her nose ring sparkled. I gave my best smile. "I am hungry, but I don't eat much," I said.

She looked at me indulgently as if I was an undisciplined child. Placing a scoop of rice on the plantain leaf, she looked at me in anticipation. I raised my hand and nodded indicating that it was enough. It was hot and her armpits were wet. Small beads of sweat hung precariously on her forehead. Large strands of fresh jasmine were coiled around her hair like a constrictor. The flowers kept falling from her hair as she moved. She had used hair oil that had a strong aroma.

As she turned to serve Maria, I took a deep breath. The combined smell of the flowers and oil was overpowering. She turned and threw a glance at me. Her long dark eyelashes seemed to promise something. The look had a mysterious element. There seemed to have been an instant connection established between us. She behaved as if she was expecting my imminent arrival. This is really weird, I told myself.

Maria didn't stop her from serving two large scoops rice. It seemed as though she wanted to prove a point to Nambiar. Once the rice was served, the old lady, who appeared to be Mrs Nambiar, came in with a steel bucket filled with *sāmbhar*.

She must have been in her mid-60s. She was a short woman and extremely fair. She wore a bottle-blue silk sari. The jasmine strands on her hair had dried up. The flowers had shrunk and turned brown. They hung on her thick black dyed hair like an apology. She wore a heavy gold chain and bangles on her left hand. An old Rolex adorned her right hand. She wore spectacles on which the Gucci logo was clearly visible. Her mannerisms betrayed an upper class upbringing. She had a quiet confidence about her and it was clear that she exerted considerable power in the family. Arguably, she was the most elegant woman I met in the household.

Nambiar dug a small hole in his rice hill and she poured the curry into it. We mimicked him. Mrs Nambiar then returned and served us *aviyal*, cut mango pickle and *pappadum*. Once the meal was over, she said to me,

"I hope you liked the meal. We kept it simple as we were not sure if you and your friend would enjoy vegetarian fare." I nodded my head in agreement. Although I was not a great fan of vegetarian food, I wiped the plantain leaf clean with my fingers to indicate that I loved it.

Maria was still battling with her large meal. She seemed to be attacking it with vengeance. She was sweating profusely, her face and lips had turned red due to the spices. She looked like a Matryoshka doll to me. "Hunger games?" I whispered to her. Her eyes were blazing. She hadn't forgiven Nambiar.

After the main meal, the younger lady, who seemed like Nambiar's daughter, returned with a steel bowl full of *paayasam*, the traditional dessert made of milk and vermicelli. It contained a liberal dose of cashew nuts and raisins. She went by hierarchy and served Nambiar first; he gulped it down in no time. He excused himself and moved to the portico.

As she served me, she looked into my eyes. While I managed to eat the dessert with my fingers, Maria was struggling. The absence of the old man emboldened the younger woman. She stood near us and forcibly served another portion of *paayasam*. It was after we finished that the other women came in to have their meal.

Nambiar was sitting on his *charukasera* or easy chair in the portico. There was a clean, white Turkish towel wrapped around it. He invited us to sit on the cane settee. He brought out his *vettilla chellam*, a beautifully carved ornamental brass box.

Opening it as if it was a jewellery box, he took out a green betel leaf and applied slaked lime on it with his fingers. Nambiar cracked a betel nut into small pieces using an ornate nutcracker. He put the nuts and betel leaf in his mouth. He completed the combination with a small strip of cured tobacco that looked like dried bacon to me. He chewed on it slowly and periodically spat it out. We sat there observing Nambiar masticate. An uncomfortable silence prevailed. Maria excused herself and retired to her room.

After a few minutes, Nambiar said, "I need a short nap. Let's meet later for tea." I continued to sit there, as I didn't want to follow Maria. Negative connotations could be drawn about our relationship.

I was flipping through old magazines when I heard the muted sound of anklets behind me. It was the lady who had served us lunch. "Bored?" she asked me. "Thought I will give you company," she said and sat on a chair nearby. She had washed her face and applied a fresh dot of red vermillion on her forehead. "So, Krish you like our place?"

Astonished at her familiarity I asked, "How do you know my name?"

"Ambika mentioned you over phone. I am Malini. Would you like to have a *paan*?"

"Been a long time. Why not?"

She pulled the *vettilla chellam* towards her. "Have it without tobacco. If you are not used to it, you may feel giddy."

I had a strong feeling that I had met her before. She put me at ease. We made small talk as if we had known each other for long. She used her fingers to apply the lime on the leaf, cut the betel nuts, rolled it together, and gave it to me. I deliberately touched her fingers. There was a certain intimacy to the act of preparing and offering *paan* to someone other than one's husband or male relative.

Though not a big fan, I accepted it. As she made one for herself, she finally asked, "Who is this girl with you?"

"A friend of mine. She is studying about Theyyam."

"That's all?"

"That's all."

I don't think she believed me, she nodded her head meaningfully. "Children?" she enquired.

"Daughter," I replied.

"Single child?" Her brows went up like a question mark.

"I would like to have more children but my wife doesn't."

A smirk betrayed her disapproval.

The *paan* reddened her lips as she sat chewing absentmindedly. She looked incredibly sexy to me. Something pulled me closer to her. Have I met her before, my mind kept pondering. "What about you?" I enquired

"What about me?"

"Do you have children?'

"No." She looked away and said softly, "Been married for 10 years."

She looked into my eyes. "My husband works for the merchant navy. I used to travel with him a lot. I was an ambitious girl and wanted to see the world. Soon, the desire for travelling diminished. I wanted a baby. I have always loved babies." Her face darkened and she fell silent for a few minutes. "I want to give birth."

There was steel in her eyes. Then they became blank and then moist.

Just then we heard the loud sound of a conch. It possibly came from a temple nearby. Malini didn't seem to hear it. A battle appeared to be raging in her mind. Her face tightened as though she had heard blood-curdling screams and loud thuds of war drums. She seemed to be analysing the pros and cons of a decision.

I asked her, "Where is your husband now?"

"Well, he is on his way and should be here by tomorrow evening. He wants to seek the blessings of the Theyyam Gods for progeny." I saw disgust spreading across her face.

"Aren't you a believer?" I asked.

"I am. But will Gods do everything?" she asked.

"Modern medicine offers effective treatments," I said quietly.

She snapped back, "I am not infertile!"

Taken aback at the aggression, I clarified, "I didn't mean that."

"Sorry, I didn't mean to be angry either. I am really sorry." She seemed scared of losing the newly established bond with me.

We sat quietly, occasionally looking at each other. I felt as though we were silently communicating with each other. From the time I had seen her, an intense desire was building inside me. The way she came across; it was a new experience.

"Do you want to see the *kaavu*? That is where we worship the serpent gods," she broke the silence.

"Sure. Why not? You can be my teacher," I smiled.

"I will see you here at 6 p.m. Let Maria remain here. The patriarch might not be happy allowing a foreigner in the sacred grove." She had found the perfect excuse. There was glint in her eyes. She seemed to be scheming.

"Maria will not be happy being left out," I said.

"Hold on," she said, "I will just be back."
She rushed inside. She came out in a few minutes holding an old paper box. Handing it over to me she said, "Do not let my father know at any cost, but this will help Maria in her thesis and keep her occupied while we are gone. This is my sister's un-submitted thesis and holds sentimental value to my father. I have to go now. Father will be awake. I have to make tea."

I went upstairs to my room. I started feeling uneasy as if an incident of significance was waiting to happen. I felt some sort of an anxiety, a fear of the unknown. I have always been a strong person and such things have never happened to me before. There seemed to be something here that was interfering with my thoughts. After grappling with it for some time, I dismissed it as my imagination or my guilty conscience. I was after all waiting to get together with another woman.

I had taken a big risk by bringing Maria to this *tharawad*. Sooner or later, this news will reach Lakshmi. It will be too difficult to justify this. I could not help these thoughts. Then I told myself, "When I reach the bridge, I will cross it." I pushed away these thoughts. At least for the time being. I wanted to have a dram from the bottle of single malt I had bought at the duty-free shop. But I fought my temptation.

At 4.30 p.m., Nambiar called out for me. I went to Maria's room to check on her. She was sleeping. "Maria, wake up." I gently shook her. She opened her eyes and rubbed them as if wipe sleep off them. "Nambiar is calling us down for tea. Let's go."

"I don't want to meet him again. Please let me sleep for some more time." Her response had a tone of certainty. I let her sleep.

I walked down to the dining table. The table had a plate full of *pazhampori* or banana fritters, a bowl of banana chips, and some cupcakes. Nambiar had started helping himself. He asked, "Where is your friend?"

"She's not feeling well. She is sleeping," I replied.

The old man was not convinced. He asked, "Is it something I said?"

"No, I don't think so. I thought Ambika would have told you about Maria. I didn't want this to be a surprise..." He looked at me intently.

"Have you been married for long?"

"Yes. Many years now." I was worried he might ask me if Lakshmi knew about Maria. Luckily, Malini walked in with three cups of strong, milky tea. She asked, "Maria?"

It was Nambiar who answered. "She is not joining us. Let's have tea." He looked at his daughter tenderly. "Krish, this is my daughter Malini." I acknowledged.

A wicked smile spread over Malini's lips. She sat beside and served us the tea. "I will have Maria's share." She took a small sip from the third cup. There were undertones to her comment.

Nambiar said, "I am going to the temple where the Theyyam will be conducted. There is very little time and lots to do. As Theyyam is a religious offering to the Gods, the arrangements have to be meticulous. I will send a word to Manikandan. He is the Theyyam veteran who can help you with your research."

"Sure. That would be a great help," I said.

"My wife will be joining me. We are going to our maternal *tharawad* where most of the relatives are staying. Malini will be here to look after both of you."

I looked at her and she placed her fingers on her lips. She didn't want me to tell him that she was taking me to the *kaavu*. That was to be our dirty little secret. The prospect of going into the thick sacred grove alone with her sent a feverish excitement in me. I lost interest in what Nambiar was saying.

Malini offered me the plate of banana fritters and said very softly, "Please try this. I made it." Nambiar seemed to be engrossed in the thoughts of arrangements for the Theyyam. He was muttering to himself and absentmindedly chewing on the fritters.

The fritters were oily and very sweet as the banana was very ripe. I complimented her, "This is the best I have had." She blushed.

Nambiar got up. He turned and looked at me. "I am going to take a shower and leave soon. Otherwise, the workers will start coming here looking for me. The fools can't do anything by themselves. They need me around always." This was the typical patriarch's attitude. He wanted to be the fountainhead of all decisions and the primal source of advice on rituals and customs. He walked towards his bedroom, leaving me and Malini to finish the tea.

Malini was back to her flirtatious self. She laughed heartily at my jokes. When her sari slipped off from her shoulders, she didn't rush to put it back in place. She was behaving like Maria had in the afternoon today. I didn't hesitate to take a good look at her well-endowed bosom. I was growing bolder and was surprised by it. I was behaving like Ajay. I was shameless.

We heard the staircase creak. Maria had decided to have tea after all. She still looked sleepy. She seemed like she had caught a fever. I touched her forehead but it was not hot. "How are you feeling?" I was concerned. Maria sat quietly beside me.

"I have a terrible headache," she groaned.

Malini's expression underwent a paradigm shift. She got up quickly and said, "I will send tea for Maria. I will see you in sometime. Don't forget your camera if you need to take pictures." She said this loud enough for Maria to hear. Malini stood inside the kitchen and stared at me for a few seconds and then moved away.

The old maid servant brought a cup of tea and placed it in front of Maria.

Maria took a sip. "This feels good. Hot tea can be a medicine for small ailments." She smiled weakly. I pushed the plate of fritters in front of her.

"I'm still full," she protested.

"Do you want to see a doctor?" I was really getting concerned.

"I am not used to being looked after. Don't worry, it could be just a headache. Where is she taking you?"

"The *kaavu*. The sacred grove where serpents are worshipped."

Her eyes glistened. "Wow! I would like to come too. There is mystery associated with such secluded places."

Though I felt bad for her, I said, "Nambiar may not approve of taking a foreigner inside the grove."

Her face fell. She said, "I feel that nobody likes me here. I feel isolated. Just because I'm a foreigner doesn't make me unholy." I didn't reply but her cup of misery brimmed over. After a brief pause, she said, "If they do not allow me to go there, why are you going? Aren't we a team?" There was anger in her tone.

"Don't you need a detailed and authentic description of the *kaavu*? A few photographs, details on the flora and fauna?" I asked her. She looked away. She obviously didn't like the idea.

The Nambiar couple came out of their room. Their driver had brought the SUV to the front of the house. As the vehicle drew away, Maria went upstairs.

I decided to return to my room to fetch the paper box Malini had given. The door to Maria's room was open. She was busy on her laptop. She looked up and said, "What time are you going to the *kaavu*?"

"Around 6 p.m. That is when the lamps are lit," I replied.

"I am working on the outline of the thesis. It will keep me

busy while you are flirting with the woman in the *kaavu.*" There was envy in her voice. I handed over the box to her and said, "Malini gave this for you."

"What is it?" she asked with disdain.

"I do not know, please have a look. She said it would be helpful in your research."

Maria kept the box aside for later and said, "Enjoy the rendezvous with Malini."

"See you soon."

"Take your time." There was sarcasm in her voice.

Picking up my camera, I quickly walked down the creaking and groaning staircase. Malini was waiting for me. She had taken a bath and her hair was still slightly wet. The two-piece costume of *settu-mundu* she was wearing made her look simple and elegant. She held a small plastic bottle filled with gingelly oil, a pack of cotton wicks and a match box. She started walking towards the grove situated at the other end of the property. I followed her, gradually reducing the distance between us.

The grove was large and looked like a small forest. It was protected by a small wooden gate.

"Such a small gate for this lovely property?" I asked Malini.

"This grove is protected by fierce spirits. At least the fear of these beings ensures zero trespassing."

Dusk descended fast and the call of the birds returning to the roost became louder. The crimson red stripes on the sky was fading away. It was dark inside and the grandfather trees looked huge and intimidating. Their leaves swayed gently with the light breeze. Nambiar had utilised the fertile soil very well. The flora constituted of mature teak, mango, jack fruit and guava trees. One large corner was dedicated to growing tapioca. This was like the Garden of Eden.

Malini held my hand and said, "Stay close to me."

She knew this landscape better than I. Though she wasn't wearing jasmine, its overpowering smell lingered on her hair. Water droplets from her hair had dripped on to her back and made the pink underskirt visible through the thin fabric of the *mundu*.

I deliberately pressed my arm against her soft belly. She didn't protest.

In the middle of the grove, there was a large old banyan tree. A concrete base was built around it and granite idols of serpent gods were placed on it. They were left open to the elements of nature. She left my hand and bent forward to place the wick and pour oil on the stone lamps. She struggled with the matches as the gentle breeze thwarted her efforts. The folds around her abdomen became more prominent and tantalising.

As she stood praying to the Gods, I looked around. The foliage around was thick. Climbers and creepers twisted around trees, creating an interwoven tapestry. Since few dared enter the grove, flowers such as jasmine, *chempakam* and *illanji* bloomed in full glory, unmolested. Their arousing fragrance wafted in the air.

By now, dusk had set in completely. The soft sounds of something moving on dry leaves sent shivers down my spine. Was it a serpent moving towards its pit? The breeze was getting colder. This was the home of the serpents and nobody disturbed them here. Obviously, I was the intruder. It was an eerie, magical world. I took a picture but the flash was too bright. Malini forbid me from taking pictures as it would attract unnecessary attention. I kept the camera on the ground.

I moved closer to her. She was murmuring in reverence to the Gods. At that moment, in the bright glow of the lamps she looked erotic. Maybe she was seeking the serpents' help to conceive. After all, the serpent, as a phallic symbol, has been associated with fertility.

As she finished her prayers, she looked at me and said, "Did you see a ghost or something? Your face is pale."

"Are there snakes in this *kaavu*, Malini?" I tried to sound normal and inquisitive.

"Of course, there are. The cobra and krait have been seen the most. They are extremely venomous but generally keep away from people," she said, matter-of-factly. "Yes, a few people have been fatally bitten by snakes in this grove. That was till father had the pathway to the idols cleared. Groves such as these are synonymous with dense vegetation. This is the sanctuary of the snakes." She seemed to love the rising fear on my face.

She continued, "Most of them who were bitten were those trying to steal fruits or coconuts. Even today, not many dare enter this place. Long ago, many intruders have died out of sheer fear. Father had a tough time finding workers to clear the path."

"Nothing can drive fear into the human mind like snakes," I said.

"Not just snakes, Krish. According to legends, the sanctity of this place is protected by fierce spirits."

The hair behind my neck stood up in heightened fear. A light sweat broke out on my forehead. Though I was an atheist, I hadn't been able to completely wipe out the possibility of the existence of evil spirits from my subconscious.

She laughed, "If you are afraid, hold me." She stood there. Like the innate craving for the forbidden fruit, the urge to have sex with her became stronger than the fear of snakes. I hugged her gently.

In the flickering light of the lamps, I saw her trembling moist lips. I slipped my hands around her abdomen and pulled her closer. Forgetting everything, I kissed her. She sat on the ground and pulled me down. As I struggled with her blouse, she lifted her *mundu* all the way up to her waist.

In this struggle, my *mundu* had come loose. She coiled around me. She didn't want prolonged foreplay and guided me towards penetration. Like a striking serpent, I entered her again and again. Though it didn't take long, she held me tight to keep me in as I shuddered in climax.

Though exhausted, she rolled me down and climbed

over me, slowly rubbing her body over mine. Desire and determination were etched on her face. She pinned me down, bit my lips, and gently thrust her nipples towards me. They were hard and salty.

"Bite me." She provoked me. Worked into a frenzy, I nibbled at her nipples and bit her breasts. She dug her nails into my flesh like a predator. Her eyes were closed as ecstasy set in. Malini was the dominant mate tonight but I didn't want to be tamed. I wound my hand around her hair and pulled her down. As we copulated aggressively, the sand and little stones crushed against my skin. The pain just intensified the experience. Brute lust generated by this intense sexual power-play gave me an opium-like high. As we climaxed, she sat on me till the throbbing subsided completely.

We lay in embrace for a few minutes before getting up to dress. The sweat made the sand stick like glue over us. The wick on the lamps had blackened and the flames were dying.

As we walked forward, I realised that I had left the camera behind. I was afraid of returning to fetch it alone. There was fear on Malini's face as well. We had no choice so we quickly ran back to fetch it.

Fear played havoc with both of our minds. Both of us didn't want to leave behind any obvious proof. Just as we reached the wooden gate, she turned and kissed me hard on my lips. There was a sense of finality to her act. She ran into the house without looking back, as though she was escaping from something.

There was light in Maria's room. She was speaking to somebody on the phone. On reaching my room, I looked in the mirror; there was mud all over my body and my shirt was dirty. I needed a shower.

I felt stinging pain all over as the warm water hit me hard. The skin around my knees was bleeding lightly. Minute particles of sand were still stuck there. I felt ashamed of myself. Had I behaved any differently from Ajay? I wrapped the soiled clothes in a plastic bag and hid them in my bag. I didn't want Maria to know.

I heard Nambiar's car come through the gate. It was already 8.30 p.m. I went to Maria's room. She was typing and didn't acknowledge my presence. I sat on the bed and remained quiet.

Without looking at me she asked me, "So, did she show you her sacred grove?" I didn't reply. So she turned and looked at me, "What took you so long? What were you doing in the pitch dark?" She sounded like *amma*.

"I came back quite some time ago. You were talking on the phone so I went back to my room."

She was still not convinced. "Did you take a bath after coming back?"

"Where is your camera? I want to see some photos," Maria asked as if she wanted further proof.

"How many questions will you ask? Nambiar has returned. He must be looking for us. Let's go down." I tried deflecting her anger by changing the subject

"Gosh! Do we need to have dinner with him? Can't we have it later, once he is done?"

"Maria, we are living in his house. We need him to take us inside the temple, introduce us to the Theyyam performers and other experts. We can't afford to antagonise him. He is doing us a favour not the other way around." I looked into her eyes and asked, "Shall we?" We went down together.

Perhaps the creaking of the stairs alerted Nambiar. He came out of the dining room and waved us in. "We just came back a few minutes ago. Come on in. How's your work going?"

I said, "We are creating a detailed questionnaire for the Theyyam expert." We sat at the table. Mrs Nambiar served us dinner.

"How come you are back early? You said you would be late? Did you not have dinner?"

"We had our dinner at the maternal *tharawad*. All our relatives have gathered there. She started feeling very uneasy and anxious, so we returned." He said pointing to his spouse.

Mrs Nambiar began, "Around 6.30 p.m., I was overcome by anxiety. A strong feeling that something was wrong. Malini is the one who has been lighting the lamp at the *kaavu* since she came here. She doesn't take anybody along with her. The *kaavu* is home for the spirits of our ancestors and venomous snakes. Many untoward incidents have taken place there. Though I believe in the magnanimity of the spirits, I am also terrified of their wrath. Nambiar dismissed my fears as my imagination. He forgets that this is an old *tharawad* and has a history..."

"Now please be quiet and serve them food." Nambiar admonished his wife.

The dinner had more items than lunch. "I packed food for you from the other *tharawad*." It was an all-vegetarian fare but I still pretended to love it.

After the meal, we sat at the portico listening to Nambiar's stories. All the while, Mrs Nambiar's fears played in my mind. How could she have known that the sanctity of the *kaavu* was being despoiled? Are the so-called spirits of the *kaavu* and serpent gods powerful enough to wreak vengeance? Don't they exist only in our minds? The more I tried to dismiss the thoughts, the more they rebounded, each time with increased severity. The thought that I had violated many taboos today started making me a little uneasy.

I excused myself and returned to my room. After maybe ten minutes, Maria followed. She came to my room and asked, "What happened to you? You look like you saw a ghost. Did something untoward happen in the *kaavu*?"

"Nothing. It's possibly the food. I am feeling nauseated," I murmured. She seemed concerned. "I just want to sleep. Should feel better in the morning," I said weakly, wanting to be left alone.

"Call me if you need something." Maria switched off the light and gently closed the door.

Despite my fears, I still thought about Malini and how things had turned out today. I had just met her in the afternoon and considering my skills at seduction, what happened today was truly a miracle. It was as though an unknown entity had been gently influencing us. This was one rare experience I would cherish all my life. My eyelids became heavy with sleep and I sank into deep slumber.

It was past midnight when I was woken up by Maria's frantic calls. "Krish, Krish, wake up. Something has happened downstairs. Let's go check."

We scrambled down the stairs. The servants were standing outside the door. I heard sobs coming from inside. I presumed it was Malini's bedroom. We went in. Malini was lying on Mrs Nambiar's lap and sobbing.

"What happened?" I asked Nambiar.

Malini looked at me. Her eyes were red and horror was written all over her face. Mrs Nambiar looked terrified too.

Nambiar, who was standing near her bed, said, "Malini seems to have seen a large serpent on her bed. The loud hiss is what woke her up. By the time we came here on hearing her screams, it had escaped."

I stood looking at Malini for some time. "Was that a warning?" A cold intense fear descended on me. Inquisitiveness overtook my fear. "How did it come in? The doors and windows were closed. Weren't they?" I asked. The consultant in me wanted to investigate, partly out of curiosity and partly out of fear.

I was taken aback by Malini's instant angry reaction. "So, you don't believe me, do you?" There was so much hate and fear in her eyes. I was not the only one responsible for what happened in the *kaavu* today. Why was she accusing me?

She pointed towards the window. I moved the curtain to take a look. Like in my room, each wooden panel was divided into four squares; the glass in one of the squares was missing.

It was Nambiar who said, "It broke a couple of days ago and I couldn't find the time to get it fixed."

I opened the door. It was dark outside. Nambiar cautioned me not to step outside. "It might be still there and strike if it feels threatened."

Now, I was getting convinced that Malini had imagined the snake. The guilt of having defiled the *kaavu* possibly weighed heavily on her mind. Her subconscious mind perhaps objectified her fear. She could have just had a nightmare and was unable to differentiate between the real and the surreal.

"Please give me a torch, uncle," I requested. "We need to know the truth." The powerful flash cut through the darkness. There was nothing outside. Maria came behind me. Despite my requests, she refused to go back to the house.

It was Maria who found what looked like snake tracks. As we went closer, our suspicions were confirmed. They were clearly wavy tracks left behind by a snake. From the direction of the tracks, we guessed that it must have escaped to the *kaavu*. We looked at each other.

Maria quickly used her feet to erase them.

"Why?" I asked.

"They need not know. Even if this was not the snake that allegedly came to Malini's bedroom, they would literally die of fear. They are highly religious people who believe in the potency of serpent gods." Maria spoke with a maturity she rarely exhibited. We went back to the room.

"See anything?" Nambiar was curious. Maria lied, "No, nothing."

Nambiar stated coldly, "We are a family that has worshipped the serpent gods diligently for centuries. We have given no reason to incur their wrath. It could have been your imagination, Malini. Anyway, do not sleep here tonight. Come and sleep with us."

We went back to our rooms. I had more questions than answers. If a snake did come to Malini's room, then why did it not bite her? Did it just come to warn her? I was equally guilty in defiling the *kaavu*. So, will it come looking for me? Or in a place where sighting snakes was common, did a snake just happen to pass by and were we making a big deal of it? Was all this really possible?

My rational mind argued against it but the sequence of events was indeed disturbing. Before sleeping, I checked under the bed, the bathroom, and even my bags. It took a long time for me to fall asleep again.

It must have been early morning when I had a terrible nightmare. I clearly saw a large black cobra coiled on my chest. As it swayed slowly, its hood was spread wide in an aggressive pose. Its forked tongue flickered in and out and I could see the thin, bright, yellow border around its glassy black eyes. They were glistening. The snake was heavy and I couldn't breathe. Then it struck me repeatedly. That is when I woke up in terror. It looked real. Very real!

I couldn't sleep again. Was it a warning? Or was it just fear playing in my mind? How come both Malini and I had the same experience? Was it because we had committed the sin together? Or was it the outcome of my expectation that what happened to Malini should happen to me too?

Fear immobilised me and I lay on the bed sweating profusely. I began to have a mild anxiety attack. There is something in this house, I thought.

I somehow pulled myself up and sat on the bed for some time. I craved for some fresh air. So I went downstairs.

Nambiar was sitting on his easy chair sipping hot tea and reading the newspaper.

URN

ambiar looked up and asked, "Are you an early riser too?"

"Not really. Yesterday's incident was very disturbing. I couldn't sleep well," I said.

"We are used to seeing snakes but they have never crossed the perimeter of the house. My wife is afraid that something has angered the serpent gods." There was worry on his face

"Belief in the divine powers of serpents is ardent in this part of the world, I guess."

Nambiar folded the newspaper. "Do you want a cup of tea?" He didn't wait for my response and called out for tea. I sat beside him. "Yes, serpent worship has a long history in Kerala. *Sarpa-kaavus* are the open-air temples of the serpents. It is man's way of domesticating and propitiating these powerful forces." Nambiar paused as his wife came with two cups of steaming tea.

"So quickly?" I asked Mrs Nambiar

"Tea is always available here. I just heated it." She seemed to want to hear what we said but Nambiar dismissed her with a flick of his hand.

"The cult of snake worship has resulted in unique ritual practices and taboos. There is a sub-culture that has grown around it. The space is considered so sacred that its desecration or *kaavu-theendal* is said to invite the wrath of the serpents that transcend generations. Humans have an instinctual fear of snakes.

"The temples of Mannarashala and Pambummekkattu Mana are the most prominent serpent worship centres in Kerala. Interestingly, Mannarashala is headed by high caste Brahman women. Women priests are rare among the Brahman community in Kerala. There are many legends surrounding these temples.

"Snakes also represent longevity and fertility. Who was the villain that caused the temptation and expulsion of Adam and Eve? The serpent is closely associated with danger, fertility and sexuality."

"But then if Eve hadn't taken the decision to eat the forbidden fruit, then we would not have been banished to earth. That decision led to our flourishing. Isn't it? So the credit for that goes to women. Isn't it?" I asked Nambiar who gave a wide grin.

The conversation was taking a very interesting turn, when I heard the gate open. Two old men walked through the gate holding faded, black umbrellas. Nambiar seemed very happy. He raised his arms and waved at them with big sweeps.

"There are no condensed answers for complex questions," said Nambiar and deliberately looked at his watch to signal that the conversation was over. I would just have to wait to hear more.

The old men, who were clad in white *mundus* and loose shirts, looked alike. "My elder brothers," introduced Nambiar. They complained about the heat as if it was customary to do so. The younger brother had a weathered look. His straight white hair was parted down the middle and coconut oil applied generously.

He spoke in a sedate, dignified voice. "Everybody's talking about it." He was obviously referring to the upcoming event. The other man, who was much older, seemed the quiet type. He just dropped into the armchair and looked into the yard without interest. He had a melancholic expression bordering on despondency. He stuttered when he said, "I don't know if I will be there for the next Theyyam."

"Keep quiet. Don't always be pessimistic," Nambiar scolded his elder brother.

"People used to have more time in their hands and participated actively in organising Theyyam performances. Now, everybody is busy," said Nambiar with a sigh. The men nodded in unison.

They had been working obsessively towards organising a memorable Theyyam performance. It was as if they were playing major roles on the world stage. They huddled together and whispered to each other. I became the outsider in their world – the lonely pilgrim!

These men wanted to leave behind glorious memories that would stay in the hearts of the people like an important monument. Nobody wants to be forgotten.

I got up and walked back to my room. The sun slowly climbed its way up. I felt the urge to take a shower. It was more of a psychological effort to scrub away my guilt and cleanse myself.

After the shower, I felt lighter. As I stepped out of my room, I heard the sound of Maria's hair dryer. I gently knocked on her door and walked down for breakfast.

The old men were sitting around the dining table deeply lost in the contents of an old register. Evidently, they were working on the budget. Empty cups of tea were in front of them.

As I sat down, without looking at me, Nambiar called out for his wife. She came out and asked me, "Hungry? Where is Maria?"

"She should be here soon."

Mrs Nambiar came back with two plates and served me some *upma* and two bananas to go with it. She asked, "Would you like some tea?"

I nodded affirmatively. "How is Malini?"

"She was really frightened. She refused to stay here and left for the maternal *tharawad* early in the morning. Her husband is reaching Kannur today."

As I started eating, Maria walked in. She looked at me accusingly and indicated, "Couldn't wait for me?"

"I knocked on your door."

"Glutton!" she whispered.

Nambiar's eldest brother looked up. He was shocked to see her and looked at Nambiar.

"She is a PhD student from the United States. Has come here to study Theyyam. Isn't it a matter of pride for us? It will spread awareness about our little village and Theyyam," Nambiar explained.

The old man was not convinced; suddenly both his brothers seem to have lost interest in the accounts. They started arguing with Nambiar in hushed tones. The three of them then left the table and moved to the portico.

Maria was astonished at their behaviour. We had our breakfast quickly. We then thanked Mrs Nambiar and went back upstairs.

Maria asked, "Why are your eyes red? Did you not sleep well yesterday?"

I told her about the nightmare. "Do you think it was an attempt at retribution by the serpent-spirits? What could anybody in the family have done to invite this? Those tracks could have been behind left by any snake passing through."

Maria tried to rationalise. "But why should you be afraid?"

I just shook my shoulder dismissively. "How's your report shaping up?" I deflected her query.

"There seems to be quite a bit of information in the papers given by Malini. I just glanced through them. I can already foresee one of the best thesis ever being submitted to my university." There was a glint in her eyes.

"Why don't you come in and have a look at the papers?" she invited.

I went to her room. She propped up the pillows on the headrest of the bed for me to sit comfortably. They smelt of her shampoo. She brought the paper box and sat beside me on the bed.

We together opened it and went through the

contents. They included cuttings from old magazines and newspapers, pages from out-of-print books, small booklets published by organisers of Theyyam as souvenirs, and a typed copy of a thesis on Theyyam submitted to the University of Kannur. The name 'Thankam Nambiar' was neatly typed on it. It was dated 1997. The papers were old and yellowing. "Be careful while handling these papers. Nambiar doesn't know that we have these with us," I warned Maria.

"The thesis seems to be extensively researched. I have saved it for the last. I wonder how this person is related to Nambiar."

"It's his eldest daughter. This holds a lot of sentimental value for Nambiar."

"He didn't mention about his daughter to us, Krish. Where is she?"

"I do not know. Please take pictures of these documents using your tablet, as I would like to return them to Malini."

I started reading the thesis. It was indeed well-written. Despite the compelling narrative, I drifted into deep sleep.

I woke up hearing my name being called out. It was Mrs Nambiar asking us to come down for lunch. Though half-asleep, I shouted back, "Coming in five minutes, aunty!"

Maria was sleeping beside me. Her hand was on my chest. She was snoring lightly. I woke her up and returned to my room to wash my face.

Worried that Mrs Nambiar would suspect that we were sleeping in the same room, I told Maria to bring the laptop along when she came down.

The SUV was missing so I presumed that Nambiar and his brothers had gone to the temple to supervise the preparations. Seizing the opportunity, I asked Mrs Nambiar's permission to join her in the kitchen.

"Come on in. You can help me with the cooking," she giggled.

She was shallow-frying *pappadum* in an old wok

shaped metal pan. It was a small kitchen that had been modernised. After complimenting her beautiful kitchen, I said, "There is so much to write about Theyyam and we wanted to hear your version too." She seemed happy that I had finally reached out to her.

"I am not an expert but I will tell you whatever little I know," she sounded humble but seemed eager to put forth her views.

I retreated, having blunted any suspicions she may have harboured. Maria was ready with her laptop. She raised her eyebrows as she didn't know what we were doing.

Raising my voice loud enough to be heard in the kitchen I said, "We can finally hear what Mrs Nambiar has to say about Theyyam. Record it so that we can use it later." I winked at Maria. "We should record her version of the Theyyam. Most of the deities in the Theyyam pantheon are women, so it is important to hear a woman's perspective." I smiled slyly.

Maria walked into the kitchen and offered to help Mrs Nambiar. In the absence of the patriarch, she behaved freely. It was Maria who served food for all of us. Mrs Nambiar was obviously happy. Maria set up the video on the laptop. We began eating. I said, "Tell me aunty. What are your thoughts on Theyyam?"

"I have grown up seeing Theyyam performances. We believe that the spirits of the Goddesses and the Gods transcend down to the earth and possess the body of the performer. They reveal their thoughts and desires by using the physical faculties of the performers.

"During the Theyyam season, people from all over congregate around these temples or *kaavus* to seek blessings from the powerful spirits.

"You know, Malini has been married for many years and is still longing for a baby. She refuses to seek medical help. She and her husband are here to seek the blessings of the Theyyam Gods. They are very powerful. I am hoping she will conceive soon." Mrs Nambiar seemed quite confident. "Do you know that most deities of Theyyam are females?"

"Yes, we do." It was Maria.

"It is only the *Devakkooth* Theyyam which is performed by a woman. Otherwise, it is the men who dress up like women to perform. Ironic, isn't it?" She sounded like a feminist. "The male performers use a breast plate and paint themselves to depict *Bhaghawathi* or the Mother Goddess."

Maria said, "Sounds like a travesty to me considering that Kerala was predominantly matrilineal."

"Hmm... Matrilineality was indeed prevalent among the Nairs and other higher castes, but not many women actually had a say in their lives," said Mrs Nambiar. I remembered Raghavan's words.

"If you do not understand the socio-political background, then Theyyam is nothing but a colourful mask-dance. But, it is much beyond that. Its stories hide the state of women in medieval Kerala and the harshness of the caste system.

"Not all, but many Theyyam deities are considered to be spirits of victims of unnatural death. Either they were murdered or died due to the inequalities and insecurities of the males. Their death perhaps drove fear into the minds of the perpetrators. They believed that the vengeful spirits of their victims would return to wreak revenge. So, in order to propitiate the souls, they were deified and worshipped. At least in some ways, females could generate dread in the minds of men."

Mrs Nambiar looked at me to see if I was upset at the allegations against my ilk. I nodded in empathy. She surprised us when she said, "Hasn't William Congreve written, 'Heaven has no rage like love to hatred turned, nor hell a fury like a woman scorned'?" Mrs Nambiar looked at Maria for a reaction; who nodded in agreement. We were surprised at her grasp of literature.

Mrs Nambiar immediately said, "I studied English literature in college."

She continued addressing Maria. "Sexual exploitation of the lower caste women by the members of the upper castes was quite common. The inky darkness of the night temporarily hid the warts of untouchability. The women they avoided in the morning became desirable at night." She wiped the sweat off her forehead and said, "Some men in our family were no different. But then they took care of these clandestine mistresses, unlike others."

I couldn't help but ask, "So the women folk knew about it?"

She fell silent for a few moments and then said, "Everybody knew. Just that nobody spoke about it."

I had touched a raw chord. Changing the subject, she said, "Malini's husband would have reached the *tharawad*. The family is gathering there in the evening. I will be leaving in some time."

I asked her, "One question has been on my mind since I came here. Why are the other family members not staying here in this *tharawad*?"

She gazed at me for a moment and said, "That's a long story. Nambiar is the best man to tell you about it."

She continued, "Don't worry, the servants will be here to take care of you. Nambiar will be here around at 4 p.m. and take you to the temple. Theyyam starts tomorrow!" She beamed.

Despite Maria's offer to help with the dishes, Mrs Nambiar told us, "Please go ahead and complete your work. We are proud to host you." She looked at Maria and said, "I hope your thesis brings out the feminine side of the story and I would love to read it. Don't forget to email me a copy."

We decided against going to our rooms till Mrs Nambiar went out. We sat at the portico discussing what she had told us. I wanted Maria to try out a *paan* but the *vettilla chellam* was not to be found. It was usually kept under the easy chair.

Maria said, "I want a break from all the reading and constant typing. Let's explore the property." It was oppressively hot, so I protested. "We will end up with sun burns. I don't want us to fall sick a day before Theyyam begins."

Maria laughed and said, "You forget one of the most famous sayings in Kerala – The one that was born of fire won't be felled by the sun! Come on Krish, be a sport. You are my strong man." Though I didn't fall for her flattery, I was bored. So I agreed.

"Wait here for a minute, Krish. Let me get my camera." She ran up the stairs, which groaned at her pace of climbing.

While coordinating my visit, Lakshmi had not forgotten to give me a brief background. She had said, "Nambiar and his brothers are joint custodians of this old ancestral property. They have spent considerable resources to renovate and maintain it for the future generations. This must be worth many millions of rupees in today's market. For them, conducting Theyyam at the ancestral temple, so diligently, is a sacred duty. So, make sure that you show great respect while covering the performance."

Like the *sarpa-kaavu*, Nambiar's property had many trees; coconut, areca nut, mango, jackfruits, gooseberry, papaya and guava, to name a few. At the back where the kitchen was, there was a big, flourishing vegetable garden. It was well cared for. Nambiar's gardener had planted okra, aubergine, snake gourd, bitter gourd, pumpkin, ash gourd and beans.

Maria walked very close to me. I told her, "Maria, let us maintain some physical distance. People in the house may be watching. For them, you are a student who has come to learn about Theyyam."

"Got it!" She walked a little away. Despite her bravado, she was struggling with the heat and was sweating profusely.

"By the way, we are lucky that nobody comes upstairs. If someone had seen us sleeping in one bed, Nambiar would have kicked us out. In no time the news would have reached my wife, Lakshmi. I am not yet ready for a divorce!"

"Well, if Lakshmi kicks you out, I will always be there for you."

Maria didn't look at me when she said that. She was changing the lens of the camera. I looked at her and said, "I am not an easy man to put up with, Maria."

"I am willing to take the risk." She focused the camera on the tree tops.

Did I really love her that much to leave Lakshmi? I was not sure but there was something about Maria. I was very comfortable around her. She didn't try to intimidate or dominate me and the barriers between us had begun to melt at an uncomfortable pace.

The trees were full of squirrels that leaped between branches with ease, like trapeze artists. Maria was clicking photographs of anything and everything. At the other end of the property stood this mango tree that looked a bit odd. Though it was green and full of mangoes, there was a particular ugliness about it. It was the only fruit-bearing tree that did not have any squirrels or any birds perched on it. It struck me as weird.

Maria was walking towards the tree. She said, "Let's sit under its shade for a while, Krish."

"Not that tree, Maria. It looks repulsive to me." I discouraged her.

"Trees cannot be repulsive, only people can be. I feel like it is calling me, Krish." She smiled sheepishly. Before she held my hands and pulled me towards the tree, I decided to follow her.

It was a relief to sit under the shadows the tree's mighty canopy threw. A light breeze on its leisurely journey absorbed the sweat and cooled our bodies. Maria lay on the ground and looked at the sky.

"Look Krish, the clouds are racing across the blue sky as if it is the autobahn. They seem to be running away from something," she observed.

"You are being poetic, Maria," I said.

"Basically, I am a poet whose talent never saw the light of the day," she said and laughed.

"This is bliss. I feel like I have attained nirvana. A sense of complete tranquillity and peace," she murmured with her eyes closed. She looked like an innocent younggirl to me. Beautiful, naughty and subtly sexy.

After marriage, rarely had I felt like this for another

woman. Something tugged at my heart. The need for each other seemed to grow stronger. I sat next to her, trying to analyse my feelings for her. It wasn't easy taking a decision like this. Procrastination seemed bliss!

Suddenly she said, "I am feeling a little weird as though the tree is trying to communicate something to me. It seems to be drawing me closer to it. Or something like that. My heart seems to be beating harder."

I dismissed this by saying, "The organ that produces your romantic hormones are working harder than usual."

"Well, maybe. But I have a strange feeling. Please, let's go," she pleaded.

As we stood up, she saw a couple of large raw mangoes in a corner. She walked towards it mumbling. "I love the sour taste of raw mangoes. See, the tree wanted me to find it," she said laughing. "Hey, come here Krish. Something is glistening here. Have a look," she called out.

"What did you see?" I was curious too.

"Looks like some sort of an old vessel to me." She was rummaging through old and dry leaves.

"Careful. There could be snakes," I warned her. "Don't touch it. Let me come over," I said and ran towards her.

"Okay," she said and stood up frightened by the mention of snakes.

"How can it glisten? Sunshine doesn't reach there. This is under the shade of the tree." I looked carefully but didn't see anything.

"I clearly saw something glisten as if the rays of the sun were being reflected over it." She was puzzled.

I did not want her to sense that I thought she was crazy. So I looked in the corner that she pointed at. Actually, I was worried about being surprised by a snake in the foliage.

Maria couldn't control her curiosity. She fetched a long stick and removed the leaves feverishly. She was confident she had made a mysterious discovery. Something that would be life-changing or worth a lot of money. She said, almost prophetically, "It feels like I came here all the way to discover this."

"There," she shouted. I could see the edge of a copper- coloured vessel covered with patina. It was still under the ground. As if descending into madness, Maria almost screamed as she went near it. She tried hard to pull it out and asked for help, "Krish, help me. This seems to be going back to the earth. I tried pulling it out but the vessel resisted, as though somebody was holding it from below."

I used a stick to dig the earth around. After a few minutes, we were able to remove all the soil around it. Maria leapt forward to extract the copper vessel. She pulled it out. We stood under the sun to examine it. It looked very old and had crude carvings around it. There were images of beings that did not look divine. At its neck were a few amulets that were covered with what looked like green mould. It was firmly shut with a lid over a red piece of cloth. We were both curious and afraid.

"Will this contain any old artefacts? Or maybe gold coins?" Maria's curiosity seemed to be on a feverish climb. Despite my overwhelming curiosity, I began to panic. She tried unsuccessfully to open it. I sensed her eagerness to see what was inside. So we tried using a large stone to force it open.

"Looks like it was intentionally shut tight so that no one could open it easily," said Maria. Her eyes had a strange glint in them that made me uncomfortable. I caught hold of the red cloth and hit the urn against the mango tree's trunk. We were like two children dying of curiosity. As we struggled with it, the urn fell from our hands on to the ground and opened. There was nothing in it except something that looked like ash.

Maria said, "What is that vapour coming out?" I looked but didn't see anything.

"It could be a figment of your imagination. The sense of discovering a mysterious object can indeed be overwhelming."

"No, Krish, I saw vapours escaping." She was adamant.

"What are you implying?" I asked her.

"Nothing, but I am sure I saw some vapours leave the urn. Or maybe I got carried away." She backed off.

"In movies, I have seen black magic rituals conducted by magicians. I have seen them using such urns to imprison evil spirits. Although I have never seen any of these personally, this looks like an urn used for black magic rituals," I said.

Maria looked at me with horror.

"These magic rituals are performed for psychological satisfaction. Such things don't happen, Maria. However, you are possibly holding a piece of history." I said this to comfort her but, subconsciously, I couldn't completely reject the idea of something evil.

The mysterious urn made me uncomfortable. My instinct warned me against taking it away from its natural resting place. I tried convincing Maria. "Leave it there. It looks like the by-product of some magic ritual. Listen to me and leave it there."

"I want to keep this as a souvenir. It will be a great exhibit at my university. This will add authenticity to my thesis and defence presentation in front of senior professors. This is an opportunity of a lifetime." She pleaded. "It is my first archaeological discovery, Krish. Please. When did you start believing in the mumbo-jumbo of black magic?"

I felt my resistance weakening. Then I told her, "Keep it, but please put it in your rucksack safely, away from everybody. I don't want Nambiar to find out about your great discovery. He may not approve of it."

She gave me a playful shove. "Let's go now before Nambiar returns."

Maria closed the urn tightly and carried it gingerly as if it was precious cargo that would change her life forever. As we walked, I looked back at the tree. I loved mango trees but this one had a sinister look about it. I had a strange feeling that it had somehow influenced us. I hated the tree.

My rational mind rebelled against my new-found uncertainty. A sense of mystery is always exciting. Sometimes, one's mind misinterprets events for a bit of thrill. Some superstitious person, in an effort to ward off imaginary spirits, must have gone to a local magician and received this as a panacea. As instructed, the person must have dug it in a place where no one would find it. He must have forgotten it after burying it under the tree. It is most probably the outcome of blind faith.

That's all, I told myself.

manikandan

As we reached the portico, Nambiar's SUV entered the gate.

Maria ran up the stairs and I sat on one of the chairs.

Nambiar got out and apologised. "Sorry, I could not join you for lunch. Organising a Theyyam performance is a hard task. Did you get bored?"

"No. Maria and I went around the property. It has been maintained beautifully, uncle," I said.

He was obviously pleased. "Yes, we all have worked hard and spent considerable money to maintain the place. It is our responsibility towards the next generation."

Nambiar asked me to join him for tea, but he didn't enquire about Maria. I didn't like him ignoring her. It was as if she never existed for him. As we sipped the hot brew, I remembered the whisky that I had saved. The time seemed right to hand it over to him as a gift.

I returned to my room to get the bottle of Glenfiddich, the 12-year-old, single malt Scotch whisky. Maria was engrossed in trying to decipher the engravings on the urn.

"Maria, please come down and hand this over to Nambiar."

She looked puzzled at my request. "Why me? I don't want to meet him."

I goaded her. "Hand this over to him as a gift from you. Alcohol dissolves barriers."

We walked down quickly.

"There is something Maria had brought for you, Mr Nambiar," I said, handing over the bottle to him.

He looked at Maria. Though it wasn't difficult to understand what it was, he feigned ignorance. "What's this?" He addressed her directly.

She mumbled, "I hope you like it."

He opened the cover, pulled out the bottle, and appraised it for a couple of minutes. A smile hesitantly spread across his face. He went to his room to stash it safely.

On returning, he said, "Bhaghyalakshmi does not agree with alcohol. She thinks it will aggravate my diabetes."

We inferred Bhaghyalakshmi was Mrs Nambiar's name. This was the first time he had referred to her by name. He paused and said, "Not that I listen to her. Little does she know that I have an occasional drink." He chuckled. He seemed to be in high spirits already.

As we sipped the milky hot tea and chewed on oily banana fritters, I asked Nambiar, "Uncle, can you tell me something about black magic?"

There was a sudden change in the old man's body language. He narrowed his eyes and furrowed his brow. His jaw tightened slightly as he asked me, "Why? What happened?" He seemed uncomfortable with the subject.

"We were researching the prevalence of black magic in Kerala. I thought that you could tell us something about it."

"This region has always been known for its dense forests with people living deep inside it. In the dark jungles, people developed their own religious beliefs, a strange mixture of animism and black magic. They were considered powerful sorcerers who had the ability to propitiate evil spirits and supernatural entities to make them obey their bidding. Though many people have shifted out of the jungles, they still practice this craft for a living."

Nambiar adjusted his spectacles as though he wanted to look into the past better. "Even members of the upper castes, who generally kept away from them, believed in the power of their mystic magic and ancient customs. They reached out to them to obtain powerful talismans that served as a protection against evil spirits and negative demonic beings such as *prētham*, *rakshassu*, *bhūtham* and *yakshi*. They also helped break spells cast by other occult sorcerers or *manthravādhis*."

Maria listened to him intently. I was glad to see a bond beginning to form between them.

"The cult of devil's worship or *chathan seva* is in vogue even today. Some of the tribal witch doctors called *odiyans* are famous for *odi* black magic. Even educated professionals approach them for conducting rituals to fulfil their wishes or simply cast a spell on rivals. The ability to unleash evil forces on one's enemies is a lovely fantasy. Isn't it?"

I asked Nambiar, "Have you or anyone in your family ever encountered a *mantravādi*?"

Nambiar looked at me intently. He looked irritated as he shook his head. He said nothing more. His body language made it abundantly clear that I had touched a raw nerve.

Nambiar broke his silence. "Let's go to the temple. Please go have a bath and come quickly." As we went up the stairs, he called out to Maria, "Thanks for the whisky."

Nambiar was waiting for us, swinging a long torch impatiently. We got into the SUV. Barely 15 minutes later, the driver dropped us of at a small crossing. "It's nearby," he said.

We walked through small, elevated mud pathways between dry fields to reach the temple. It was a small structure located in the middle of a *kaavu*. I was expecting a big temple since important religious functions were held there. The decorations were simple with very light green tender coconut leaves.

I told Nambiar, "I was expecting a bigger structure."

"This is our family temple. Our maternal *tharawad* is just a few yards from here. As you notice, this is in the midst of a sacred grove. Unlike the *sarpa-kaavu*, this is relatively sparsely vegetated. Long ago, this was a wooded area."

Nambiar stood at the entrance of the temple and continued, "Traditionally, Theyyam is held at the *kaavu*. Look around and you will see trees such as *pala*, *chempakam*, and banyan, which we believe are the earthly abode of the Gods and the spirits. Generally, *kaavus* were densely wooded areas and not generally frequented by people. In a way, the fear of the wrath of the spirits ensured their conservation." Nambiar didn't seem to believe in the existence of spirits or maybe he was agnostic.

There were many oil lamps ready to be lit. A temporary shed was erected where the Theyyam entourage was camping. We peered into the temple to look at the idol.

I asked, "Uncle, are we allowed take a picture of the idol?" "Idol?" he said, laughing. "There is no idol in a Theyyam temple."

"Idolatry is primary in Hinduism. Isn't it?"

Nambiar looked at me with a professorial look. "Yes, but Theyyam is peculiar in that aspect. It is the ceremonial weapons of the deity that are worshipped. Look inside, the room is empty."

He was right.

"The sword, the shield, and the other items you see placed outside temporarily are the items that are worshipped."

The sword was long with a curved scythe at the end. It had small metallic balls attached to them. The colourful round shields seem to be made of wood.

"Let me introduce you to Manikandan, the veteran Theyyam artist. I have already informed him about your arrival. He will spend some time with you to explain the socio-cultural background of the Theyyam, and its stories." He called out loudly, "Manikandaa..."

An old man came running from the shed nearby. He stood slightly bent, with both hands folded. He avoided looking at Nambiar's face.

"Manikanda, these are the people who want to learn about Theyyam from you. Spend a couple of hours with them and tell them all that you know." It sounded more like an order than a request.

He said with extreme humility, nodding his head vigorously, "Oh!"

"You can address him as Mani," Nambiar suggested to us

Mani was a lean, tall man who must have been in his seventies. His skin was the colour of ebony and his hair was white with no black strands among them. He had a gold bangle on his hand and was clad in a dirty white *mundu*. His upper body was bare.

Nambiar turned to us and introduced him, "Mani is a veteran of Theyyam and is one of the people who has performed for the longest time in our temple. If he doesn't know something, then nobody knows it." The words hit the right chord and Mani seemed to grow in stature and confidence.

Nambiar came close to me and whispered, "He will take you to the riverside away from the din. I will also send across some toddy to keep his excitement levels high."

"Toddy? Aren't they supposed to be fasting?"

"Mani is too old to perform. He is considered the guru. If he spends a day without drinking toddy, that day you will see the crows fly upside down." He smiled and said, "Don't forget to taste it yourself and give some to Maria as well. Meet me here around 9 p.m."

Maria looked at both of us. As we followed Mani, she asked, "What was going on? You men seemed to be conspiring."

"Nambiar was suggesting that we get you married to Mani's son," I said and broke out laughing, leaving Maria red-faced.

Mani led both of us towards a small old temple located

on the banks of the river. He sat outside on a boulder and we on the steps of the temple. The priest was getting ready for the final puja of the day. A few people were standing outside, waiting for the puja to begin.

Mani said, "Let's do this quickly?" His humility seemed to have vaporised. "I have to go back to the *kaavu* to supervise the performers. I am their guru and they need constant supervision. They are such amateurs."

I guessed that he actually wanted to go to the nearby toddy shack. I told him calmly, "Don't worry, Mani. Nambiar will send somebody here with your *kallu*." Mani put up a fake protest, "No, no, that is not what I meant." He gave me a gummy smile.

We were all sweating. However, the unrelenting wind provided some relief from the heat and humidity. The river was meandering lazily. The undercurrents weaved patterns on the calm façade, betraying concealed turbulence. There was a patch of reeds around the river banks. We heard small splashes as fishes jumped to catch flies resting on the plants. A few green frogs sat like statues with the bags under their mouths constantly moving as if they were blowing silent bagpipes. The toads croaked periodically like they were exchanging long-distance gossip.

The birds were chirping. The dominant ones seemed to be bullying the weaker ones for a more comfortable perch. A lone heron stood immobile on one foot trying to dupe the fish below. They were all predators in one way or the other. Behind the semblance of calm, hidden death awaited the prey.

I could see small *vanchi*s crisscrossing; people in them were throwing their nets repeatedly to catch small fish. The fish would most probably be sold to the toddy shack in exchange for liquor. The people in the shop's kitchen would turn the fish into spicy curry that the drunken men would relish.

The tributary of the Kannur river was the lifeblood of the village. People bathed in it, and washed their linen, cattle and taxis. Basically, it bore the dirty brunt of the populace.

Mani sat down and gazed at the water, possibly pondering where to begin. He ran his hands across his legs as if imaginary ants were running up and down. He slapped his legs occasionally to kill a mosquito. The sky was beginning to darken but the transition was painfully slow.

"We humans can infer complex meanings from almost anything," I said, looking at Maria. She replied with a heavy sigh as if my comment didn't have a purpose or motivation.

The tyranny of silence overcame Mani. He smoothed the wrinkles on of his *mundu* with a few gentle passes of his hands. This seemed like an unconscious effort to dust layers of accumulated memories. He was wondering where to start. It was not easy to have two adults sitting around him, desperately seeking information.

A young man came running towards us with a large cloth bag. The sight kick-started Mani. The man greeted Mani but handed the bag over to me and said, "Nambiar sir sent this for you." Saying so, he left abruptly.

The bag contained four bottles of *kallu* and two large packets. As we opened the packets, the aroma of strong spicy crab curry and mussels spread. Maria looked at the bottles filled with florescent white liquid and asked, "What's that?"

"It's *kallu,* or toddy, the local alcoholic brew extracted from the inflorescence of the coconut tree. It goes well with spicy curry. Traditionally, this task is executed by the people from the low-caste *Ezhava* community." Once again, I played the role of the expert.

Mani couldn't hold his excitement at the thought that not only did he save money but could also have good quality toddy. He pulled two bottles towards him, impatiently opened one, and took a gulp. The expression on his face seemed as though he had attained nirvana.

Maria had a sip of the brew and remarked, "This tastes real good. It has got light froth."

"Don't go by the taste. It can give you a real kick," I told her.

The spicy mussels brought tears to Maria's eyes. She smacked her lips together, which by now had turned red.

Mani literally ate through all the crabs and finished the first bottle. He coolly walked to the river and washed his hands. Maria wondered aloud, "What is his digestive system made of?"

He asked, "Shall we start?"

"Please do, but I will need periodic short breaks to translate for Maria."

He nodded.

"So, sip your brew when I am translating and don't get drunk too soon." Despite looking mildly offended, he cradled the bottle.

Mani's face was devoid of any emotions as he seemed to go through his mental files. Maria looked at him, trying to decipher his thought processes. Mani looked at us with his drowsy drunken eyes.

He began, "People today know Kerala as one of the most beautiful places in the country. Tourists come from all over the world to experience the greenery, beaches, food, or simply drench themselves in the monsoon. Little do they realise that Kerala has had a very difficult and complex past. It was one of the most asymmetrical societies, I would say."

He paused for a second and then spoke like a militant, "The deplorable caste system was the bane of Kerala. Though it was prevalent all over India, it appears to have been enforced with particular harshness here. The Aryans dominated and disrupted a predominantly self-contained, well developed society. The Dravidians, tribals and the hill people were living harmoniously before their arrival. The caste system was partly responsible for negating the profits and economics of spice trade. It never let Kerala prosper as much as it should have."

There was anger and bitterness in his voice. He looked exhausted from the tirade. He picked up a few blades of grass absentmindedly and chewed them as I translated his words for Maria.

She nodded and said, "Traders and colonialists crossed choppy seas to undertake the long and risky journey to Kerala. She must have been quite a seductress." Maria winked. She asked, "Billions of dollars' worth of spices would have been traded. Where did all that money go? I don't see the effect of so much money having come in."

Mani was popping left-over mussels into his mouth like peanuts. "Keralites love gold. So most of the traders came laden with gold to buy spices. Surprisingly, the demand for pepper was so high among Romans that Pliny, the Elder, complained that trade with Kerala was draining the Roman treasury."

"Most of that gold went into making ornaments for the Malayali woman. That obsession continues," I said.

"Krish, I love gold too," Maria said. "Can you get me a chain?"

I retorted. "And what? Tie it around your neck as a symbol of marriage?"

"Please do." She was being mushy.

"A white bride? Not a bad idea." I smiled. "Just that Lakshmi may not agree to it."

"We will negotiate with her."

"Bigamy is not legal in India, Maria." We laughed together.

"Getting back to the subject, ancient Egyptians used spices from Kerala to make perfumes and oils for mummification," said Maria.

"That means, we Malayalis had a role in helping them become famous," I said.

"Who?" she queried.

"The Egyptians."

She smiled.

Mani was feeling left out and desperately wanted to intervene. He coughed loudly and cleared his throat. Once he got our attention, he began again, "By the end of the eighth century, people from the other parts of

India, who called themselves the *Nambuthiris*, started settling down in and around Kerala. Over a period of time, around 32 settlements came up. It was a slow but steady incursion of the Aryan population. All they brought with them were strong religious and socio-cultural beliefs."

The old man nodded sadly. He spat hard on the ground and continued, "These so-called Aryans despised the inhabitants and treated them like savages. They treated our Gods with disdain."

His face twisted as he uttered, "Their hold strangulated the society." He took a long sip from the bottle. "The caste system and the accompanying concept of pollution was implemented to humiliate my people. The touch or even the shadow of the untouchables or members of the lowest caste was considered so polluting that it needed purification rituals. Thoo!" He spat again and used profanity to express his disgust.

"*Mairu*! These people called us despicable!" His voice was becoming louder and his discourse was getting aggressive.

"In the caste hierarchy, Brahmans were at the top. Members of the Kshatriya or warrior caste had to maintain 12 feet distance from the Brahmans, the Kammala 36 feet, and the untouchables, such as the Paraya, had to maintain 60 feet distance from the Brahmans."

Just like his mood, darkness set in. Mani switched on the light fixed on the temple wall. It was suddenly bright.

Maria was surprised and asked, "Was there no justice?"

I couldn't help but laugh. "They all colluded. A case of the fence eating the crop for its own nourishment." She said, "The society suffered sadistic tendencies, eh? Suffering in silence without the ability to react must have been difficult." There was genuine sadness in her eyes.

"Haven't things improved substantially, Mani?" I asked. I didn't want Maria to think that we still lived in a caste-ridden society.

"Of course, things have changed quite a bit. One of my nephews got married to a Nair girl. He is a software engineer, settled in the US. They worked together. Despite the family's reservations about his caste, the girl's insistence ensured that the marriage took place smoothly," said Mani.

"Caste tension has eased but not gone away completely. It will take time. What hardened over centuries will take at least decades to soften," he said in a low voice, as though somebody was eavesdropping.

I told Maria, "When I wanted to marry Lakshmi, the caste issue did crop up. Her family did harbour apprehensions. But social status and potential economic prospects reduced that friction. Societal inequalities lose their power when the context erases itself. There is a new caste system in place now – it is based on financial capacities rather than caste positions." I continued, "So Mani, how did your forefathers cope with that kind of life?"

Mani was drinking the toddy as though it was an electrolyte and he had just finished a five-mile run. He looked up and said, "What could they do? They suffered."

"This was one of the reasons why Naxalism and militant communism took roots in modern Kerala. Till then, Theyyam helped a lot. Just like we believed in the power of the spirits, the upper caste members feared their wrath," Mani guffawed.

"Theyyam partly served as a frontline defence mechanism against the tyranny of the caste system. In simple terms, the upper castes, despite trashing our Gods as demons and unclean spirits, were terrified of their wrath. Albeit temporarily, during the Theyyam season, we got relief from the reign of casteist terror." Mani reached out to his toddy to rehydrate himself. He finished his bottle and looked at mine longingly.

Maria listened to the translation and said, "Wow! That's interesting. Indeed, a clever move. But how did it all originate?"

I pushed my bottle towards him and said, "Mani,

Maria wants to know how Theyyam originated." I didn't let him take the bottle. Not yet!

"Honestly, nobody really knows. And that includes me. Like all folk performances, Theyyam also went through many social mutations and adaptations. However, the performers revere our guru Manakkadan Gurukkal as the father of Theyyam." Mani reached for my bottle.

"Wait, Mani. This is for you. But don't finish this." I gave him the bottle but forbade him from drinking.

As a surety, the upset Mani took the bottle from me and cradled it in his lap. "Oral history assigns a 1000 vintage years to Theyyam," he said.

Mani took out a packet of *beedi*, a thin cigarette filled with tobacco and rolled in a *tendu* leaf, and lit one. Momentarily, his face vanished in the mist of thick tobacco smoke and reappeared like a spirit.

He continued with renewed energy, "Manakkadan Gurukkal was our teacher and belonged to the lower castes. He was also a poet, medicine man, and, most importantly, the guru of Theyyam. People venerated him for his magical powers. His fame reached the king, who was astonished that people from lower castes could have intellectual abilities."

Mani pulled hard at his *beedi* and said, "In order to unravel the mystery of high cognitive abilities in a low caste person, the king summoned Gurukkal to his palace. He challenged him to create and perform 39 Theyyams. Gurukkal undertook the formidable task, as the king had challenged the pride of the lower castes. That night, the palace grounds reverberated with the sounds of the drums and, in the light of the torches, fiery Theyyams were performed to the astonishment of the onlookers. By morning, the king was satiated. It was a victory for the low caste masses."

Maria asked me, "So, what is the big deal?"

I translated her query to Mani.

Mani looked at her as though she was a little child. He said, "Theyyam is a ritual art form. All deities have their own legends and songs that are recited to propitiate them. Each of them has distinct costumes and props. How can somebody suddenly create 39 unique Theyyams and perform them? That is an impossible task unless the person was an extraordinary genius."

Maria shook her head to indicate that she refused to believe this exaggerated version. I reminded her, "Remember, the guru also had magical powers."

Maria said, "Are you suggesting that he must have used magic? You don't believe in magic, do you?" I didn't answer her query. Maria continued, "Maybe he hypnotised the king? But how did he hypnotise the whole crowd?" Her attempt to answer ended up with more questions.

Mani didn't drink. He was observing our body language carefully. He knew that Maria wasn't convinced with his story. In an effort to dispel her doubts he said, "The legend also says that to further test his capabilities, the king asked Gurukkal if he could raise him to heaven. After tying the king with a rope, Gurukkal raised him to heaven for him to have a glimpse."

This explanation made the story more unbelievable. I defended Mani. "Antiquity of stories adds to its believability. These stories may have been crafted and extrapolated into the life of a revered local guru. Mani seems convinced about their veracity."

Maria smiled and said, "Hold on. Let me read you something." She swiped through her tablet and read out, "This is from Thomas Carlyle's book 'On Heroes, Hero-worship, and the Heroic in History'. He writes, 'And then consider what mere time would do in such cases; how if a man was great while living, he becomes tenfold greater when dead. What an enormous camera-obscura magnifier is tradition! How a thing grows in the human memory, in the human imagination, when love, worship and all that lies in the human heart, is there to encourage it.' That explains the phenomenon. Doesn't it?"

"Don't forget about the element of hero-worship here," I said.

"Talking about hero-worship, Carlyle writes, 'I consider hero-worship to be the grand modifying element in that ancient system of thought. What I called the perplexed jungle of paganism sprang, we may say, out of many roots: every admiration, adoration of a star or natural object, was a root or fibre of a root; but hero-worship is the deepest root of all; the tap-root from which in a great degree all the rest were nourished and grown'."

"Theyyam itself has strong roots in hero-worship, Maria. Let's hear what Mani has to say."

Mani didn't drink. Maria had hurt his caste pride and doubted his guru. "Gurukkal is supposed to have passed away in Manakkadu region at the age of 32. His tomb is located between Adi Muchilottu *kaavu* and a Shiva temple and even today lamps are lit to respect the great legend." He wanted to convert Maria from a sceptic to a believer.

Maria said, "Wow! Like the rock stars who passed away young, eh? He must have been quite a rock star of his age? See, here we are, after many centuries, still talking about his alleged exploits."

Mani shook his head as if he understood and said, "The right to perform one of the most important Theyyams, namely the Muchilottu *Bhaghawathi* Theyyam, is restricted to a performer from the guru's family."

Mani was visibly getting tired, yet we couldn't let him go. Once the Theyyam performances started, it would be difficult to get hold of him. Maria helped. She said, "Mani, I love your stories. Tell me more."

I tried to translate but Mani raised his hands to indicate that he had understood. Maria took her bottle and clanked it with Mani's bottle and said, "Cheers!" They took long sips, as though they were long-lost companions.

Mani said, "Most of the prominent deities in the Theyyam pantheon are women and worshipped as Mother Goddesses."

Maria used her tablet to film Mani so that she would

not miss the minutest details he was providing. Mani felt like a movie star. He tried to look his best. He said, "*Bhadhrakali* is the most prominent among all Mother Goddesses in Kerala. She is worshipped in various forms. She is so popular that she has been adapted as the guardian Goddess of small villages and towns. Just add an *amma* suffix to the village's name and she becomes the guardian Goddess of that village. This adaptability is also one of the reasons for her prominence in Kerala."

He paused and pointed with his slender hands towards the sky. He then said, "She watches over us constantly from there. Though she is a Mother Goddess, she is indeed a fierce deity and famous for slaying the demon *Dharika*. She is very affectionate but is equally feared for her wrath. Like all Gods, she loves to be flattered."

Mani then told me, "Might as well finish the toddy as it will turn sour due to fermentation." He took a large gulp and continued, "She has a dual personality and uses her abilities to vanquish evil and bestow blessings. She is the Goddess who can cure diseases such as smallpox, help in having children, and be their saviour. Demons fear her so her support is invoked during exorcisms."

"*Bhadhrakali* appears in various manifestations of Theyyam. Some of them are patron goddesses of various communities. For example, *Muchilottu Bhaghawathi* is the Goddess of members of the Vaniya community, *Veeranchira Bhaghawathi* of the Nairs, *Pullooru Kali* of the Thiyyas, *Karinchamundi* of the Yadavas, and *Udira Kali* of the Pulayas." He rolled out information as though he was reading from written notes.

Maria looked at Mani with admiration. She said, "What makes his description and analysis important is that he didn't learn these from a book. It is all coming out of his experience. Impressive."

Mani said, "Now, let me tell you the story of *Muchilottu Bhaghawathi*, one of the most important Theyyam deities. Her parents were orthodox Brahmans. They had difficulties in conceiving a child and prayed to the Goddess. When she was born, they attributed it to divine help. She was an extremely intelligent child who easily defeated some of the best of Brahman scholars in debate.

"As she grew up, the parents of the 'virgin' girl started seeking suitable alliances. She insisted that she would only marry a man who defeated her in a debate. As word of her beauty and intelligence spread, many Brahmans came from afar to win her hand. They all participated in the debate. She defeated them one by one.

"As expected," Mani said, "to be defeated by a woman was difficult to reconcile with. The men hatched a plan. They dared her to answer their questions. As she cruised, along came the two trap questions. They asked her, 'What causes the greatest pain?'

She answered, 'Giving birth.'

Pat came the next one, 'Tell us, the greatest pleasure on earth is?'

She replied, 'Sex.'

This was the answer the men were waiting for. They ostracised her saying that unless she had experienced both, she would not have been able to answer the questions convincingly. 'She is not a virgin but an immoral woman,' they said.

"Despite trying her best, the members of the audience refused to be convinced. This was public humiliation. She was not only thrown out of her house but also the community. She cried and wandered eventually and reached the Echikulangara temple. She prayed to God Narayana and contemplated her future. The story is long, but, in short, she was left with no choice but commit suicide through self-immolation. She procured oil for setting herself afire from a prominent member of the Muchilottu Nair community. Eventually she became a Goddess and was venerated as the patron of the community. She was thence known as the *Muchilottu Bhaghawathi*. She was included in the pantheon and is celebrated in the *Muchilottu Bhaghawathi* Theyyam."

The translation made Maria react harshly. "The rascals… they cheated her! This was clearly a case of entrapment."

I said, "But then they eliminated a powerful female rival. Such tricks have always been used to deal with strong-willed and intelligent women."

She snapped back, "What a sham!" She was very angry and asked, "And what happened to her tormentors? Did they live happily ever after?"

Mani shared her anger. He said, "After she became a Goddess, her tormentors died a slow, painful and humiliating death due to small pox, leprosy or lunacy."

That made Maria happy. She said, "Good for them. Revenge is a dish best served cold. So this Goddess also has two sides, that of a protector and an annihilator."

"Let me also tell you the tragic story of Kadankottu Makkam. She was the only sister to 12 brothers who loved her dearly. They pampered and fulfilled all her wishes. The wives of these brothers resented this. When she got married and went to live with her husband, they were happy to get rid of her. Makkam got pregnant and, as per custom, she returned to her maternal home for delivery. She gave birth to two beautiful children. This triggered jealousy among the childless sisters-in-law. They plotted her murder."

Mani continued. "Makkam's brothers had gone for war and when they returned from the battle field, their wives accused her of having an illicit relationship with a lower caste oil merchant. Outraged at her for having dishonoured the family, they brutally slayed Makkam and her children and threw their bodies in the well. According to local legend, they were reborn as divinities. The brothers and their wives realised their mistake. In fear of her wrath and in search of redemption, they created Theyyam forms for them."

Maria was upset. "Sometimes women can be their own arch enemies. But why the children?"

Mani sensed her anger and said in a more reconciliatory manner, "Not all Theyyams are the idolisation of women who died violent unnatural deaths. *Padakkethy Bhaghawathi* is an example. She is supposed to have come to Malabar on a boat. She had six brothers whom she loved very much. She grew into a beautiful woman and her brothers arranged for her marriage. To prepare for the feast, the brothers went to the forest to hunt for deer. However, their rivals demanded that the limbs and the heads of the deer be given to them. When the brothers refused, they were killed brutally. When she heard about the murders, she discarded her ornaments, dressed as a hermit, and killed all the murderers. She thus transformed into a war Goddess. There are many war Goddesses in the Theyyam pantheon."

It was getting late and Mani seemed keen on returning to the temple. He said, "Let's go. It is getting late." Although he had consumed three bottles of toddy, Mani walked steadily across the narrow path between the fields.

As we walked back, Maria asked, "Aren't there other types of Theyyam?" She was a little tipsy.

"Yes, there are but the most important ones are the female deities." Mani swung small arcs across the path with his torch. He told Maria, "There are only two things that I am mortally afraid of. Snakes and the *yakshi*." Mani walked briskly, leaving us behind.

I held Maria's hand and we walked slowly towards the temple. As we approached the temple, we saw Nambiar waiting for us. Mani informed him, "I have told them all that I know."

Nambiar nodded in acknowledgement. We walked together towards the car. "So, how was the session with Mani? I am sure Mani regaled you with all his stories?" Nambiar enquired.

"It was worth the time. The toddy helped," I said. Nambiar laughed and said, "I know." As we sat in the car, Nambiar asked Maria, "Hope you are getting quality content for your thesis."

She replied, "Thank you, sir. All we need is an expert who can now interpret the performance for us." Nambiar thought for a second and said, "Professor Nambhuthiri will be joining us tomorrow for the performance. He is my old classmate and an expert. He travels the globe lecturing on Theyyam and folklore. I will introduce you to him."

"Thank you, sir." Maria sounded genuinely grateful.

Nambiar said, "Rural geographies are smaller than urban ones. Everyone here knows everyone."

Maria then asked, "Sir, who is a *yakshi* and what does she look like?"

Nambiar was taken aback by her question. He laughed and asked, "Where did you hear about *yakshi*? Did Mani introduce you to one?"

She said, "Mani is mortally afraid of it."

"Ha! Ha! Ha!" Nambiar couldn't help laughing. He said, "*Yakshi* is a mythical, malevolent being who is supposed to feed only on human blood. It prefers the blood of younger males and is described as a very beautiful being. Attired in a white sari, the *yakshi* leaves her hair open, she wears strands of jasmine or *pala* flowers, and chews betel leaves. The *yakshi* is supposed to be so seductive that any man who sets his eyes upon her wouldn't be able to resist. After mating, she drinks the blood of her victim and pushes him down the palm tree where her abode is. She targets the lone traveller, especially in the night. She calls out to her victim from behind. The only way to survive is to run without looking back. Many years ago, the fear of the *yakshi*s was so strong; many young men were found dead under palm trees. Most would have died of sheer fright just by believing that they were being followed by the *yakshi*. But those deaths added to her legend."

The car entered the gates of the house. Nambiar said, "Let's have dinner. I am famished." We had a simple dinner with the elderly couple. Maria asked Nambiar, "Why is it that young women don't stay here in this *tharawad*? Is it because this is an old house?"

He avoided looking at her and said, "Yes and no. Let's talk about it later?" He was obviously stalling. Maria took the cue and refrained from pursuing the matter further.

Nambiar was tired and he wanted to go to bed early. We went back to our rooms. Maria said, "Let me change into something more comfortable."

I stood by the window looking outside. The inky

black sky was full of stars that twinkled like diamonds. There was this lone star that looked like an oversized solitaire.

The wind ruffled the leaves and swayed the trees gently. During my teenage years, I believed that hideous beings lurked stealthily in the dark. I may have overcome the fear but it still coiled in a dark corner of my mind. I remembered Nambiar's description about the *yakshi*.

The sticky intoxicating smell of the *pala* flowers wafted through the windows. The scene outside was kind of eerie, like the setting of old Malayalam horror movies. I was engrossed in my imaginative thoughts. Suddenly, I felt the overpowering fragrance of jasmine and the sound of soft footsteps from behind. It added to the fear and sent my heart racing. This was a bizarre night!

I was afraid to look back. A gentle touch on my shoulder sent shivers down my spine. For a moment, I believed it was a *yakshi* that had come to kill me. I screamed.

Maria cupped my mouth quickly and said, "So you thought it was the *yakshi*?" I turned back and said angrily, "Maria, you scared the hell out of me."

"Seriously? With you around, it is the *yakshi* who should be scared!" Maria said and laughed.

"Where did you get the jasmine strands? They don't go well with your gown."

"Courtesy Mrs Nambiar."

"You now look like a…" I didn't complete the sentence.

"Whore?"

"No. You actually look like a *yakshi*." I would never address Maria as a whore.

"*Yakshi*? Aren't they supposed to be sensual beings?" The smell of jasmine was strong.

Something stirred inside me strongly. "You are possibly sexier than the original." I gathered my courage.

"I am thirsty and in desperate need to suck blood," said Maria and ran her fingers across my neck. She stood on her heels and pressed her teeth. With the other hand she caressed my cheek.

"She drinks blood after mating," I said.

"Got the sequence wrong," she said and smiled wickedly looking into my eyes. I felt her warm breath on my face. She came closer and her lips touched mine, sending waves of excitement through my body. We kissed gently at first and then the tongues, like slimy snakes, desperately reached out to each other. She arched her hips and her bosom pressed hard against my chest. She knew how to start a fire.

I ran a finger across the contours of her breast making her nipples pucker up hard, like raspberries. She opened the top of her gown and let me gaze at her breasts. I lifted and tossed her on the bed. Not that I could turn back but I managed to mumble, "I am not carrying any condoms, Maria." She was too aroused to answer.

Like a good girl who wanted to be violated, she held me tight. Her movements gathered speed and her moaning grew louder. Shocking pleasure rocked my body.

Both of us were drenched in sweat. Maria kept her face on my chest. She asked me, "Are you feeling guilty?"

"No."

"You just committed adultery."

"Hmm... now that I have sinned...?" I gently held her face and kissed her again triggering another round of ecstatic love-making.

We slept in an embrace. Neither of us wanted to let go of the other.

day of the theyyam

I t was a busy day at the Nambiar household. After a hurried breakfast, we all went to the maternal *tharawad*. Maria and I had carefully packed our bags with all that we needed for the photo-documentation of the Theyyam. This was a one-time opportunity for both of us. The old building was packed with people. Almost all the relatives of the Nambiar family seemed to have arrived from all over India and abroad.

We were treated like special guests. Around noon, Ajay called. He was at the Kannur railway station and was very upset that I hadn't gone to pick him up. I had actually forgotten that he was arriving that day. When he had called yesterday, I was not very keen to have him here. Despite his professed lack of interest in Maria, he would be an unwelcome person intruding my relationship with Maria. She had become an indispensable part of my life. I told him to take an auto rickshaw and reach the place. In all sincerity, I wished that he would lose his way and return to Kochi in anger. But then, that was not to be. I saw him trundle through the crowds carrying his overnighter.

Maria was very upset when she heard that Ajay was coming. I requested her not to create a scene in the house as all eyes were on us. She was very reluctant when I requested her to show him the library where we were to stay. However, she played the role of a hostess very well.

Dr Nambhuthiri was with us throughout the day. He was very excited at the prospect of being our guide. He seemed to be taken in by Maria's childlike curiosity.

Considering the crowd and the resultant business prospects, many small vendors had set up shop outside the house. The balloon vendor was the busiest, driving the children into a frenzy.

The pre-Theyyam ceremonies had begun. Both of us got to work, determined not to miss any of the rituals. Maria used the handy-cam and I wielded the still camera. Between the two of us, we would be able to build a large inventory of content. That was the plan.

After the ceremonial lamp was lit and the process was initiated, we walked towards the temporary shed which the Theyyam artists where using as their green room. A dark, rugged old lady in wrinkled and soiled clothes came towards us. I had already noticed her 'reading' the palm of a few people using a large magnifying glass. It was obvious that she was a soothsayer and was looking forward to earning a decent sum of money from the already charged crowd. Just before she came to us, she stopped, adjusted her spectacles, and stared at both of us.

She trooped towards us and said with a gummy smile, "So you both came back?"

I asked her, "Do you know us?"

"You have been here before." She spoke reasonably good English. I was surprised at her flair but Maria's face became taut.

"No, we have never been in Kannur before," I told her rudely.

This was perhaps her time-tested trick of gathering attention and earning some money.

"That was a long, long time ago, children," She insisted confidently, as if she had met us personally.

"Gosh! C'mon, don't say such fantastic things. You

are scaring the lady," I told the old woman in Malayalam.

She looked hurt. "You have a history here. Your lives seem to be somehow intermingled with Malabar's history."

The old woman paused and looked at Maria for her reaction. Maria had a very serious look on her face. I think it was a deja vu moment for her. I remember her telling me about the Romanian gypsy's comment about her having been a princess in Kerala. Her face seemed to freeze slowly.

"I know you wouldn't believe me. Show me your palms."

I wanted to walk away but Maria held my hands, signalling me to stay with her. She extended her right palm and indicated to me with her eyes that I should hear what the old woman had to say. Albeit reluctant, I complied with her request.

The old woman looked at the palms with her magnifying glass and ran her fingers through Maria's lifeline. She gently shook her head. She seemed bewildered at what she saw. For me, she was just another charlatan trying to make a few rupees by playing with people's minds.

She looked as if she had seen something disastrous. Then she asked me to show her my palms. I reluctantly extended my right palm. She looked at them and then placed both our palms together. The smile on her face vanished. The look on her face wasn't positive.

"What happened, grandma?" I asked her impatiently.

She looked up and suddenly there was apprehension on her face. It had turned white with fear. She seemed to look at somebody. It was Ajay who was standing behind us. The old woman abruptly got up and walked away. She refused to take any money from me. None of us could understand what made her act in such a manner.

I definitely didn't appreciate Ajay following us everywhere. Somehow, he didn't quite fit in the environment. He was not only an outsider but an intruder.

That brief encounter seemed to have left Maria a little bewildered. "She spoke reasonably good English, didn't she? Who would have known that somebody in shabby clothes could speak the language so well?"

"She must have had some education or actually must have picked up the language from the English speaking tourists. Who knows?"

"She seemed to know something. I felt as if she could see the past and the future." Maria seemed fascinated with the old woman.

"Forget about this. You will always find people like this with fantastic stories. They just dispense hope and false expectations in return for a few currency notes. They can create powerful notions of a fool's paradise and make them seem real and tangible. Some of these guys have a better perception of human psychology than even trained professionals. Their beliefs have a placebo effect. Please don't take her too seriously," I gently admonished her.

Though I tried to calm her, fear played in my mind too.

"But why did she go away abruptly? Did she see something that she couldn't speak about?" Maria seemed to be getting a little worried.

"Let's catch-up with the Theyyam artists in their green room before they start their performances," I shrugged my shoulders, caught her hand, and playfully pulled her towards the shed.

Dr Nambhuthiri was standing outside the shed talking to people from the Theyyam entourage. "What was the old lady telling you?" He seemed to have been watching us. I told him the gist and he said, "Hmm… One of the oldest residents of this area, she knows almost everything about here. Despite her age, she retains a strong memory. She can tell you stories about anything and everything here."

"Maria here believes that she can see into the past and the future."

"Well, she is respected and equally feared. Some people believe that she practices black-magic. She is also famous for her accurate predictions."

"Didn't I tell you?" Maria looked at me accusingly.

"You have seen the world. Tell me honestly, do you believe in all this mumbo-jumbo?" I asked Nambhuthiri.

"Sometimes, it is difficult to dismiss certain phenomena. I try my best to remain an agnostic but it is not always possible to ignore what appears to be paranormal. Let's talk about this later. Don't you want to see the Theyyam make-up?"

The shed was a hub of activity. A few men were sitting on the mud floor and making the headgear for the Theyyam. They were fashioning it out of coconut leaves and cloth.

The person who was to perform first was lying on the ground with his head on the lap of the make-up artist. His face was painted orange and it stood out oddly against his ebony black body. The make-up artist had filled orange, red, yellow and black colours in coconut shells. He was using a short piece of stick to draw intricate designs and apply paint.

"What type of colours are you using?" I asked the make-up artist, in Malayalam.

"We make it ourselves using natural ingredients." He was concentrating on his masterpiece and didn't seem to be in a chatty mood. I turned to Nambhuthiri and asked, "Why these bright colours?"

"Of all the five senses, it is believed that vision is the most powerful and sensitive. The accessories that a Theyyam performer wears are also very bright and colourful. Imagery is the key factor here. Theyyam is a revolutionary, folk art. Its imagery conveys subtle rebellion. The performers represent the masses from the lower castes who are seeking release from psychological captivity. Predominant use of red and other bold, energetic colours are meant to excite and stimulate the crowd."

"The intricate designs drawn on the face of the Theyyam performer obliterates his original personality and helps the crowd believe that the performer transforms into God. The wearing of spectacular costumes enhances the illusion of being a divine being. Otherwise, these people are not allowed anywhere near the abode of higher caste members but during Theyyam they are allowed inside. Temporarily they are treated like Gods. The get-up, thus, is an important factor."

Soon, Nambhuthiri got busy helping Maria interact with the members of the Theyyam troupe, by being her translator. I sat nearby and watched the expertise with which the make-up was being applied.

Around 2 p.m., the Theyyam performances began. The actual performance was preceded by a few rituals. Certain deities were assigned the privilege of *thottam* songs that were sung aloud to propitiate the spirits.

Thottam songs fall under the genre of ballads and contain legends related to the deity. These songs were an invocation to God to descend and possess the body of the performer. The artists, while reciting the *thottam*, wore simple costumes and minimal make-up. After this was over, brightly dressed Theyyam performers danced at regular intervals. The performances were held alternatively at the *kaavu* and the *tharawad*.

The actual transition of the performer into God happens during a curious process called *mukha darshanam*, when the performer stares into a small handheld mirror. What he sees in the mirror is not himself but the reflection of the deity. This is when he tips over; he is possessed.

This transition appeared to be a metaphysical experience. Most of the deities carried weapons and looked like angry beings. Their facial make-up, ornate headdresses, and other accompaniments made them look fierce. The performance itself was not graceful but masculine and aggressive. The performer sometimes leapt in the air. Overall, it seemed to be physically challenging performance.

There was loud music and firecrackers were burst at regular intervals. I saw a temple employee holding large rockets in his hand. He lit them and sent them into the air. The overall atmosphere was indeed mesmerising.

Theyyam was a spectacular compound of rhythmic music, pounding acoustic instruments, aggressive dancing, tribal rites, rituals and customs. In its execution, it seemed to be highly exaggerated and dramatic.

After every performance, the devotees thronged the Theyyam performer and spoke to him about their expectations and anxieties. For them, the performer was a 'talking' God. He received offerings, including cash, and mumbled answers to them.

Maria was keen to consult the performer. Despite my reservations, she pulled me towards the 'God'. I requested Nambhuthiri to join us to translate the mumblings. When it was our turn, I gave a 100 rupee note to the Theyyam. He looked at us and seemed to tremble. He kept muttering excitedly and seemed to search the crowd. Nambhuthiri interpreted his muttering to us. "The Theyyam is saying that you have to be careful. You have to be careful."

Nambhuthiri asked the Theyyam, "Why? What will happen?" The Theyyam performer then saw Ajay looking at us from a close distance. He pointed his fingers towards Ajay and repeatedly said, "Let God help you, let God help you. Terrible, terrible." He gave us all a pinch of *kuri*, which is a mixture of rice powder and turmeric. His face twisted and gnarled. He then looked away as if he didn't want to interact with us anymore.

The first phase of the performances ended by 10 p.m., after which simple, vegetarian dinner was served at the community kitchen set-up at the corner of the property.

Everybody looked for a place to rest till 2 a.m., when the next round of performances were to commence.

Ajay was lurking behind us and Nambhuthiri asked me finally, "Who is this person following us? He looks like he is troubled."

"He is a friend who came to watch the Theyyam."

"He doesn't look like he is enjoying it. He is constantly staring at you and Maria."

"Mr Nambhuthiri, what made Theyyam survive after so many centuries?" I asked, bringing the topic to an end.

"See, Theyyam is radically distinct. Its deities are modelled on ancestors and people who lived here and were celebrated as heroes. Theyyam has social roots and it is a people's ritual or let me call it a social festival.

Normally, people worship their Gods in the shrines where idols and sacred items are kept. In Theyyam, you see, Gods are performing live in front of their devotees. Christian missionaries dismissed Theyyam as a devil dance. While some call Theyyam rustic theatre, I like to call it the 'theatre of the oppressed'."

Nambiar came looking for us. He suggested that we rest in the library and promised to wake us up at 2 a.m. to watch the final performances.

Ajay, Maria and I went to the dingy room. We had no choice but huddle together on the floor. Ajay chose his place in such a way that Maria ended up being sandwiched between us. I was too tired and slipped into sleep. As promised, Nambiar woke me up and I called out to Maria. We let Ajay sleep as he didn't seem too interested in the performances. The truth is that we didn't want him around us.

It was around 2.15 a.m. and the performances were more magnificent than before. They were held under the light of burning coconut leaves and earthen lamps. Some of the Theyyam artists jumped into the fire or walked through burning embers. We felt as though we were being transported to another world. We watched the performances transfixed. Like the king in Mani's story, we were satiated!

Around 9.30 a.m., all the performances and related rituals were over. People started dispersing. Nambiar insisted that we have breakfast. He handed us the keys to his house and said, "We as a family will have to be here for few more hours. Please go and rest in your rooms. The driver would drop you home."

I asked Maria if we should call Ajay. She angrily said, "Leave him here. He will find his way to back to us."

"But Maria, isn't he our guest? He will miss breakfast."

"He is no child, Krish. Let's go," she insisted. I secretly liked her hatred for Ajay.

We left him sleeping in the library and went to Nambiar's house for a well-deserved rest.

blood

Theyyam was over. Despite the challenges of organising, it had gone very well. The performers had packed up and the temple and its premises looked like an empty battlefield. The family members who had come from relatively nearby areas started returning home. Only the ones who had come from far were around. For the three old men, this was very satisfying. Maria and I were planning to return to Kochi.

This trip had given us more than we had bargained for. The inputs from Mani, Nambhuthiri, Nambiar, his spouse, and the Theyyam performers were key to this trip. We also had old documents, many hours of video footage, and hundreds of photographs. This was enough for Maria to write an easily defendable thesis and for me to publish a coffee table book.

This trip had also bought Maria and me emotionally closer and made us a close-knit team. The feeling that Maria loved me unconditionally became stronger. It would not be easy to live away from her and a long distance relationship was also not the best alternative. To be away from Maria was unthinkable. I did contemplate divorce but I wasn't ready to take a firm call. Lakshmi wasn't such a bad person that I should leave her. My mind was torn between the two women. Unable to arrive at a decision, my mind roamed like a vagabond.

Back at the Nambiar residence, we both crashed in our respective beds and slept like logs. It was the loud ringing of my mobile that woke me up. By the time I reached for my phone, the ringing stopped. I decided to return the call in a few minutes. I walked down the stairs to make black coffee for myself.

Ajay was sitting on Nambiar's recliner in the portico. He was fidgeting with his jack knife, opening and folding it absent-mindedly. Looking up he said, "So, you guys left me behind?" He was angry.

"After waking up, I searched for both of you. I wanted to be dropped back but the old man said that he needed the car. All he did was to give me directions to walk back here." Ajay was very upset and edgy. "And when I got here I see you both deep in slumber. Did you ever think of me?"

Thank god. If I had agreed to Maria's suggestion that we sleep together, all hell would have broken loose. Good sense had prevailed.

Ajay kept murmuring to himself. I think he was abusing Maria and me. "It is not too far," I defended but he didn't seem to listen. "You were sleeping soundly. That is why we didn't want to wake you up. You had come after a strenuous journey, after all. We didn't abandon you, Ajay." I tried to console him. "And, please put away that knife of yours." I was beginning to get irritated. He complied.

This jack knife was a gift from his father during one of his rare trips. Whenever Ajay was in rage, he would play with it or use it to scrape or stab something like a piece of wood. He had scraped some hate words under the desk in our school as well.

"Do you want some coffee?"

"No, what I need now is a drink!" He was being rude.

I rummaged through Mrs Nambiar's kitchen to search for a saucepan and coffee. Finally, I managed to make three mugs of hot steaming coffee. I handed a mug to Ajay and went up carrying the other two. "Hold on, I will just join you." I pre-empted Ajay before he followed me.

Maria was stretched out on the bed with the blanket pulled up to her nose. She didn't respond to my calls and I shook her hard.

Her eyes were red. She put her hands around my neck and said, "Sleep near me."

"Ajay is downstairs."

"Gosh, when did he return?" She abruptly got up from bed. I gave her the hot mug of coffee. "Thanks. What is he doing?"

"He's just sitting there. Nambiar had called. I guess it is to invite us for lunch at the *tharawad*."

"I don't want to go anywhere. Can we eat here?"

"You sure about that?

"100 per cent."

Nambiar's driver had come to pick us. That is when I remembered I had not informed Nambiar. I called him immediately.

"Uncle, we three are planning to have lunch at a local restaurant. Hope that is okay with you?"

"Sure, ask the driver to drop you at the restaurant near the temple. They serve good food, typical of Kannur."

Maria refused to come with us. "Get something packed for me."

As I went down, Ajay was waiting. He had a strange look on his face. The restaurant wasn't too far and we sent the driver back to Nambiar. We ordered food.

Ajay was unusually silent. He kept drinking water as if he was trying to quench a raging fire in his belly. We ate silently.

When I ordered food to be packed for Maria, he asked, "Why didn't the princess come with us? Why do you have to take food for her?" There was an unusual bitterness in his voice. This was not the Ajay I knew. We were walking back when I stopped at a small shop to buy a bottle of cola.

"When did you start drinking cola? Thought you never touched it?"

"This is for Maria."

I had actually planned to seek his advice on the relationship that had developed between Maria and me. But considering his behaviour, I dropped the idea.

The sun was trying hard to scorch the earth. The heat and humidity seemed to add to Ajay's agitation. As we walked back silently, he lit a cigarette and dragged it on feverishly.

Just as we opened the gates, Maria walked down the stairs. She said, "Did you best friends forget me? I am famished."

The sight of Maria changed Ajay completely. A charming smile spread over his lips. We walked to the dining room. She said, "Smells good. What did you buy?"

"*Porotta* and beef curry. Go get a plate and a glass from the kitchen."

"Why glass? Is there beer? I feel like a drink." She shouted from the kitchen.

We all sat around the dining table. I watched her eat and poured her a glass of cola.

"I am not used to being pampered," she said, smiling. "I would like to retain my independence. Don't spoil me."

Ajay was dying to make small talk but he struggled to find a point to begin with. It felt he was having a tussle to get Maria's attention.

He stepped out of the dining room only to return with a bottle of rum. When he asked Maria for a glass, she merely pointed towards the kitchen. He probably expected her to fetch one for him. Ajay got a glass for himself and mixed a large drink.

Since Ajay had heard Maria's desire for a drink, he took a long sip and asked, "Any one need a drink badly?" Maria and I looked at each other. Taking her glass, I poured a small drink, mixed cola with it and sipped. "It's been sometime... normally a whisky person. Desperation can make me drink anything." There was something sensual in drinking from her glass. I whispered to her, "Drinking from your glass makes the drink headier."

Maria fetched another glass for herself. Alcohol

lightened the mood. Somehow, I ended up drinking the most. Ajay was back at his witty best trying to make Maria laugh with his risqué jokes. There was much gaiety.

We finished the bottle in an hour or so. I felt very sleepy and yawned. We went to our rooms. Ajay curled around the corner of my bed. In deep sleep, I thought I heard a heated argument between Ajay and Maria, but concluded that it must be a dream.

I woke up to the calls of Nambiar. "Krish… Krish… Come down."

"Coming uncle. Give me a minute," I shouted back.

Ajay was lying beside me. He was wide awake. "Didn't you hear Nambiar?" He seemed agitated and dismissed my query with the flick of his fingers.

I walked to Maria's room. She was lying down on her belly. I called her, "Maria! Nambiar is back. He's calling for us." Her eyes were red as she looked towards me. "Were you crying?" I asked her, sitting at the corner of her bed.

"No…. me? Cry? It's just the lack of sleep." She was defensive. Though I wasn't convinced, I let it go.

"Do you know how to make tea?" I asked.

"Not the way you want. But I can make you great coffee," she said.

"Show Nambiar and his brothers the magic of your coffee."

She didn't move, so I gently pulled her from the bed.

"Lazy bum," I said playfully.

We walked down. The creak of the bed in my room suggested that Ajay was getting out of it to join us.

"He is always hovering around you. Why doesn't he give us some privacy?" Maria complained.

"We are splitting tomorrow and then he wouldn't be a bother. Let it go." I tried to soothe her.

"Don't tell him where we are staying in Kochi. I don't want him around anymore," she said.

"So much hatred? What did he do?"

"Honestly, I don't like him." She paused. "Not anymore. He is revolting."

Nambiar and his brothers were sitting at the portico. Nambiar looked at me. "Sorry uncle. We wanted to eat non-vegetarian food so we couldn't join you at the *tharawad*," I apologised. The three brothers broke out laughing. The eldest one said, "Sometimes you new generation guys can be foolish. Since Theyyam was over, the women had prepared non-vegetarian food and there was plenty of whisky." They laughed again. It seemed as though the men were high.

"It is rare that I am allowed to go a little overboard," said Nambiar.

Maria asked them, "Do you want to have some coffee?"

Nambiar said, "Sure. I guess it will be the first and last coffee from you since you guys are leaving tomorrow. Can you figure out where to find what you need in the kitchen? Every woman guards her kitchen as if it were her kingdom."

The three brothers broke out into laughter again. They were just looking for some reason to laugh. It was good to see Nambiar in a lighter mood.

Maria stood with her hands on her hip and told them with mock seriousness, "A woman knows her way in the kitchen. Even if it is not hers." Nambiar and Maria seemed to have started liking each other. I sat with the old men. Nambiar asked, "So, what time is your train tomorrow?"

"Maria and I are flying to Kochi tomorrow," I said.

Ajay looked at me. "Thought all three of us could go by train? Wasn't that what we discussed? I don't even have a reservation ticket." He paused for a couple seconds and asked me, "Why didn't you get me an air ticket too?"

"We had already booked the tickets before you planned to join us," I lied.

"And what about the plan for train travel? Didn't Maria mention last week that she would like to experience unreserved journey in the train?" He was upset that he was being cut off.

"Did we invite him? Let him travel in the unreserved compartment. I cannot spend a few hours confined with him," Maria had hissed when I broached the idea to her.

"Trains are a great way to travel in India. They are not only cheaper but bring you closer to the Indian way of life," Nambiar said and the old men nodded.

Ajay got up and walked into the kitchen. There was a shuffle inside the kitchen and Maria quickly walked out with a tray carrying four small cups of steaming coffee. Ajay followed her. She gave me an angry look.

Maria gave the coffee to the old men and as I reached out for a cup, she said, "This is for Ajay. Please get your cup from the kitchen."

"Here," she said smiling and offered the coffee to Ajay. He looked perplexed.

Maria followed me to the kitchen. "Why did you let him come into the kitchen alone?" She stared at me.

"Did he do anything?" Silence was her answer. "You do not seem to understand. Let's join them," she said and went to the portico. This was the first time I saw a woman hating Ajay so much. At least, as far as I knew. I liked that.

Nambiar looked at Maria and said, "Good coffee." She beamed as though she had received a gold medal.

"So, Krish. What do we do? This is the final night where we are all together. We have to celebrate tonight," Nambiar was unusually enthusiastic. He continued. "I have a plan. Let us take a bath in the river and go to the *tharawad* for some good non-vegetarian food. We will then return to savour your single malt. Narayanan here has some great cigars that his son presented to him. We will enjoy ourselves. What do you say?"

"Not a bad idea. We are game." I looked at Maria. Maria initially hesitated but when Ajay offered to give her company, she readily joined us. We all left for the river in the SUV. The old men played in the river like children. They cracked jokes and laughed among themselves. They were good swimmers and made fun of me as I sat on the banks with Maria. I took their jibes in my stride. Ajay swam across the banks like an Olympian. I realised that he was trying to impress Maria. The atmosphere was charged with happiness. I remembered *amma*'s words – "Too much happiness invites sadness."

It was already dark when we reached the maternal *tharawad*. Many of the relatives had gone back to their homes. We were just a handful of people left. Nambiar introduced a tall lean man as Malini's husband. He had the dignified look of a seasoned seaman. A fair man, he had a warm smile on his face. Malini was not to be seen anywhere.

I felt like a victor. I had the feeling that Ajay had described earlier. This poor man had no idea what his wife and I had been up to in the serpent grove.

We had a great feast of spicy chicken curry, mussels, fish, *chapattis* and rice. Mrs Nambiar and Maria hugged each other. Their eyes turned moist. Mrs Nambiar extended an invitation to Maria to visit their home again the next time she visited Kerala.

Malini too came and hugged Maria. She stood holding her husband's arm and gave me a farewell look as though we would or should never meet me again. Was I jealous? I could not deny that she had given me memories that would be difficult to forget. The smell of her sweat would linger in my mind for long.

To make conversation, I told her husband, "I saw you seeking the blessings of Theyyam. May your wishes be fulfilled." He smiled and thanked me as I stole a glance at Malini. If his wish was fulfilled, I would be the one who actually 'blessed' his spouse. She didn't react. There was no guilt or remorse on her face. Her expression was that of a confident woman who got what she wanted by hook or crook. Did she use me or was I the fool? I was not sure but she had given me an experience I would remember for a lifetime.

Nambiar said, "Let's go." He went to his brother and

whispered something in his ear. Narayanan shook his head and pointed to the small bag that he was carrying.

Once we returned to his house, Nambiar suggested that we sit under his favourite mangosteen tree. There was a gentle breeze. Ajay and I carried the chairs, including Nambiar's recliner. The seating area was 25-30 feet away from the house.

Maria refused to join us citing that she wanted to work on her thesis and told me, "I can use the solitude."

All of us gathered under the tree in a small circle. Ajay sat facing the house and I sat across him. Nambiar and Narayanan brought out the bottle of single malt, a case of whisky tumblers, an ice box, two bottles of mineral water, and a large plate of lightly fried cashew nuts. The other brother brought a rechargeable lamp with him and placed it in the middle of the table. The bright light illuminated the area where we were sitting.

Narayanan took out a travel humidor and a long match used to light cigars. He said, "My son gave it to me last month when he came from the United Kingdom on vacation. I was waiting for an occasion to smoke these."

Narayanan poured small portions of the golden liquid into each of our glasses. He said, "Add water or ice depending on your preference."

Nambiar asked, "Do you think your girlfriend would enjoy whisky?" I guess he was trying to catch me unawares to understand the true nature of our relationship. I lowered my voice and looked straight in his eyes. "She's more like my student, Mr Nambiar. She is not my girlfriend. She is a responsibility for me." I was on the guard as I knew that Maria's presence would be communicated to Lakshmi sooner than later.

Nambiar quickly went on a defensive, "I was just pulling your leg." Despite the sincerity in his voice, I was sure he wasn't.

"Bhaghyalakshmi does give me company once in a while. Go

ahead, give her a drink. We will wait for you here,"

he said. He poured a large drink, added a few cubes of ice, and handed me the tumbler.

Maria was pouring over the thesis that Malini had handed me. She had pulled the curtains across the windows. "I was dying to talk to you. This thesis contains detailed history of this *tharawad*. Pretty scary stuff. There are answers for some of our questions about the urn. I need to talk to you, Krish," said Maria.

"Of course. Once I come back." I didn't take her too seriously. "Nambiar sent this for you." I handed the tumbler to her.

"Your single malt? I don't want to get drunk while I read this," she protested.

"The best things are savoured slowly. Enjoy the drink."

She got up from her chair, took a gulp, and said, "Nice!" "Can we talk for a few minutes? Nambiar's daughter seems to have left behind a warning for us through the thesis." She pleaded.

"I will return as soon as possible. They will be waiting for me. If I spend more time with you, it will be misinterpreted." I told her about Nambiar's indication of her being my girlfriend.

"But, I am your girlfriend!" She said with her characteristic hands-on-hips stance.

"But he needn't know that."

She looked deep into my eyes. "Come back soon." She kissed me hard and said, "This is to remember me, always!"

"I will, I promise. The whisky is already doing its magic!"

I started towards the door and she hugged me from behind and said, "I love you, Krish!" This was the first time she had explicitly conveyed her feelings to me.

I looked at her and said, "I love you too, Maria. Always!"

She softly bit the back of my neck and said, "I am

your personal *yakshi*! If you ever stop loving me, I will kill you." The tone had a ring of obsessive intensity that sounded like a warning. No woman had ever professed her love for me. Not like this. Not with this intensity. It was an unusual experience. I turned back and asked, "What if you stop loving me?"

"I would rather die than do that," her eyes glistened.

"I have to go. The men are waiting."

They were indeed waiting. Narayanan extended a cigar and a well-used cigar cutter. Ajay took out his zippo to light the cigar.

Nambiar curtly said, "Don't do that. They are Cohíba Espléndidos, costing in excess of $30 each. Your cigar will smell of petrol. Haven't you enjoyed a cigar before?" He had a disgusted look on his face suggesting that Ajay was about to commit a cardinal sin. "Let me show you how to savour a cigar. Look at me and do likewise."

Ajay didn't appreciate the hostile response. He was wise enough though to follow his counsel. The connoisseur lit a matchstick and slowly rolled the cigar while puffing it.

Despite his inhibitions, Ajay imitated the cigar-lighting ritual to please the old man. He was becoming more sensitive to the preferential treatment the old man gave me. He gave me a wary look. He had perhaps not realised that I had gone way ahead of him socially. The gap between us was becoming more obvious to him.

All of us lit our cigars. Nambiar asked me, "Are you into cigars?" He considered me somebody who was used to good life. "Occasionally. I prefer the Aniversario series." He shook his head in approval.

Ajay diluted his drink with soda. For somebody who was used to gulping down alcohol, he surprisingly nursed his first drink for around 20 minutes before refilling his glass. He kept looking at the house and sucked the cigar hard. He wanted to finish it quickly. He was clearly uncomfortable in our company. He seemed preoccupied with his thoughts.

After waiting for another ten minutes, he finished his drink and got up. He said that he wanted to return to the room.

I asked, "What happened?"

"I want to go to bed early. The last week at work was really hard. I logged in more hours to be able to get a couple of days of leave just to be here." He walked away.

I don't think he was speaking the truth. Something was clearly bothering Ajay. I dismissed any further thoughts and decided to enjoy the company of the eminent old men.

Nambiar seemed relieved at his exit. He was in a talkative mood.

"You know, Krish, all three of us worked as professionals abroad. Since we are clad in white *mundus* and loose shirts like the local people, people mistake us for ordinary peasants. I was in Singapore while my brothers worked in the United Kingdom," said Nambiar.

Narayanan added, "And we like it that way. None of us wanted to settle abroad. This is our soil and we want to spend our remaining time here."

The rich flavours of the aged whisky and the earthy taste of the cigar smoke added to the euphoria. The rush of the last couple of days had been tiring. The men were talking and laughing at each other, reminiscing old stories. We were all slowly getting drunk. I watched the thick smoke from the cigars rising to the sky and dispersing into nothing.

All of a sudden, Nambiar asked me, "Remember, you had asked me a question about why women do not generally stay in his house?"

I nodded. "You said you would tell me about it at a later point in time. Is this the right time?" I asked in anticipation of a great tale.

"Hmm… There is a long story behind it." He then looked at his brothers as if seeking their approval.

"Our grandfather used to be the advisor to the local ruler. This was many, many decades ago. He was a very educated man and proficient in the queen's language. The English were the colonial masters then. They exerted considerable influence on local affairs with the objective of consolidating political power and maximising earnings for the crown. Ruthlessly exploitative, the English were in the process of turning a flourishing international economy into a colonial economy. They plotted to acquire monopoly rights to the most profitable trades. They were pitting rulers against rulers to create a monolithic political administration in order to advance their economic and politico-strategic objectives. At the court, everyday a new battle erupted between the native ruler and the representative of the English government. New agreements were couched in legalese and the ruler depended on my grandfather to negotiate agreements with them. The English initially always targeted our grandfather with temptations and then subtle threats. They wanted him to be on their side. However, grandfather considered them *mleccha!*"

"*Mleccha?*"

Nambiar continued, "In ancient India, this term was generally applied to foreigners. Those days, anybody who came from outside the region could be considered a foreigner to the land. During the period, colonialists were termed *mleccha* to indicate that they were uncouth barbarians. Technically, they were treated as untouchables but these people could not be treated the same way as other untouchables. Untouchability was more mental than physical in their case. Despite being political masters, people wouldn't partake food with them nor invite them to their abodes. "

Nambiar went on. "Once grandfather helped the ruler negotiate a complex treaty with the English. The terms were in favour of the state and its implementation resulted in improved financial status for the ruler. He was extremely happy and felt indebted. The very next day, in the court, grandfather was honoured with a title, a thick gold chain, and this property."

"This seems like an important piece of history."

"Yes. We all used to dismiss these stories as mere old tales, till my daughter pieced together a riveting story a few years ago using old records etched in Palmyra leaves. These were abandoned in the basement till she found them. She had chosen Theyyam and the history of this *tharawad* as the subject of her thesis."

"Where is she now?" I asked.

Nambiar's face dropped. Narayanan patted on his shoulders gently and said, "She passed away before submitting the thesis."

"How?" I should have controlled my curiosity.

Narayanan said, "Nobody knows. She died suddenly in her sleep. Though we were not able to identify the exact cause of death, using the family influence we got it certified as cardiac arrest for an official closure."

"Our doctor told us unofficially that she possibly died of fright." It was Narayanan

"Fright?" Narayanan just waved his hands and I felt it wise not to pursue the subject further.

Nambiar recovered from his sadness. He finished his drink and said, "Who can stop the wheels of destiny?"

I said, "So you were talking about your grandfather…"

"Yes, let me complete the story. Grandfather was very thrilled. He wanted to build a large house on this property that would match his ascending stature in the royal court. He took my grandmother to proudly show the property and described to her the details of the large mansion that he would build there. This was to be the legacy for his children and grandchildren. Grandmother was overjoyed. But as they walked around the property, she began feeling uncomfortable and complained of a choking sensation and she fainted.

"A worried grandfather and his servants took her home in the bullock cart. Though she started feeling better after leaving the property, the village doctor was summoned. Despite his years of experience, he was not able to point out the cause.

"In the night, she woke up screaming. She had high fever and was shivering. Grandfather was worried and he summoned the doctor again. All he could do was place crushed herbal leaves on her body to bring down her fever.

"The doctor had his doubts. He asked grandfather, 'Why don't you check more about the property before planning to settle down? Something during the visit seems to have triggered the illness in her'.

"At night she woke up due to recurrent nightmares screaming, *'Ayyo...* Don't kill me.' She couldn't remember anything when she woke up. Grandfather was very disturbed. He couldn't sleep a wink that night.

"In the morning, as she served him his customary tea, she confronted him, 'What happened to me? The women said that I was screaming and crying yesterday night. I don't remember anything.' Grandfather dismissed it saying that she had high fever and the medicines given by the doctor should cure her. 'There is nothing to worry,' he consoled her.

"But his mind continued to be turbulent. The words of the doctor bothered him. He left for the palace to meet his closest friend, the finance minister. He narrated the incidents to him. Together they met the head of the lands department to take his opinion.

"The official looked at grandfather and asked him if this was regarding the land allotted to him. The land had not been officially allotted to anybody for a very long time. According to rumours, this was the massacre site of a large number of political prisoners. They were horribly tortured before being beheaded and buried there *en masse*. This had allegedly happened around a century before.

"Their crime was that they had conspired against the king. They were betrayed by the daughter of the prime minister who was in love with the crown prince. Due to the king's opposition, the future king could not marry her. Apparently she was an ambitious woman and believed that the king's death would help her become queen. It was she who had drawn up the scheme and enticed the General of the Army to participate in its execution. He was promised untold wealth and power.

"Eventually, when the plot was discovered, she betrayed them all, except the crown prince. She escaped death but was banished from the land forever. The general accused the woman of using him. He screamed vengeance on behalf of all his compatriots. He promised that he would come back from the dead to wreak revenge on her. The general and most of soldiers were tortured to death."

I suddenly had a feeling that this story was familiar, but I couldn't recollect when and where I had heard it.

Nambiar continued, "The massacre took place in secret and the corpses were buried in an unmarked site somewhere within the property and the incident itself was not officially recorded. Despite the secrecy, rumours about the incident spread among the people. Even today, nobody knows if it is the truth or just a fantastic story. However, what we know for sure is that the land remained uninhabited and a mini jungle slowly grew around the site. Nobody went near the place for fear of blood-thirsty spirits of the massacre victims. This was till a sorcerer and his disciples chose to settle there.

"The sorcerer was known to possess the ability to conjure evil spirits and make them do his bidding. It is alleged that he summoned the spirits of the victims of the massacre. They were willing to do his bidding provided he helped them take revenge against the king, his family and the prime minister's daughter. Despite reports from the spies, the king was afraid to take action against the sorcerer."

Nambiar looked at me. He said, "Those were different times, Krish!" I nodded in understanding as I wanted to hear the whole story.

"Finally, the officials managed to bribe one of the disciples who eventually poisoned the magician. The soldiers moved in and killed all the disciples including the one who did their bidding. Their bodies are also buried in this land. However, this incident was recorded and the dead were described as rebels. The jungle dried up soon.

"It's only the old timers who have heard about these incidents. Many vagabonds and drunkards used to end up dead in the vicinity of it. There was a fear psychosis generated and people started avoiding the area.

"The official asked grandfather if he saw any trees in the property. Grandfather said, 'There was only a large mango tree. Other than that just grass and weeds.' Nobody knows the veracity of these stories. But, why take chances?

"According to the records there are more than 20 dead bodies of the 'rebels' buried somewhere within the property. Now that you had an experience, you should be cautious."

The official discouraged my grandfather. 'I cannot return the land to the king. He would feel insulted,' grandfather said.

"Despite the finance minister discouraging him, grandfather was not willing to let go of the property. He had already fallen in love with it. 'Don't return it, just don't build your abode there'."

Nambiar paused for a drink before continuing, "Due to grandfather's desire to find a solution for the unconfirmed presence of evil spirits, his friend suggested that they meet a sorcerer that he personally trusted. That evening, they both went incognito to the dwelling of the sorcerer. They kept the trip a secret from everyone including the king. By the time they reached, it was twilight. They heard the chanting of mantras from inside. As they stood outside, they heard a deep voice call out their names. The voice invited them to come in. 'Do not hesitate to come in.' A startled grandfather asked the minister if he had informed the sorcerer about their arrival. The unnerved minister shook his head in denial. The atmosphere was turning bizarre. Grandfather wanted to leave at once but the minister held his hand and stopped him.

"As they entered the ashram, they saw a man wearing tiger skin with ash all over the body sitting alone, chanting mantras. As they stood quietly behind him, he said without looking back, 'That land is not good to inhabit. It is the abode of murderous spirits.' Grandfather was shocked and disappointed.

"The man got up and turned towards them. His face had scars all over and dreadlocks that had not seen water for a long time. He reeked of cheap liquor and slowly rolled himself a joint.

"The minister spoke, 'My friend has been given that property as gift by the king. He wants to build a large house and live there.' The sorcerer looked at grandfather and simply said, 'Fool! Haven't you heard? *Vinaash kale, vipreet buddhi* (When the time of destruction comes, the victim aids it by behaving like an idiot).'

'We need your help, sir!' The minister pleaded on behalf of his friend.

'Why are you adamant that you should live there? That place is cursed! Women cannot live peacefully in that place! They would die unnatural deaths.' None spoke a word.

"Disappointed, the men turned back. Then the sorcerer spoke, 'Let me see what I can do. Incarcerating those spirits would be a tough task. They are thirsty for revenge. Please leave behind some money and I will see you the day after tomorrow at twilight. Meet me there and ensure that you bring no women with you.'

"Grandfather took a small pouch of gold coins and left it at the feet of the sorcerer. He said, 'Stop.' He went inside, took something, uttered some mantras, and handed it to my grandfather. 'Tie it on your wife's right arm. Let it remain till the puja is over.' He abruptly returned inside. It was an amulet wrapped in a red cloth.

"It was quite late by the time grandfather reached home. There was loud shouting coming from the house. As he rushed in, he saw grandmother in a state of possession. She was talking loudly in the language of the lower castes and shouting expletives at the servants. It took five people to control her and tie the amulet on her body. She lost consciousness but the experience shook my grandfather. She slept well and the incident never repeated itself.

"As twilight set in, the sorcerer and his pupils arrived at the site and began their puja. Apart from my grandfather and his friend, nobody else was allowed to witness the secret ritual. The spirits seemed to have put up a horrible fight but by dawn the sorcerer was able to incarcerate them in a copper urn. He tied powerful amulets around the neck of the jar to keep them securely imprisoned."

A cold shiver ran down my spine. I felt as though somebody was watching me and a sudden fear overtook me.

He continued. "The sorcerer said that these spirits could not be eliminated but he had held them captive in an urn. He could not say with certainty if any of them had escaped the powerful ritual. His disciples buried the urn deep in a corner of the property. The sorcerer asked grandfather to keep everybody away from the area. 'Curiosity can be the harbinger of trouble. So, keep the location a secret and do not ever mention about this ritual to anyone.' He warned him again.

"Before leaving, he warned, 'These beings are powerful and will try their best to escape. They are vengeance-thirsty beings. So, please take my words seriously. As long as the urn remains buried, this place and all of you are safe. However, watch out for women who have crossed the seven seas.' He didn't elaborate and left."

Nambiar finished explaining.

Then the eldest brother Narayanan said, "Though these stories are scary and captivating, none of us really believe it. Powerfully rendered stories devour us and leave influences that transcend lifetimes." He spoke like a philosopher.

"What happened to you, Krish? Your face is pale," Nambiar was staring at me with a worried look.

I stumbled over my words, "I think we found the urn!" "What?" All three men looked at me in disbelief.

"A couple of days ago, under the old mango tree. It was Maria who found it."

Silence descended and everybody looked at each other in sheer horror.

Narayanan kept repeating, "The prophecy! The

prophecy!"

Time seemed to stand still till Narayanan almost fell from the chair screaming and pointing at something, as though he had seen a ghost.

Turning around to see what it was, we saw Ajay standing beside us. Engrossed in the story, none of us had seen him come. Nambiar raised the lamp.

Ajay had blood all over his face and clothes. It was a frightening sight. My first impression was that something had happened to him. We all abruptly jumped from our chairs. He looked like a zombie with his bloodied face bereft of any emotions. He kept staring at me blankly. He didn't respond to any our questions.

Panic seized me. "Maria, where is Maria?" I shouted at Ajay.

I don't know if it was a smirk on his face or if it was my imagination. He just turned and walked towards the house. My legs grew heavy and I was the last among the group to reach the house.

There was blood on the wooden steps of the staircase. I was overcome with absolute apprehension about what lay beyond the door. I could hear the soft voice of the Theyyam performer eulogising the virtues of the *Bhaghawathi*. Maria had recorded the *thottampattu* yesterday.

The state of the room was shocking. Blood was splattered everywhere. The bed sheet and her night gown were drenched in it. There were small pools of blood on the wooden floor. The lifeless body of Maria lay on the floor. Almost instinctively, I took her hand and felt for her pulse, desperately hoping that some life would be left in her. It was cold and it seemed to penetrate my body.

Her gaze was cold and hard as an ice cube. There was a deep gash on the right side of her cheek. This seemed to have been meant to disfigure her.

The buttons of her night gown had been ripped apart. Her thighs were exposed although her underwear was intact around her waist. There were many wounds on her body. Her fingers looked like claws trying to hold onto something desperately. She looked like a grotesque doll!

A faint smell of her perfume and blood hung in the room.

Ajay's favourite jack-knife lay near her feet. The urn had been kicked away in anger. Its lid was missing.

I felt an emotional cyclone of extreme hatred, loss and anguish rising inside me. Ajay just stood staring at her body. He had the look of confusion, one of bewildered fear. I wanted to reach out and strangle him but I felt numb.

Nambiar suddenly lunged at Ajay, seized him roughly by the neck, and hissed savagely on his face "Demon!" Ajay didn't put up any resistance but the other two old men pulled Nambiar away.

I saw Narayanan making a frantic call.

I stood there for a moment and then stumbled out. I desperately needed something solid to lean against. Walking towards the stairs, I sat down crying uncontrollably. My blood pressure shot up and I could hear what felt like a dull, monotonous beating of a drum in my ears. I felt my strength ebbing away slowly.

Living without Maria seemed pointless to me. I was overcome by desperate loneliness. I heard the faint sirens of an ambulance as it made its way through the quiet roads.

I felt terribly sleepy. My mind was shutting out. Denial had always served as a wonderful strategy in some of the worst times of my life. I tried to convince myself that this was just a nightmare.

Tomorrow when you wake up, things will be back to normal, I told myself.

I slipped into a crazy, hopeless and desperate dream in which I kept falling helplessly from a precipice, repeatedly.

confession

When I woke up, it took some time for me to comprehend that I was in a hospital. Through unfocussed eyes, I made out the IV bottle hanging on a metal stand. I groaned in an attempt to move. A nurse hurried towards me and called out to the attendant, "Please inform the doctor, the patient is awake."

She propped me up with pillows. I saw my bloodied clothes and slippers in the corner. Yesterday's memories returned with full force; anxiety surged and I felt breathless. It was as if a heavy rock had been placed on my chest. I started screaming in a desperate attempt to escape the stifling memories. The doctor injected something into the IV bottle and I slipped back into a dreamless slumber.

It was afternoon when I woke up again. My hands felt immobile and I whimpered in protest. The nurse came and looked at me with sympathetic eyes.

"Just relax! The doctor will be here in a minute."

"Untie my hands, please. Why am I in the hospital?" I asked the nurse.

"You were brought in unconscious yesterday. When you were admitted, you were in shock," she replied dispassionately.

The doctor came and peered into my eyes and felt my pulse. He was a middle-aged, short, dark, bald and podgy person. I didn't like him. He had a stethoscope hanging from his neck, like an appendage. He looked at me as if I was a curious specimen.

"Do you want to sit down?" he asked softly. "You were thrashing around in the bed. That is why we had to restrain you." He pulled a red plastic chair and sat near me. "Do you remember what happened yesterday?"

"Yes, I do."

Grief swept over me, but, strangely, I was able to cope with it. I was coming to terms with the tragedy.

"You lost consciousness yesterday. After all, it was a very tragic incident," he said.

"I need to go, doctor."

"You have to stay in the hospital. I can't take any risks. We would like to keep you under observation. If you co-operate with us, you should be able to leave soon," he reassured me and instructed the nurse to remove the IV needle.

I felt very weak. The nurse insisted that I eat something. She helped me brush my teeth and handed me a plate of rice gruel. Food was the last thing on my mind but she stood beside me with a stern look. Perhaps it was the authority exuded by her uniform that made me comply. Eating had never been such a burden before.

I asked the nurse if she had found my mobile phone. "Yes. But have your medicines now."

"I am not sick."

She thrust a couple of pills in my hand and a bottle of water. "Have." That's all she said before handing my phone to me.

There were two missed calls from Lakshmi. I returned her call and the first thing she asked was, "Are my parents there yet?"

"No. I haven't seen them. When did you know?"

"Nambiar informed Ambika," she said. "The news has been broadcast by all local channels. OB vans are camped near Nambiar's house streaming live news. Policemen are swarming the place. This is turning into a high-profile case. I am trying to book a ticket at the earliest. Now take rest." She didn't ask me any questions.

"I just want to get out of here soon," I whimpered. The battery, which was already low, died out on me.

The sedatives started working and I crawled back into bed.

When I closed my eyes, the image of Maria lying on an ice slab in the morgue haunted me. I couldn't relax. Where would she be now? Though she was dead, I felt responsible for her body.

I desperately wanted to talk to Nambiar. But the phone was dead and the charger was at the *tharawad*.

"Madam, is there a phone that I can use?" I checked with the nurse.

"Not in the room and I can't take you to the reception. The doctor would be angry."

Perhaps it was the desolate look on my face that made her offer me her mobile phone.

"Not more than a minute."

Nambiar didn't take the call though I called a couple of times. I returned the phone to her.

He called back after a few minutes and the nurse handed the phone to me.

"Speak softly," she warned me.

When I answered the phone, he asked, "Whose phone is this?"

"The nurse's phone. How did you know it was me?" He chose not to answer my question.

"Many people were calling on my phone to enquire about the incident. So, I avoided taking calls. Just that you called a couple times…"

He sounded sombre. "How are you, Krish?"

"Where is Maria's body now?" I didn't answer his question. "In the mortuary. The police wanted to have a word with

you."

"For what? Did I do something wrong?" I always tried to avoid policemen. They made me uncomfortable.

"They just want your statement. Don't worry, the inspector is a relative. Krish, I wanted to consult you on the most important thing. What do we do with her body?" His voice was bereft of emotions.

"She had once mentioned that she would like to be cremated in Kerala. I think we should respect her wish. How about the electric crematorium of the Kannur municipality?" I couldn't think of any other option.

"We are partly responsible for her fate. Aren't we?" Nambiar said hesitatingly. "We should honour her in her final journey."

"What's on your mind?"

"Let's cremate her in the *tharawad* itself. What do you say?" he asked as though seeking my permission.

"I think we could do that. She will have a final resting place." I agreed.

"We will meet tomorrow morning?"

"Yes."

"That's enough. If the doctor knows about this, I will lose my job," the nurse started panicking. She almost pulled the phone from my hands. "The police would be here to meet you around 3 p.m. today," she said cradling the phone.

"Can I watch TV?"

"No. The doctor has strictly forbidden that. He wants you to rest and not get agitated. The channels are full of news about yesterday's incident. They are sensationalising the murder." She sounded like a matron.

I felt mentally desensitised and plopped into the plastic chair and closed my eyes. After sometime, the nurse called out, "Sir, sir, the police inspector is here to meet you."

"Police?"

"Yes. The inspector wants to have a word with you," she said.

The inspector walked in with a bunch of papers tied to a typical red government file. He had two stars on the shoulders of his khaki uniform.

I never really liked policemen. Newspapers regularly reported police brutality and custodial deaths in Kerala. I saw them as insensitive people intoxicated with power. More than respect, they evoked fear in me. I wondered many times if they hadn't heard of scientific interrogation techniques as they were known to use third degree torture on undertrials.

When I tried to stand up, he said, "Okay, okay. Please remain seated." I obeyed.

He removed his peak cap and sat near me. A short dark-skinned person, he seemed to have forgotten all about exercising many years ago. His belt seemed to groan as it tried to accommodate his considerable girth. He must have been in his late 30s but looked much older. The double-chin attested for a sedentary life. I was afraid that the plastic chair would give away under his abundant weight.

He began. "I am the sub-inspector of the station. Also a distant relative of Nambiar." His tone was mechanical. I was getting the feeling that I would be arrested.

"Am I a suspect?" I expected him to bring out the handcuffs like a magician.

"No, you are not, but you are a prime witness. All I need is your statement. I am here to listen to you. Tell me everything that you know about this case." He looked like somebody who had seen the worst of humanity and yet tried hard to present a humane face.

I explained everything that happened after landing in Kochi.

The inspector said, "So, you saw an American woman at a shack and then at the synagogue the next day. She comes with you for dinner that very evening. You get so close that you push your wife to arrange to see Theyyam. And then everything ends in disaster. Doesn't it sound a little unnatural?" I didn't like the way he looked at me. I merely shrugged my shoulders.

"Who was Ajay? How closely did you know him?" he quizzed.

"He is my friend from school."

His questions became more pointed. "What kind of character was he? Tell me everything you know about him," he probed further.

"All I know was that his mother brought him up as a single parent. His father rarely visited the family. He was a bit wayward and never listened to his mother. She was constantly worried about him getting into bad company."

As I went over my memories, I realised that there was not much that I knew about Ajay. What I knew was collated from what he had said or what I had deduced. I had very little first-hand information about him. The policeman was looking at me while flipping through the pages on his file. He seemed to be verifying my story. That made me uncomfortable.

"After his mother's death a few months ago, he seems to have gone berserk. He was in and out of relationships. He also worked in a local travel agency because he would get to meet foreign female tourists. He claimed to have developed intimate relationships with many of them."

Just then I saw my in-laws walking in. They seemed very concerned at the sight of the policeman but chose not to interfere.

The inspector told the nurse, "I would like to take him to the canteen for a cup of tea." She seemed hesitant. "I need to talk to him in private. Let the doctor know." The nurse nodded her head very slowly.

We walked towards the canteen. I refused when the inspector offered me his hand as support. I wanted to be seen as fit and independent. We sat in a quiet corner. He ordered tea for both of us. The attenders of patients were vying with each other to get the attention of the waiters and they made a lot of noise. Two cups of hot tea were placed in front of us quickly. The uniform helped.

The tea was very strong and sugary. But I loved its smell and taste. It had been more than a day since I sipped tea. It tasted divine.

It was me who broke the silence. "How's Ajay?" Despite his unpardonable crime, I still harboured some sympathy for him. I didn't have much anger left in me.

Despite his bold manners and swagger, I always saw Ajay as a troubled person. Was he suffering from delusions of grandeur or persecution? Or were they interchangeable states in his case? Or did one trigger the other? His exaggerated feelings of vanity were nothing but a cover for his deep insecurities and inferiority complex. I don't think he ever realised the extent of damage he was doing to the lives of others. Deep inside, he had some goodness and I had been the beneficiary of his largesse many times. His life was a constant battle in search of an identity. For me, he was a psychologically flawed character who deserved some sympathy. Most people don't understand characters like him. All he ever faced was revulsion from all those he dealt with. I probably was the only exception.

"Ajay?" The inspector asked as though he hadn't heard me clearly. "I have been a policeman for many years. But I have never encountered such a case before. I have a strange fascination for abnormal psychology." He gave me a long look. "I try to decipher the thought processes of criminals. Not many policemen in Kerala have my reputation for cracking difficult cases."

I was getting impatient to know about Ajay. "So you were telling me about Ajay?"

"Yes, yes. Let me explain." He spoke like a talkative child adamant on putting forth his viewpoint. "Unravelling the details of this case would be a feather in my cap and add to my already considerable reputation." He revealed his motivation. "Getting back to the point," he said, "I was the one who arrested Ajay. He was very silent throughout the journey to the station. In the lock-up, he just sat staring at the wall, seemingly debating with himself. He seemed to be in such a disturbed state that we decided to leave him alone.

"To be honest, the constables were a little apprehensive considering the nature of his crime and since he was covered in blood. It is with great persuasion that he changed those clothes. Around 3.00 a.m. in the morning today, Ajay insisted that on seeing me. He refused to interact with the constables.

"Despite being woken up from deep sleep, I rushed at the opportunity to hear the murderer. He started with a request for tea and cigarettes. I took him out of the lock-up to a small room used by the constables as a dressing room. He wanted total privacy. So, I had to personally write the confession."

The inspector continued. "He told me that the story of his life was his confession. Ajay insisted that I convey his story to you."

This is what Ajay said:

'I had a very difficult childhood growing up with a mother who was abandoned by the man she loved the most. He never gave her a formal divorce. It was my mistake, I came into this world earlier that I should have. Despite my father's insistence, my mother didn't want to abort me. It was perhaps a difficult decision for my mother. She chose me over her husband.

It is true that my mother sacrificed her life and ambitions for me, but it was her decision not mine. She constantly implied that I was the cause of all her misfortunes. Whenever she was angry and frustrated, she would curse me and called me 'the son of a devil or Satan'. I didn't know if she was abusing me or my father. But somehow, I began to like the persona of the devil that was being attributed to me. (Ajay laughed fanatically saying this.)

Ironically, my anger was directed towards my existent mother rather than the non-existent father. Why didn't she simply abort me or kill me when I was an infant? Why sacrifice, then repent, and complain all your life? Sometimes, I derived a secret sense of satisfaction for being the cause of her misery. Subconsciously, I was angry at everything female.

I always felt jealous when I saw happily married couples. Marriage is an institution that had caused me much trouble.

That is why I chose to have intimate relationships with married women. I treated them well to the point that many pleaded me to marry them. They had no compunction leaving their husbands for me. This was the cruel satisfaction that I was seeking. Their husbands had no clue that I was taking what was rightfully only theirs. I never saw a woman for more than a fortnight. But their marital relationship could not be the same again.'

The policeman constantly referred to his notes to refresh his mind.

'Till I met Maria, I found a sense of power and control in sin. Maria was different. She was the second woman for whom I fell.' Ajay hadn't answer the inspector's question about who the first woman was.

"Was it Lakshmi?" my mind raced behind the answer.

I was astounded to hear the policeman reveal that Ajay and Maria were acquaintances. They had given me an impression to the contrary.

"Ajay now spoke like a mad man," said the officer.

'She came to Kochi after booking a cheap travel package. Though short of cash, she was hell-bent on completing her thesis on Theyyam. Instead of just covering the performances as an outsider, she wanted an intimate perspective. She was very ambitious and wanted to join her university as the rural sociology faculty. The woman seemed obsessed with becoming a celebrity. Something like a female Indiana Jones.

'Hopelessly in love with her, I wanted to marry her and settle in her country. Despite many opportunities, I refrained from having sex with her. Like a fool, I was willing to wait. Now I know that she had manipulated me to find somebody who could sponsor her trip. (I could imagine hatred gathering like dark clouds in his eyes.)

'Without ever verbalising it, she reciprocated my love or so I believed. Helping her fulfil her dream became my need. I was planning to propose to her once she was back from Kannur.

'When Krish told me that he was coming on a short vacation, I latched on to the golden opportunity. Coming from an old Hindu family, he had the contacts and the resources to take her to a *tharawad*. I planned their meeting as if it was a sheer coincidence.

'The bitch! (Ajay spat out angrily.) The born actress played along in trapping that naïve idiot, Krish. From the day he landed, I had gently dictated his itinerary. We delivered such a beautiful drama at the shack. I bribed Babu at the shack so that he would leave two tables empty in such a manner that she could sit across us. Krish was a fool. He did not suspect anything when he met her again at the synagogue. He fell for the trap. However, I didn't expect them to bond so quickly. This is where I went wrong and my life took wrong turns.

'Krish was an average student at school and I never expected him to make it big in life. He was a classic nincompoop when it came to women. He was so scared of women that he used to worship popular girls in our class. While I didn't reach anywhere in life, he slowly and steadily climbed up the ladder. I was jealous about his marriage to Lakshmi.

'Lakshmi had all that I desired in a woman. She was a strong beautiful woman with a great pedigree. Something about her triggered an infatuation in me. Contrary to my expectations, Krish actually won her heart. I don't know why but she disliked me from the beginning.'

I stared at the policeman blankly when I heard this.

'It was difficult for me to forget Lakshmi and all I wanted was to see their marriage break. When Krish and Maria left for Kannur, I gathered I could use this opportunity to create fissures in Lakshmi's mind. So, I had more reasons for bringing Maria and Krish together.

'While this wouldn't automatically mean that Lakshmi would love me, I wanted to see her unhappy. (Ajay gave a wicked smile. He seemed to be enjoying his role as a home wrecker.)

'Before meeting Krish, Maria liked to spend a lot of time with me. She would sit close to me and hold my hands. She was very affectionate. For a change, I controlled myself despite being aroused by her presence. I didn't want to upset the applecart of my future plans. My heart longed for that woman. But before I could spend more than a fortnight with her, she was on the train with Krish heading towards Kannur.

'Things didn't go the way I planned. My calculations started going awry. I called Krish once they were in Kannur. He sounded excited. He gushed when he spoke about Maria and thanked me profusely for having taken him to the shack where he met her. He promised me a big party once he was back.

'Without Maria, I started feeling lonely. I called her many times but then she never let a conversation exceed more than a minute or two. She would find a reason to end the call quickly. I could sense rejection but I was in denial.

'There was something amiss. My mind started conjuring up images of Maria and Krish getting intimate. Though I believed that Krish, the hen-pecked husband, was not a threat, my sense of security was beginning to crumble.

'The more I tried to forget about them, the harder it became. I wanted to be in Kannur to ensure that Maria's mind would not sway towards Krish. When I requested for leave, my boss refused. The bastard took that opportunity to get back at me for my lack of respect to him. In a fit of rage, I shouted at him and left the office.

'When Maria did not respond to my calls, I reached out to Krish. I got the location of the house before letting him know that I was coming over to Kannur. As suspected, his behaviour changed the moment I said I was coming. He tried to actively discourage me.

'I was always confident about my seduction abilities and this man, whom I considered an imbecile when it came to women, had started to threaten my skills. My mind was in turmoil and I experienced an inner rage like never before. I reached out to an old college mate who practices psychiatry at a private hospital. I think he said that I was suffering from a milder form of melancholy and gave some medicines from his stash of samples. He said the medicines would calm me down but I had to use them regularly for some time.

'He made me feel like I was mentally unstable. What hurt more was his advice. 'Why don't you learn to love someone and finally settle down, Ajay? You are still like the wandering mendicant seeking the elusive miracle herb. Once you have a family, your mind will settle down. You are a victim of your own vicious thoughts. An insecure person's mind is a devil's workshop.' This sounded at once like a diagnosis and a prescription to me. I didn't like the way he spoke. But in retrospect, his words turned almost prophetic.

'That night, I couldn't sleep despite the medicines. So I called Gracy. Despite her repeated calls, I hadn't been with her since I met Maria. She is one of the horniest women I have met. Though she was initially angry for not responding to her desperate calls, she readily invited me home. Having sex with me was her way of getting even with her husband.

'She always made me feel like a love god. Her constant praises worked like an aphrodisiac for me. The bitch thought that she was my only lover. But that night, I couldn't get an erection despite her goading me. I got out of bed in anger and frustration. While I sat drinking her husband's whisky, Gracy looked at me and taunted me that I seemed to have lost my potency. A sudden rush of rage overtook me and I pushed her into the bed. She put up a stiff resistance but I violently completed the act. She pushed me away, spat on me, and told me never to return. I heard her sobbing hard as I left her house.

'She wanted it and I gave it to her. Didn't understand why she was crying. The bitch!

'I drove home. Something had snapped inside me. I just jumped into bed but I couldn't get sleep. As I lay in there, I thought about all the women I had slept with. For the first time, I thought about their husbands. I was guilty of encouraging infidelity in women. I had never treated anyone like the way I treated Gracy that night.

'I felt guilty for not having been empathetic with my mother. A concoction of grief, guilt and helplessness was forming in my head. I realised why Krish had once called me a person with a narcissistic personality disorder.'

The inspector stopped and looked at me. I told him, "I had no idea that I had been responsible for causing so much turbulence in Ajay's mind. He had known me for so many years. All he had to do was to tell me that he loved Maria. But he chose to use me to further his love for Maria."

My mind was slowly registering the machinations of Ajay. I had never associated him with cunning thoughts. What hurt me most was that Maria had been a willing accomplice. At least till she ensured that she could witness a real Theyyam performance. I don't think she faked her love for me. Perhaps this knowledge would lessen the pain of losing her in such a brutal manner.

The inspector was referring to his notes again. He read out the contents like a story.

'I decided to be in Kannur the next day and boarded the unreserved compartment of the train going towards Kannur. Nobody had come to the Kannur railway station to pick me up. When I called Krish, he asked me to take an auto rickshaw. I didn't have much difficulty in reaching the house as every local seemed to know it. Krish greeted me warmly and introduced me to Nambiar. That old man was a snob!

We took an instant dislike to each other.

'There were a lot of people in the big house. A man was reciting out loud what sounded like a prayer. Maria was taking a video of the man screaming. Dressed in a Kerala set-sari, with jasmine in her hair, she looked like a very fair Malayali woman. She looked really beautiful and I felt a strong urge to embrace her. She reached out and shook my hand and said, 'Welcome to the land of Theyyam.' Her response cooled me down and my worries began to vanish. I thought that I had been worried for no reason. She still liked me.'

'Krish said, 'Maria, why don't you show him the room?' She looked at him bashfully. 'C'mon, Ajay.' She seemed to deliberately maintain a safe distance from me. The room looked like an old library with many old books with layers of dust on them. There was no furniture there except cotton bedrolls heaped in the corner. She stood beside an old almirah and told me, 'Thank you Ajay. This is turning out to be a great trip. We met a lot of people who gave us detailed information. This would not have been possible without your help.' She smiled. I went forward and told her desperately, 'Please stay for a few minutes. I want to talk to you.'

'There are too many people here. The Theyyam is set to begin soon. Let's get some lunch. We will meet in the evening sometime?' Saying so, she walked away briskly.

'Devotees had started gathering around the house. Maria and Krish took me to the kitchen for a spartan lunch. The first round of Theyyam rituals started around 2 p.m. and continued till about 10 p.m. Krish and Maria shared the task of documentation. He used the camera while she filmed the performance from various angles. Being Nambiar's special guests, they had all the freedom they wanted. There was also an old man whom they addressed as Nambhuthiri; he acted as their guide. Their camaraderie made me uncomfortable. My heart swung between hope and despair.

'Between 10 p.m. and 2 a.m., there was a break in the performances. We all had a simple vegetarian dinner and retired to the library. The house was full of relatives and friends. The performances were divided between the house and the nearby temple. So the crowd kept moving here and there.

'The family members were lying down wherever they could find some space. Some of them came and took the bedrolls stacked in the library. Everybody wanted to rest till the next performance. Even some of eminent and elderly members of the family were seen sleeping on thin mattresses on the floor. We three went to the library and managed to find some space in the midst of old papers and book piles. I wanted to chat but they both wanted to catch-up with sleep.

'I lay in such a fashion that Maria was between both of us. I thought with Krish asleep, I could initiate a conversation with Maria. She turned towards Krish feigning sleep. Isolated in my own world, I tried to make sense of what was happening to my life. Sleep was playing truant. Maria started to snore gently and put her hands around Krish. I couldn't stand the sight so I waited for some time and then slowly turned her towards me. I kept her hands on my chest. It felt like heaven.

'In that position, sleep came to me quick. It was after a long time that I went into deep sleep. By the time I woke up, it was already 10 a.m. I couldn't see Krish or Maria. I saw Nambiar chatting with a small group of elderly men. I asked him where my friends were. He said that they had returned to his house. The driver was standing near the SUV. Instead of offering to drop me at his house, Nambiar merely asked the driver to give me directions. I could see some people having breakfast at the makeshift kitchen but nobody offered me any food.

'As I started walking, my overnighter felt heavy. The house wasn't too far but the insult hurt me. It was hot. When I reached the house, I couldn't find anybody. I walked upstairs and found Krish sleeping in the first room. Luckily, the door wasn't locked. I didn't bother to check where Maria's room was. I left my bag there and returned to the portico. I sat there smoking cigarette after cigarette. I was very upset that the two had left me alone. Hunger fuelled my anger.

'When Krish woke up, we went for lunch at a nearby restaurant. Krish was beginning to fuss about Maria. Although I was not sure whether they were having an affair, I was beginning to get intimidated by their affection towards each other.

'I wanted a drink badly to cope with the uncertainty. After we had a few drinks, we decided to catch up on lost sleep. Krish went to sleep quickly. Maria had returned to her room. I thought it would be a good time to talk to her and went into her room. On seeing her, I asked her what was brewing between Krish and her. She told me that it was none of my business and tried to shoo me away. We shouted at each other. I wanted to strangle her but I controlled myself. In desperation, I went back to Krish's bedroom. I was very, very upset. Even if she didn't love me, I was okay. But the way she defended her relationship with Krish hurt me more. I became the outsider. Strangely, the more she rejected me, the more I wanted her. Now, I wanted control rather than romance.

'In the evening, when I sat with Krish and the old men for drinks and cigar, I had made up my mind for a final confrontation. A tormented mind and a broken heart together form a deadly combination, don't they?

'My mind was like a sea, a raging sea. I knew that destiny had provided me with the opportunity to meet Maria. Yes, I was confident of making her understand the depth of my love for her.

'In the night, when Krish and the old men continued drinking and relishing their cigars, I felt the desperate need to meet Maria. I didn't want to get drunk and waited till everybody got into the groove. When I reached her room, she was studying some sort of an old vessel. I could hear the voice of a man reciting a eulogy to the Goddess from her laptop. She looked up and was astonished to see me alone. Her first question was, 'Where is Krish?' She seemed agitated and afraid all at once.

'I just need a few minutes with you, Maria. Don't you think I deserve it?' I pleaded with her. She calmed down and invited me to sit on the bed.

'She listened carefully as I spelt out my deep love for her.

I told her how badly I wanted to marry her and spend the rest of my life with her. I tried to convince her that no woman has ever made me feel like this. I thought she would understand my predicament.

'There was no reaction and she merely asked me in an even tone, 'Have I ever told you that I loved you, Ajay? I do like you and am grateful for introducing me to Krish.' Almost instinctively, my hand went into my pocket to feel the coldness of my jack knife.

'I am a wanderer, Ajay and do not want to be tied down with the threads of a marital relationship.'

'So, what is Krish for you? What does he have that I do not?' I couldn't help comparing and I wanted an answer. She chose not to reply.

'Take your time, honey. But, you are mine.'

She looked at me mockingly, 'Don't you understand?'

Her firm rejection made me lose hope. For a moment I felt like I was shrinking. I felt inferior to Krish and everybody in the world. I reacted sharply. 'Are you rejecting my love?'

'Love? Are you capable of that emotion? What you need is a woman's body,' she snapped back.

She surprised me when she tore the buttons of her night gown and opened it. 'You can have my body, Ajay. But not my heart.' I felt nothing at the sight of her breasts.

She lay on the bed and said, 'Come, indulge in lust. We become even after this. No debts to repay.'

'Krish is a married nincompoop and you like him.' I felt a burning sensation in my eyes.

'He is a good man. Yes, I love him though I would not marry him either. But how does it concern you? You are just jealous!'

As I looked around, my eyes fell on the old vessel kept on the desk. She taunted me again, 'Do what you want with my body just once and go away,' She reminded me of Gracy. I took the vessel and threw it at her. It hit her bosom. She screamed at me and called me a loser. Strangely, she didn't try to run. I turned up the volume of the eerie song emanating from the laptop.

'My hands literally trembled with anger. I jumped on to the bed, pulled out a pillow, and pressed it on her face. I kept trying to smother her but she fought back like a possessed woman. That's when I remembered the knife. I took it out from my pocket and stabbed her. I could hear her muffled cries but she continued to resist. Blood spurted out like tiny fountains and the pillow turned red. She eventually grew tired. I removed the pillow to check if she had died. She was still muttering something and I slashed her cheeks to disfigure her. In her feeble attempts to escape, she fell from the bed.

My anger wasn't abating and I stabbed her till I was tired.'

The inspector paused and said, "At this moment, Ajay stopped and cried inconsolably. I looked at him sympathetically as he was nothing but a child now. Ajay then continued…"

'She simply wouldn't die. She pleaded with me in a low voice to end it. I stabbed her again and again to end her misery. Along with her, the embers of my anger died down too. As remorse took over, I sat next to her weeping. It was over! Everything was over! There was a sudden calmness, with only the eerie song playing in the background. The only two emotions I experienced then were that of self-loathing and revulsion.

'By the time I reached Kannur, my mind had already turned into a tinder box ready to explode at the slightest provocation. I had perhaps concealed my disturbed mind from everybody including myself. But I had never planned to kill her. I couldn't be in that room anymore and my mind was dazed. I had ended up killing the woman I loved the most. Sir, I want you to promise me that you will narrate all this to Krish.'

By the time the inspector completed the story, I was angry and upset. I thought Ajay wanted to leave behind a legacy. The reason he narrated the story was because he wanted to be pitied. He portrayed himself as the victim in the entire story, I thought.

The inspector looked outside as if he was observing the minute details of the world. I reached out to him and nudged him, "So, where is he now?"

The inspector said, "There was a strange glitter in his eyes. It was a mixture of fear and determination. In hindsight, I should have known. I thought that he was just playing with my psyche. But he was not. Had I known, I would have stayed."

"And then what happened?"

The inspector was unwittingly building the suspense. "I know that you went through emotional hell yesterday," the officer said.

I was losing my patience and told him wryly, "I am fine. Please tell me everything. I am not a kid. I survived yesterday, didn't I?"

The inspector looked hurt. He probably thought I was being insensitive. "I left for home after that. I couldn't bear his presence in the police station. He had left me deeply disturbed."

He said, "I had just reached home when I was called back to the station by one of the constables. He kept saying that something terrible had happened. When I reached the station, the constables were standing around the cell. He had killed himself!"

It hit me like a hammer blow.

"What? What happened to him?" I couldn't comprehend it. "You mean Ajay? He died? How? He was in the lock-up, right?"

The inspector looked at me guiltily and said, "We weren't expecting any trouble. He made a noose from the strands of his clothes. He hung himself from the window."

My heart sank. "It must have taken some effort to die that way. But the man was determined. His body has been sent for autopsy. I am aware that this could be considered an extra-judicial killing and I could be suspended. But more than the legal repercussions, it was the corpse that scared me. His bulging eyes stared at me as if they were asking me to fulfil his wish. I have grown up listening to stories of demons and evil spirits. I have seen dead bodies before but I was mortified of this dead prisoner. I wanted to fulfil his wish so I rushed to meet you and deliver his confession."

There was fear in his eyes of the inspector. I leaned back. Ajay was a confused and tortured soul, I thought. His conscience was perhaps burdened with accumulated guilt that needed purging. Perhaps he was also afraid of Maria's vengeance. Did he believe that Maria would return in a malevolent form and exact revenge?

My thoughts shifted to Maria. "Where is her body now?"

"It is at the mortuary and would be released after the autopsy. Do you want to reach out to her near and dear? The body could be repatriated to her country." The inspector sounded like a lawyer now.

I told him, "I had a word with Nambiar today. We will be cremating her body in that property."

"After all this?" he asked.

I just looked at him. "What was her fault?"

The inspector offered his support. "I will help in getting the body released as early as possible."

I returned to the room where my in-laws were waiting. They looked worried but chose not to burden me with questions. My father-in-law had bought some food for me. They soon left the hospital as the visiting hours were over.

I ate dinner quickly. Then I propped myself against the pillows and reminisced the trip. It had been memorable, in more ways than one. Maria had inadvertently led me into a magical world of Gods and spirits and helped me explore the complicated psychological landscape of my own people in a way I had not imagined before.

Maria was possibly killed due to Ajay's unrealistic expectations. He proved that unbridled desire for a woman can turn a man into a demon. Man can sometimes be more violent and vengeful than evil spirits.

My mind weaved several patterns around the recent happenings. It seemed as though a carefully calibrated cycle had been initiated. Right from my meeting with Vishnu and Maria to the intimate encounter with Malini; everything seem to be part of a synchronised plan.

Were we the key players in the failed coup that took place many decades ago? Did the spirits of the victims of the massacre come back to exact their final revenge? Did they use Ajay to execute the general's fatal threat or was Ajay the General? Was Maria the prime minister's daughter and I the prince in the story? Did I inadvertently become the catalyst for bringing the woman from across the seven seas? Maria's 'accidental' discovery of the urn and the release of the trapped spirits seemed to be poetic justice. Was the gnarled mango tree possessed by spirits or did malevolent spirits live on the tree? Did the spirits finally execute their blood-thirsty plan?

Though these could be nothing but a series of accidental coincidences, it was difficult to dismiss them. The pointers were too stark to ignore. For a believer, it would be a game of destiny. A revenge executed by the inhabitants of the underworld.

For Nambiar and his family, the prophecy had come true. The world is full of surprises and mysteries that are difficult to unravel. I chose to deny these pointers as there was no empirical evidence that consultants like me seek. But then has there ever been any evidence of happenings like these involving divinities or spiritual beings? This was my way of coping with the enormity of the catastrophe.

My mind then started to worry if Malini had been impregnated. I dismissed the thought. I often boasted to my wife that it wouldn't take much effort for me to impregnate a woman. I told her, "One shot, one kill." That's all it took for a potent man like me to cause pregnancy. Now I was hoping that the fantasy of potency would be just that. No single encounter can result in pregnancy, I tried hard to convince myself.

I woke up in the morning and was surprised to see Lakshmi standing beside the bed. I was really happy to see her. "When did you come?"

"I landed early morning today. I thought you needed me now more than ever."

I threw myself into her arms. I fought hard not to cry. As always, her presence gave me confidence and strength.

She helped me brush and forced me to have breakfast. The doctor came for a check-up before signing the discharge papers. He said, "There is nothing to worry. Time is a great healer."

When we sat in the car, I told Lakshmi, "My job is not complete. Take me to Nambiar's house. I need to be there for Maria's cremation. I need to say goodbye one last time."

Her reaction was cold. Lakshmi, unlike her instinct, did not question me.

The scene at the house was starkly different from what it had been the day we arrived in the house. It was very gloomy. A large group of people stood talking among themselves. Broadcast vans from different television stations were parked outside the compound and journalists were waiting for the corpse to arrive.

Nambiar was sitting in his recliner with his head tipped back. His hands were crossed in his lap and his fists were clenched tightly. The tragic events had proven traumatic for him. He seemed to have suddenly grown older. His lips quivered as he greeted me, "How are you now?" There was genuine concern in his voice. I didn't reply. He looked at me with deep tenderness and pity.

He said, "We cut the old mango tree for cremation. I don't want it to serve as a reminder of the tragedy."

"Let it burn away," I said with disgust.

"Yes. Let the fire consume it," Nambiar whispered. "All along, there was something creepy about that tree." We seemed to share our hatred for the tree.

He pointed towards Maria's belongings that were left in a corner of the portico. The ambulance with Maria's body arrived quietly. The inspector came out and waved at me. Along with Nambiar, I went forward to fetch her body. It lay wrapped in coarse white cotton. It must've have been dissected horribly, I thought. There were small specks of dried blood on the corners of the shroud. The body seemed to have bloated up. It was heavy.

Nambiar, the inspector, an attender, and I lifted the stretcher and shifted the body on to the funeral pyre created from the logs of the gnarled mango tree. Although it was wrapped in a shroud, the cameramen were all over the place trying to take close-up shots of the corpse. I hated photographers more than before. I tried to push them away. Lakshmi was watching me intently.

"Who will be the *kartha*?" the head priest asked.

"I will be the *kartha* and perform the final rites. She has nobody else," I said.

"How are you related to her?" He seemed cross. He probably was a stickler for following religious norms.

Nambiar stepped forward and whispered in his ears. The priest was unhappy about letting me perform her last rites. After a couple of minutes of arguing, he finally relented.

"Go, take a bath wearing a single piece of cloth," he barked. I ignored his rudeness, removed the shirt, handed it over to Lakshmi, and walked towards the pipe just outside the portico. I filled a bucket with water and poured it over my head.

I walked across and touched Maria's feet. Before she was gone, I had to apologise to her personally. I stood for a few seconds and whispered my apology. If I had been vigilant, I would not have let Ajay go into the house alone. I could have prevented it from happening.

The junior priests sprinkled holy water on the pyre. The priest muttered mantras and I repeated after him. I lit the pyre and it caught fire fast, fuelled by clarified butter.

Nambiar, who was standing beside me, asked, "What will you do with her belongings?" He was trying to tell me something. I stood there thinking about it. I went to Lakshmi and asked her, "What do we do with Maria's belongings?"

"Where are they?" she asked.

I pointed towards the portico and said, "The laptop bag, the rucksack & her cloth bag. That's all she brought with her."

"Wait here."

Lakshmi returned with the bags. She indicated with her eyes to throw them into the fire. I was hesitant. "A lot of research is on her laptop, Lakshmi." She stood there without responding. Her eyes were cold and determined. She wanted to get rid of everything associated with this trip.

"You have enough on your mind, Krish." I was afraid of her wrath. It also struck to me that anything that belongs to Maria could be the source of constant tension.

I threw the bags into the pyre. Everything that Maria owned, along with her body, was consumed by the fire. Just like that, there was nothing left behind except her memories. She simply vanished from my life. Just like that.

"It will burn for a few hours. We will return later," said Lakshmi. She held my hands and led me away. We didn't speak anything in the car on the way to the hotel that she was staying in.

It was late afternoon when we returned to the *tharawad*. The body had finally burned. The priests had collected a handful of ashes and a few pieces of bones that had survived the fire in a small urn. Nambiar requested them to bury the urn in a 'suitable' place. Nambiar's servant went with them to do the needful. They left no traces to identify the location of that urn.

A concerned Nambiar asked the head priest, "Do you think there will be trouble?"

He said, "No. She will not return a malevolent spirit."

"But she died an unnatural violent death. Didn't she?" Nambiar was still feeling insecure.

"All dead persons don't return. Just to be sure, we will conduct the necessary puja. Just do a *bali tharpanam* next year. She will attain moksha. This was the last part of the drama. It had to end this way. That's destiny. Who can change destiny?"

As we turned back, I told Nambiar, "I am sorry to have caused all this."

He said, "Didn't you hear the priest? Who can stop destiny? This was to happen. According to the priests and astrologers that Narayanan consulted, she took the brunt of the anger of the spirits. She seems to have been their ultimate target. Don't worry. Please go peacefully and try to forget what happened. What is destined will happen and it just happened in front of you." He gave me a weak smile. None of us bade goodbye to each other.

We returned to the hotel. "I need to rest, Lakshmi. These events have taken a toll on me."

"Sure, we are leaving early in the morning. I don't want you to spend any more time than absolutely necessary in Kannur."

I felt as though a big burden had been lifted from my chest. By the time I woke up in the morning, I saw Lakshmi had packed all the bags and we were ready to go. I got ready quickly and we left for the airport. As the plane lifted off into the skies, I had this strange feeling that I was reaching the abode of the spirits and celestial beings. I looked out of the window almost instinctively as if Maria would be there to bid me goodbye. Life would not be the same again, I knew.

Glossary

Word	Meaning
Achhan	Father
Amma	Mother
Antharjanam	Ladies of Nambhuthiri caste; who stayed inside the houses
Auto rickshaw	A three-wheeled, low-powered vehicle used for short commute.
Avatar	Manifestation of a deity in a physical form on earth. According to Hinduism, Vishnu, the supreme god, took nine different human forms at various stages to help humanity. The 10th avatar is yet to happen.
Aviyal	A thick mixture of vegetables andcoconut, seasoned with coconut oil and curry leaves.
Ayyo	An exclamatory word used to express strong feelings that include fear, shock and surprise.
Bali kallu	Flat granite stones on which rice balls are kept as an offering to the departed souls. The crows are said to eat the offering on behalf of the departed souls.

Bali or balitharpana	A ritual performed in memory ofthe departed. People believe that the departed souls attain mokshaor salvation from the eternal cycle of rebirths.
Beedi	A thin leaf cigarette filled with tobacco
Bhadhrakali	Another manifestation of Goddess Durga
Bhagawathi	Mother-goddess
Chai	Tea
Chaiwallah	Tea-seller
Chapattis	An unleavened flatbread (also known as roti), it is the staple food of North India. Made of whole wheat flour and cooked on a tava or flat skillet.
Chappals	Slipper
Charukasera	An easy chair
Chathan Seva	Devil worship
Chempakam	Micheliachempaca or joy-perfumetree. The flowers are cup-shaped, fleshy and highly fragrant.
Dakshina	A voluntary offering, donation or payment for the services of a priest.

Darbha	A type of grass considered sacred by Hindus; it is used during religious ceremonies.
Durga	The Hindu Warrior Goddess who combats demonic forces; also depicted as the Goddess Parvathi, the wife of God Shiva
Ganesha	The Hindu God with the head of an elephant, known as the remover of obstacles; son of God Shiva and Goddess Parvathi
Garam	Hot
Guru	Highly experienced and regarded teacher
Guruvayoorappan	(lit) Lord of Guruvayoor. A form of the Hindu God Vishnu, and the presiding deity of the Guruvayoor temple in Kerala, India
Henna	The leaves of the henna tree areground into a paste and applied on the hands or legs in intricate designs during special ceremonies. The paste leaves behind a deep orange mark.
Hundi	A collection box normally kept in a temple. Devotees drop coins, notes or, in some cases, small pieces of jewellery, into this box as an offering.

Idli	A savoury cake made by steaming a batter consisting of fermented black lentils and rice.
Illanji	Mimusopselengi is a medium-sized evergreen tree that has fragrant flowers. Also called Spanish cherry, medlar, and bullet wood.
Jimikki	A bell-shaped earring with filigree work.
Kaavu	A thickly wooded sacred grove where serpent spirits or other gods are worshipped.
Kaavu Theendal	Desecration of a sacred place
Kallu	Toddy / palm wine, an alcoholic beverage created from the sap of palm trees; also, a slang for any local alcoholic brew.
Kanyadhaanam	A Hindu ritual in which the father gives his daughter in marriage to the groom by placing her hand in his.
Karimeen	Green chromide (Etroplus Suratensis), also known as the pearlspot. Commonly found in Kerala's backwaters, this is an expensive fish and considered a delicacy.
Karingali	A medicinal plant; small pieces of its bark are put in boling water and used for drinking.

Kartha	This word has multiple meanings but in the context of this novel, it means chief mourner who performs the death or funeral rites. Normally, karta is somebody who is related to the dead person.
Kasavusettu - mundu	Traditional clothing of women in Kerala. It consists of two pieces of cloth in white or off-white colours. When a gold border is added, it is called kasavusettu- mundu.
Kolussu	Anklet or ankle chain
Kulipinnal	A simple loose hairdo done on wet hair.
Kuri	Holy powder or paste usually applied on the forehead; usually ash, or sandalwood paste, or paste made out of a mixture of rice powder and turmeric is used.
Lakshmi	The Hindu Goddess of wealth and prosperity
Mairu	A curse word in Malayalam.
Malayali	People from the state of Kerala who speak the Malayalam language.
Mandapam	The place where a wedding is conducted.
Mannapedi / Pulapedi	Fear of lower-caste men 'defiling' or ritually 'polluting' women from the upper castes

Mannas/Pulayas	Members of lower caste in Kerala, earlier considered untouchables
Mantra	Sacred utterances chanted or sung as an incantation/prayer in Hindu religious rituals. It is believed that mantras have spiritual powers and invoke the support of the gods and other divine beings.
Manthravadhis	Occult Sorcerers
Masala dosa	Dosa is a fermented crepe made from rice batter and black lentils. The masala dosa is made by stuffing the dosa with a lightly-cooked filling of potatoes, fried onions, and spices. It is popular in South India.
Mleccha	A term for a non-Indian barbarian, a foreigner in ancient and medieval India; used generally in a derogatory sense to mean inferior, impure, uncouth etc.
Moksha	According to Hindu religious beliefs, the soul of a departed person undergoes rebirths in various forms based on their deeds in the previous birth. Bali tharpanam is one of the rituals that frees the soul from eternal rebirths and helps it reach heaven.

Mukha Darshanam	The act of watching the reflection of a face (in this case, one's own) normally in a mirror.
Mulachi Parambu	(lit) The land of breasted women; named so after Nangeli,the lower caste woman who protested the breast tax, who lived there
Mulakkaram	Breast tax, imposed on lower caste Hindu women in earlier times if they wanted to cover their breasts in public
Mundu	A single piece of garment wornaround the waist (like a sarong).
Murapennu	A boy's father's sister's daughter or mother's brother's daughter considered as his potential bride.
Nadaswaram	An acoustic double reed instrument, famous in the southern states of India. It is considered auspicious to play the nadaswaram during special functions such as weddings.
Namaste	A traditional form of greeting with folded hands.
Nambhuthiri	Hindu Brahmins (the highest caste) from Kerala, India
Odi	Black Magic as practiced by Odiyans
Odiyans	Tribal witch doctors

Paayasam	A traditional dessert made of milk and vermicelli
Pala Tree	Alstonia Scholaris or Indian Devil tree
Palakkadan	A person belonging to Palakkad in Kerala.
Parangis	Inhabitants of Kerala who have Portuguese ancestry; possibly a corruption of the word *'Firangi'*
Pazhampori	Banana fritters
Pongala	A ritualistic offering of porridge made of rice, sweet brown molasses, coconut gratings etc.
Pappadum	A thin, fragile, crisp disc-shaped food typically served with rice. Made from seasoned black gram dough and is popular in Kerala. Though it can be cooked with dry heat, it is normally fried in oil.
Porotta	A layered flatbread typical of Kerala. Made of maida, a finely milled, refined and bleached wheat flour. Predominantly eaten with a spicy non-vegetarian curry.
Pretham / rakshassu Bhutham / Yakshi	Types of demonic beings
Puja	An act of worship or religious ceremony to invoke the blessings of God.

Sadya	A traditional vegetarian feast served in Kerala during special occasions such as weddings.
Sahagamanam	(lit) accompanying the Lord. Immolation of a widow in her husband's funeral pyre, also known as satī
Samadhi	The act of consciously and intentionally leaving one's body.
Sāmbhar	A lentil based vegetable stew.
Saraswathi	The Hindu Goddess of knowledge
Sari	Along piece of fabric elaborately draped around the body, -traditionally worn by the women of South Asia.
Tendu	Coromandel ebony or East Indian ebony (Diospyrosmelanoxylon). It is a species of flowering tree. Its leaves are wrapped around tobacco to make the Indian beedi, which is also called the poorman's cigarette.
Thaali	A small pendant suspended on a thick yellow string or a gold chain and tied around the neck of a bride. This is an insignia to proclaim that the wearer is married.
Tharawad	Ancestral home, could belong tomaternal or paternal side.

Thottampattu	Eulogy sung to propitiate the gods and goddesses. The songs talk about the origin, legends and virtues of the divine entity.
Thulasi	A kind of basil considered sacred by Hindus.
Upma	A common south Indian dish, cooked as a thick porridge from dry roasted semolina or coarse rice flour.
Vada	A deep-fried snack made from lentils, chillies, onions and curry leaves.
Vanchi	Dug-out canoes
Vettila Chellam	A brass carry case, primarily used to store betel leaves and betel nuts.
Yama	The god of death according to Hindu mythology